mademoiselle
CHANEL

mademoiselle
CHANEL

PIERRE GALANTE

Translated by Eileen Geist and Jessie Wood

Henry Regnery Company • Chicago

Research and interviews for this book conducted with
the assistance of Manuela Andriota and Philippe Orsini.

Library of Congress Cataloging in Publication Data

Galante, Pierre.
  Mademoiselle Chanel.

  1. Chanel, Coco, 1883-1971. I. Title.
TT505.C45G35   746.9'2'0924 [B]   72-11173

Published by Henry Regnery Company
114 West Illinois Street, Chicago, Illinois 60610
Manufactured in the United States of America
Library of Congress Catalog Card Number: 72–11173

Contents

Part I

1.

Gabrielle and Her Secrets

IN THE gardens of Montreux Palace, which slope gently down to the banks of Lake Geneva, an elegant old lady was seated on a wooden bench. She had chanced to stop there on this sunny, leisurely afternoon in December 1970. The warm sun made her otherwise unseasonable clothing—a navy blue suit with white collar and cuffs, blue and white hat, dark glasses—quite practical. Only the bare trees, whose black branches stretching up to the blue skies were reflected in the water, and the leafless skeletons of the bushes that lined the deserted paths revealed the lateness of the year.

The old lady answered the queries of the man seated next to her with monosyllables and silent pauses. Then, suddenly, she became animated. Her strong, square hand with its scarlet nails ran lightly over her pearl necklace, her fingers resting occasionally on a single pearl. When she found the exact word she was looking for and had spoken it, she would—almost with regret, it seemed—let go of the pearl.

While the two were sitting there, a small, brown-haired girl, under whose red coat a skirt and sweater of the same color could be seen, came down the path. The old lady looked questioningly at the child. Her curiosity became more aroused when the little girl settled down near her and began to play with a doll dressed in tawdry rags. Bending down, the old lady spoke to the little girl with a smile that suddenly erased her wrinkles, illuminating her face with a youthfulness to match that of her still svelte figure. Even in her later years, Coco Chanel liked to say: "I could still wear the clothes I wore as a young girl. Cut off my head, and I'm twenty years old!"

"What is your name?"

"Isabelle," the child timidly answered.

"Lend me your doll."

With the flabbergasted child watching, the old lady deftly undressed the doll. Then, taking up the bits of rag one by one, she wrapped them around the disarrayed doll, pinning one to the other with hair pins, which, with a gesture that was clearly habitual, she plucked from her own hairdo. Finally, she handed back a very elegant doll to the smiling child.

"Do you like her now?"

"Oh, yes."

"And what's your doll's name?"

"Gabrielle." The child hugged Gabrielle, now miraculously made presentable by the kindness of this distinguished and slightly intimidating lady.

The old lady's smile suddenly froze, and her face slipped back into the wrinkles of old age. As if brushing away invisible dust, she passed her finger behind one lens of her glasses and slowly traced the curve of her upper eyelid. Her thin, brightly painted lips murmured, "Gabrielle," then lapsed into a silence that seemed interminable. Her eyes stared into the distance or into nothingness, perhaps looking back into her memories.

"Come. It's beginning to get cold. Let us go back to the hotel." Gabrielle Chanel—"Coco" to her few close friends and to millions of women—slowly walked back up the alley alongside an Iranian journalist, Freidoune Sahebjam.

"She had tears in her eyes," he told us. "A month later I learned of her death."

A year earlier.

In the much-photographed salon, with its Coromandel screens, precious objects in gold, bronze, and rare woods, old bindings, polychrome porcelains, and white gardenias scattered over the low tables, a voice, hoarse, now raucous, now shrill, ranted and raved:

"What a bitch. . . ." Those present tried frantically to save the situation.

"Mademoiselle . . . you must calm down. This is not good for you."

"Shut the hell up. I tell you she's a bitch. Why do you defend her? Maybe she came to see you, too. What did you tell her, eh? Tell me!"

"Oh, Mademoiselle, how can you say such a thing?"

Shocked, her ladies-in-waiting showed their disapproval.

Turning to Serge Lifar,* her confidante, Coco brandished a letter, the object of her wrath.

"My dear Aunt. . . . Recently we were visited by Mademoiselle Edmonde Charles-Roux, who is doing research for a book about you. I am writing you now to ask what I should tell her. . . ."

"And," Serge Lifar related later, "she was livid with rage. She had no idea of what she was saying. She kept repeating as if gargling her bad language, 'The bitch . . . the bitch. . . .' "

The "bitch" had a name well known in the fashion and literary worlds, a name as distinguished as her diction, her person, her circle of friends, and her origins: daughter of an ambassador, former editor-in-chief of French *Vogue,* novelist, winner of the Prix Goncourt, a pacesetter of Parisian society even though a distant and reserved person. In short, the kind of person who normally does not come under fire—except from Coco Chanel—when such a lady has the "preposterous" idea of writing the life story of one of the most famous women in the world.

A few days later, almost calm, Coco confided to Carmen Tessier, the leading gossip columnist of the French press:

"But I know Edmonde well! Why didn't she come to see me?" Why, indeed? Doubtless because Coco would have told her only as much as she had told Louise de Vilmorin: "I was born in Auvergne"—and even that was untrue.

Why did all those who tried to collaborate with her, at her own request, on her memoirs—Maurice Druon, Georges Kessel, Yves Salgues, and Gaston Bonheur, all well-known and brilliant writers—fail?

---

*Serge Lifar, the world-renowned choreographer, for years was one of the stars of Diaghilev's ballets.

When we interviewed Gaston Bonheur, a poet, writer, and journalist, we asked him to explain the reason for these failures:

"It was around 1950 that, invited by Coco to La Pausa, her villa on the Côte d'Azur, I tried to organize Chanel's memoirs. She dreamed of her memoirs but dreaded seeing them down on paper, in black and white—forever.

"I think the first thing that struck me about her was that she reminded me of a boarding-school girl. It was partly due to her severe-looking clothes—the little boater she rarely took off—and to the monastic atmosphere she tried to impose upon La Pausa. It was the kind of house where everything was extremely clean, imbued with a sort of odor of sanctity. One felt that there was some link between her childhood memories and something very deep within her that stamped her whole way of being, of dressing, of living, all of which seemed to spring from a strict boarding-school code.

"Perhaps Chanel had a Cinderella complex toward the little girls brought up in châteaux or toward the perfect little girl she never was but would have liked to have been. This accounts for her proud solitude, so characteristic of the school-boarder.

"As to her memoirs, I understood almost immediately that it wouldn't work. The business of writing memoirs is rather romantic since it is usually based on anecdote, and the trouble was that Chanel stubbornly refused to relate anecdotes. She would say: 'Anecdotes are vulgar. What do they mean? They're unimportant.' She saw herself as such a classic figure that she could only express herself in maxims. She wanted her memoirs to consist of thoughts boiled down to three lines.

"Unless one were La Rochefoucauld himself, I couldn't quite see how it would be possible to help her in her desire to write her memoirs. Also, she refused to remember.

"There were two possible reasons for this attitude. To remember would be to evoke a real life when what she really wanted was to forget it in favor of a refined past, an edifying and, most of all, an enlightened life. She also had a sort of 'English attitude,' the result of her Anglomania, which decreed 'no personal remarks.' Talking about oneself was vulgar and 'not done.'

"Furthermore, one never developed a close relationship with her because she never gave up her role of lecturer. She never let herself go. Sometimes she could relax a little, but never enough.

"She was much more like the founder of an order than a personality of Parisian life. One could very well have said about her: 'Mademoiselle Chanel founded the order of the Sisters of Beauty.'

"I started to write what I was able to get out of her. The death of Diaghilev in Venice, for instance. This was a perfectly recountable episode because, in her eyes, Diaghilev's death had ennobled him. It was literature. It was part of the events that could be talked about without sounding like a concierge.

"If you asked her to tell you all about how she threw the jewels given to her by the Duke of Westminster into the sea, she gave you a dissertation on the emeralds but refused to talk about the episode itself.

"I tried talking to her about her childhood, in chronological order. She didn't tell me a thing. She became evasive. She always very cleverly evaded the real to dwell on what she wanted to talk about. When I talked to her about her father, she would say with great vagueness: 'I remember once, in an inn. . . .' Then she would ramble on about the decor, the paper flowers, and a red scarf. She'd go off on a tangent leading to her pet subjects: lessons in elegance, in manners, in the art of living. You could not get her into a corner for she fled just as the mythomaniac flees. She escaped from the particular to the general."

Without her cooperation, writers and journalists have exhausted a fabulous bestiary to describe Chanel. She was a little black bull for Colette, a swan for Jean Cocteau, and a sparrow for Truman Capote. Pierre Laval, the statesman, saw her as a young lamb dressed up as a woman. In short, there were as many different animals with which to describe her as places for her to be born.

From the start, one is confronted with paradox and mystery when one looks into the career of Coco. As if fearful that a past she despised would catch up with her, she seldom told the truth when asked about her early life. What she could not hide, however, were the records.

In fact, on August 20, 1883, Mme Joséphine Pélerin, an employee of the poorhouse of Saumur, appeared before M François Poitou, acting deputy-mayor of the city of Saumur, in the department of Maine-et-Loire (far from Auvergne, where she claimed to have been born), to register the birth of a female infant, born in the poorhouse on August 19 at four o'clock in the afternoon. The parents of the child were Henri Chasnel, tradesman, twenty-eight years old, from Nîmes, department of Gard, and Eugénie Jeanne Devolle, tradeswoman, twenty years old, from Courpière, in the Puy-de-Dôme (Auvergne). The child bore the name of Gabrielle.

So much for the "mystery" of Coco's birth, but what were the facts underlying the bare statistics? An examination of her family is revealing. Her grandfather, Adrien Chanel, originally from Savoie, was the twelfth of a family of thirteen children. He married a young Protestant woman, Virginie Fournier, in Nîmes.

Mme Adrienne Valet, née Chanel, a first cousin of Coco to whom she bears a marked resemblance, is married to a mining civil engineer. They live in Paris near the Marais on the fourth floor of a middle-class apartment house. In her sixties, and well-preserved, she is the mother of three children and the grandmother of a little boy who is her pride and joy. She has devoted her life to her children. "That's maybe why," she said, "I didn't always see eye to eye with Coco."

She related to us what she knew of her family:

"We were real gypsies, always traveling. My grandfather, who was also Coco's, bought fabric rejects from silk manufacturers in Lyon and sold them through itinerant vendors. Then he followed the vendors all over the country in order to recover his money and claim his profits. Finally we settled in Vichy."

On November 19, 1856, in the absence of Adrien Chanel, an employee of the Nîmes poorhouse reported the birth of a child named Henri-Albert (Coco's father). The acting deputy of the registrar's office made the following entry on the municipal registry: ". . . Virginie Fournier, nineteen years old, wife of Adrien Charnet, twenty-four years old (no other information), gave birth," etc.

Charnet, not Chanel. It was not until twenty-two years later, on January 21, 1878, by decision of the court of first instance of Nîmes, that it was finally decreed that "birth certificate No. 1805, dated November 19, 1856, is to be corrected and that the family name of Charnet will be replaced in the future by that of Chanel, which is the true name."

Coco never bothered to have the spelling of her name corrected—despite the fact that her name, Chanel, was spelled Chasnel on her birth certificate—and the date of her death was inscribed in the margin of her birth certificate as follows: "Chasnel, Gabrielle, deceased in Paris, 1st arrondissement, January 10, 1971."

What kind of childhood and youth did Henri Chanel have? We know that like his father he was a tradesman, wandering from city to city; that he lived in Saumur at 29 rue St.-Jean for a while—at least he was there on August 19, 1883, the date on which Eugénie Jeanne Devolle gave birth to Gabrielle Chasnel in the city poorhouse.

That was the first of Coco's wounds: born in the poorhouse, like her father. But there was a second wound, much more subtle, unexpected, and severe: her parents were married fifteen months after her birth. The Chanel-Devolle marriage certificate, number 29, is dated November 17, 1884. However, Gabrielle, as we have seen, was born on August 19, 1883: an illegitimate child.

Indeed, by the time of their marriage, Coco's parents had already given birth to another daughter, Julia-Berthe. This daughter later married but died young, leaving a son, André Palasse. Coco cared for her nephew, unofficially adopting him.

Very little is known about Eugénie Jeanne Devolle, daughter of Auvergne peasants and mother of Coco, except that her parents were dead when she married Henri Chanel, that her family was relatively well off, and that before her marriage in the Courpière town hall she appeared before Maître Fayon, notary, accompanied by her future husband and his parents to draw up a marriage contract—itself an indication of some standing.

We are indebted to the present notary, Maître Jean Croquez, successor to Maître Bonfils, who in turn had succeeded Maître Fayon as notary, for making available to us a photocopy of this contract. We cite only its essential contents:

Appeared before me, Maître Jules Joseph Fayon, notary in Courpière:

1) M Henri-Albert Chanel, traveling tradesman, living in Issoire,

Oldest and legitimate son of M Adrien Chanel and Mme Virginie Fournier,

Acting in his own name, and accompanied by his father and mother,

Hereinafter known as the party of the first part,

2) M Adrien Chanel and Mme Virginie Fournier, his spouse,

tradesmen, domiciled in Clermont-Ferrand, 8 rue Saint-André appearing here in order to assist their son, the future husband,

Also as party of the first part,

3) Mlle Jeanne Devolle, without profession, domiciled in Issoire, native of Courpière,

Oldest and legitimate daughter of François Devolle, deceased, and Mme Gilberte Chardon, deceased [born on May 8, 1863, Jeanne Devolle had just turned twenty-one at the time she signed this contract, in November 1884],

Acting in her own name,

Hereinafter known as the party of the second part.

The above-named parties declared that the conditions under civil law of the proposed marriage between M Henri Chanel and Mlle Jeanne Devolle are as follows:

First,

The future spouses declare that they elect as a basis for their union the regime of individual property, in accordance with the provisions of Articles 1530 ff. of the Civil Code.

Second,

The bride-to-be is to provide the following dowry:

1) clothes, linen, bric-a-brac, and furniture for her personal use, the whole comprising her trousseau of which a detailed description is not here given, in view of the fact that such property is by its nature sufficiently distinguished from that of the husband-to-be;

2) various household articles, furniture, housekeeping utensils, etc., the whole being estimated by the two parties as having a value of five hundred francs;

3) a sum of five thousand francs in cash or claims which is her legal property, as she has duly established.

The above dowry will be given over to the husband-to-be on the day of the celebration of the proposed marriage; the marriage certificate will be the acknowledgment of this transaction by the wife-to-be, and no other document will be necessary.

Third,

The future spouses do mutually and reciprocally bequeath by these presents to the surviving spouse, as each respectively agrees: the usufruct of all the real estate and personal property belonging to the first deceased, without exception.

The surviving spouse will be entitled to such usufruct during his lifetime without obligation to provide security therefor or to make use of such property and capital, but on condition that an inventory be made. In the event that the spouses have children, this bequest will be reduced by one-half, subject to the same conditions as to usufruct.

Such are the conditions agreed to by the two parties.

Jeanne Devolle brought to her husband a dowry of five thousand francs, furniture, and linen: in 1884 a far from negligible dowry. Yet it was small satisfaction for Coco. First, she could not avoid the physical circumstances of her birth and the legal stigma of illegitimacy. Second, her father was a waster and the dowry was soon gone. And, finally, Coco also had to bear a third wound: her mother died of tuberculosis a few years after Coco's birth, leaving, besides Julia-Berthe and Gabrielle, three other children, Antoinette, Lucien, and Alphonse.

Then, shortly after her mother's death, yet another wound was inflicted, probably the deepest for a sensitive child to endure. Having turned the boys over to public welfare and the girls to his family, Henri Chanel disappeared.

Born in the poorhouse, an illegitimate child, without a mother, and abandoned by her father—such was Gabrielle's early history. Yet Coco never admitted even to herself what effect this early life, with its inherent loneliness and sense of death, had on her. She refused to accept her tragic years as having finality or significance, even when she was condemned to the humiliations of a turn-of-the-century orphanage.

"Some day my father will return from America a very rich man," she would say. Later, to some, Mademoiselle said:

"My father was a southerner from Pontex, a village near Nîmes. My mother started to have labor pains in the train and that's how I was born in Saumur in the home of people my mother had met in the train compartment."

For others, she was the daughter of a rich wine merchant from Béziers who had left for America after the death of his wife.

Yet her imaginative fabrications were only for show; inside she knew the true story behind her birth. The secret trauma of Coco, even when she was a rich and famous woman, was her childhood.

Silent in the face of her biographers, she rarely opened up even to her more intimate friends. André-Louis Dubois,* one of

---

*André-Louis Dubois has served as prefect of police of Paris and as ambassador to Morocco. Currently he is president of the Fédèration nationale de la Presse française.

the rare beings with whom she never fought, told us the following anecdote:

"The most mysterious thing about Chanel's life was her childhood. She rarely talked about it, and one never knew exactly where she lived as a child.

"Sometimes she let drop tidbits of her childhood memories, or she might recall a certain decor: 'Trains, trains. . . .' She talked constantly about trains, sometimes even claiming to have been born in a train. Why this obsession with trains?

" 'Because,' she said, 'my uncle was a stationmaster. In fact, that is why we always traveled very grandly, in second class, for we had free tickets.' "*

Yet despite her lack of candor, sometimes she would describe a memory quite precisely, quaintly, or poetically depending on her mood. Occasionally, she went too far for good taste, as, for instance, when she confided to Carmen Tessier, the famous French columnist and wife of André-Louis Dubois, details of an episode that could have been inspired by René Clement's famous film, *Forbidden Games:*

"We lived near a cemetery. For me a cemetery was not a sad place. I loved it and went there as often as possible. It was where I felt most at ease. I had my dead, my tombs; two or three were my favorites. My family tried to keep me away from there by saying: 'Your parents aren't buried there. You don't know those people. . . .' But that made no difference to me. I brought them flowers as often as I could, and forks, spoons, or anything I could steal at home. I spread my loot around the tombs and arranged it. I loved doing it. Then one fine day, the family discovered that various objects had disappeared. Everything was put under lock and key, and, since I had nothing to take to my dead, I forgot them."

Death, it seems, was never far from Coco's experience; later, one sad and moving reminiscence of childhood was linked to another.

In no way, in fact, was Chanel's childhood, even when we can untangle it, "normal"—a fact that is amply demonstrated by her account of her "aunts."

---

*There was, of course, still a third class in those days. The family did not travel first class, for the uncle held a modest rank in the hierarchy of railroad employees.

"I was brought up in Auvergne by two elderly aunts. They had promised to bring me up but not to love me. They condemned me to sewing on my trousseau."

"They were two old ladies, very bourgeois in appearance," remembered Céline, Mademoiselle's personal maid. "Mademoiselle described them as two very severe but well-off ladies, in whose home she refused to learn the piano."

These aunts, who, in some versions, turned out to be cousins of her mother, are completely unknown to any of Mademoiselle's living relatives, among them Mme Valet. Did they exist? Or were they merely figments of Coco's imagination, concocted in her eagerness to forget the orphanages she subsequently lived in and the aura of disgrace that surrounded such establishments? The record, as one pieces it together, suggests they did *not* exist.

But if there were no aunts, what happened to Gabrielle? Coco's grandmother Virginie, to whom Henri Chanel had entrusted Coco and her sisters and who at the time was living in Vichy, had enough to do with her own children, the youngest of whom, Adrienne, was only two years older than Coco. Consequently, Gabrielle probably was not, at first, taken in by her father's family.

Thus between the ages of six (when her mother died) and twelve (when she entered boarding school), Coco endured considerable privation and, to her, intolerable indignity. Later she claimed this was the period of the aunts: Auvergne. That is what she said, and she said little more. Yet since her mother was from Auvergne, she probably was taken in not by some fabricated aunts but by the Devolles prior to going to live with the Chanels.

If this is the case, Coco almost certainly spent the "Auvergne" period of her childhood—the six years between the ages of six and twelve—in Issoire, although one can find no trace of her stay there. In 1884 when the Chanels, Coco's parents, appeared before Maître Fayon, notary at Courpière, to sign their marriage contract, they had declared their residence to be Issoire. It was also in Issoire that Mme Valet's mother, a native of that city, married a Chanel, an uncle of Coco. Our researches led us to Sauxillanges, a large village less than ten miles from Issoire with a population of 2,500 in 1900 (in 1971, the population was 1,200). There, before the turn of the century, the Sisters of the Good Pastor ran an orphanage, which today has been moved to Clermont-Ferrand.

In Sauxillanges, Mlle Eugénie Guerrier, in her mid-seventies, white-haired and very chatty, whose mother was a milliner in the region, thinks she remembers the young Gabrielle. "She wasn't shy," Mlle Guerrier told us, "certainly much less so than the village girls. She had a quick eye for the boys, even though she lived with the Sisters of the Good Pastor!"

According to Mlle Guerrier, it is quite possible that Coco made her professional debut working for Mme Claude Guerrier, her mother (the milliner), staying only a short time. Next Coco seems to have been employed by the Mlles Boyer and Cusson, dressmakers, who also lived in Sauxillanges. The latter as well as Mme Guerrier were famous throughout the region and had a large clientele. At least twice a year, all three went to Paris to look at what was being done in the big fashion houses and undoubtedly upon their return recounted everything they had seen and done in the capital. Unquestionably, what she heard was enough to make the young Gabrielle Chanel dream.

There was also Aubazine, in Corrèze. "I sometimes heard an uncle, an aunt, or a cousin ask: 'Where are the girls?' and my mother would answer, 'At Aubazine,'" Mme Valet told us. The "girls" were Coco and her sisters. Aubazine was originally a convent, a masterpiece of twelfth-century Romanesque architecture. After 1789 the monastery was not inhabited by monks or nuns. Only one sister of the Order of the Sacred Heart of Mary was charged with overseeing the convent, and with the help of a few laymen she took care of about fifteen orphans, who replaced the monks in the remaining buildings.

At twelve came a change; the Chanels took over.

"When Coco was twelve years old, she and her sisters were placed in a religious boarding school in Moulins. Part of this establishment was for students who paid and another for orphans who could not pay," Mme Valet told us.

The children with parents lived in tolerable conditions; the plight of orphans was far different. Coco and her sisters fell into the latter category, for though the family—the grandparents in Vichy and the aunt and uncle Costier in Varennes-sur-Allier—could take the girls during the holidays, it did not have the financial means to permit them to escape the unheated dormitories and separate refectory tables.

Moulins was a subprefecture and an elegant garrison town. Coco lived there most of the time between the ages of twelve and twenty, until 1903, a long stay cut by holidays in Vichy and Varennes-sur-Allier, by an escapade in Paris, and possibly by a short stay in Sauxillanges.

The mother superior of the convent in Moulins told Coco's father's sister, Julia Costier, who had come to take Coco to Varennes-sur-Allier for a summer holiday, that she was without illusions regarding Coco's character and declared:

"You know, I shall never see her again. I'm sure of it." Mme Valet, who recounted this anecdote to us, is not certain of Coco's age at the time but guesses that she might have been about sixteen or seventeen.

In Varennes-sur-Allier, Coco's young aunt Adrienne, a very beautiful young girl who was betrothed to a rich, old, and ugly notary, joined her.

One Sunday afternoon at the height of the village fair, Adrienne, intoxicated by the youthful cries and laughter around her, by the music and the rataplan of the drums, suddenly said to her niece, Coco, who, in those days, was called Fifi after a songbird owned by her grandfather: "Let's go to Paris!"

To Paris was the cry. Discovering a small carnival in progress, Adrienne and Coco quickly earned a little money by selling confetti for a merchant. Who could resist buying a bag of confetti from two such pretty girls? They traveled to Paris first class, holding second-class tickets, until the train conductor insisted that they pay the difference between first- and second-class fares. Thus the two girls found themselves with practically no money even before reaching the capital.

What happened in Paris? "They stayed with friends," Mme Valet said. "After a few days, they returned to Vichy. Adrienne did not marry the notary and Coco did not return to the convent in Moulins." Was this the point at which Coco went to Sauxillanges for one or two years?

Coco never spoke about this period of her life. The speculation, ranging from gossip to priceless legends, shows only that Coco was unsettled about her life ambitions. Only one thing is certain: a young girl, almost twenty years old, could no longer believe in the return of a rich father from America.

Coco, her sister, and her aunt Adrienne sang for a while in an elegant café in Moulins, much frequented by officers.

Little more is known about Coco's youth. A young girl, beautiful and poor, waited in the smoky atmosphere of a "café-con-cert." For what? Her destiny? Fortunately, destiny was close at hand.

In 1903, a model recruit in the Chasseurs d'Afrique, Etienne Balsan, a dashing young man of twenty-five, was nearing the end of his military service in Algeria. Less than a century before, his ancestor, of modest origins, had moved from Mazamet to Châteauroux, a wool center, where he founded a wool cloth factory. The Balsan firm had quickly become one of the most important in France, and the family began making brilliant marriages with the noblest of families.

Etienne was the youngest of three brothers. Since childhood, his turbulence and imagination had set him apart. Sent to England to finish his studies and to learn to respect authority, he succeeded in bending the schoolmasters to suit his fancy. He also developed an irresistible love for horses, so when he returned to France, it was out of the question for him to go into the family textile business like his brothers, Robert and Jacques.* Etienne began to train young horses in the fields around Châteauroux and rode in races for gentlemen riders. He had two obsessions: fresh air and horses.

Then he volunteered in the Chasseurs d'Afrique, a fine regiment full of young men from good families—like Balsan—who were often as not dandies, effetes, which Balsan was not. Soon the simple trooper was much talked about, as his nephew and present head of the family, François Balsan (son of Robert), a member of the Overseas Science Academy and an explorer, has recounted to us, with fiery enthusiasm.

"Uncle Etienne was an anti-snob. Which in those days meant that a little peasant girl, a working girl, or a singer in a cheap café-concert could be just as pleasant company as a well-born young lady. Uncle Etienne saw no difference. . . . During his military service, while on guard duty in front of the Governor's Palace one hot day in July, he put down his rifle and his shako, unbuttoned his coat, and went to sleep in the shade of the sentry box. A civilian who was passing by thought it proper to remind

---

*Jacques Balsan distinguished himself as a fighter pilot during World War I and participated, along with Doctor Gross, director of the American Hospital in Neuilly, and William K. Vanderbilt, in founding the Lafayette squadron. In 1921 Jacques Balsan married the daughter of William Vanderbilt, Consuelo, after her divorce from the Duke of Marlborough.

him of his duties. He made a grave mistake! Told off in no uncertain terms, he didn't pursue the subject.

"The civilian was none other than the governor. Without
delay Balsan was sent to the stockade and assigned the most unpleasant jobs. This lasted until one winter day when almost all
the horses had chilblains. No veterinarian capable of curing
them could be found. Balsan went to the colonel and bet him
that he could cure the horses.

" 'If I succeed, have me transferred back to France. It's all I
ask,' he said.

"The colonel was very skeptical. The veterinarians all laughed
at the presumptuous young trooper. But thanks to a recipe he
had learned in England, Balsan cured the horses. The colonel
honored his promise. Balsan was transferred in 1903 to the cavalry unit stationed in Moulins. He spent the remaining months of
his military service there."

Moulins was the most popular cavalry garrison in France.
There were lots of café-concerts for the entertainment of the military. In one of these our three local young ladies performed: she
who was to become Coco Chanel, twenty years old, one of her
sisters, Antoinette, and their aunt, Adrienne. Since they were
poorly paid, the owner permitted them to circulate around the
room after the performance. Naturally their charm worked
wonders, and well-to-do customers, officers for the most part, did
not hesitate to show their generosity.

So it was that the trooper Balsan, brilliant but undisciplined,
met the young Gabrielle Chanel. Later, with the passing of the
years, the entire press dubbed him "her handsome officer." Coco
never denied it.

2.

Coco and Her Belle Epoque

Coco and Balsan were attracted to each other almost immediately. He had just terminated a youthful affair with Emilienne d'Alençon, a celebrated demimondaine, and the little provincial girl brought him a whiff of fresh air. For her part, he easily persuaded her to follow him to Paris when his military service ended.

For all his reckless abandon, Etienne Balsan loved the outdoors and physical exercise and preferred the life of a country gentleman and breeder of horses to the idle life of the fashionable dandy. His inheritance from his father, who died in 1896, and from his mother, who died in 1902, had given him an enviable financial situation, and in 1903 he set up a racehorse training center at Lacroix-Saint-Ouen and established a home at the château of Royallieu near Compiègne.

Horse races replaced the tournaments of olden times for this modern chevalier and his companions, Jules de Saint-Sauveur and the Barons Edouard* and Robert de Nexon, and they flung themselves into these races with great zest. Paris was not far away, and they went there for a ball from time to time, but they rarely stayed late in the drawing rooms of the aristocratic houses

---

*Edouard's friends usually called him Maurice.

of the rue du Faubourg St.-Germain. They stayed at the Ritz, but nothing in Paris could capture the fancy of these dashing young men, not even the young girls, of whom the Duchess de Gramont,* one of the great names of European aristocracy and a lively and pungent memorialist, has left this cruel portrait:

"No stupidity, artificiality, conventionality was spared us: foolish tunes, stupid plays, dull and banal conversation, repulsive clothes. The well-brought-up young girls were dressed in pale, washed-out colors, shabby fabrics. All the touching up that heightens attractiveness—jewels, powder, rouge, and perfume— were strictly forbidden them. They barely avoided smelling bad."

At the château of Royallieu, where she lived, Coco would contemplate these young girls when Etienne Balsan occasionally entertained them, but she did not watch for long. She escaped very quickly, dressed in breeches and a man's jacket, to the forest of Compiègne, where, soon joined by Etienne, she rode like a dervish, legs astride—this was in 1903!—for seemingly endless gallops.

"My, but your girl friends are terribly unattractive," she would say.

"But, Coco, she's the daughter of the Marquis de. . . ."

"What difference does that make? She's badly dressed."

Later she was to say: "I was mortally timid." But the Chanel spirit always quickly surfaced. At first intimidated, she soon reacted with the withering scorn for which she was to become famous. It was not long before she looked down on the people who had once filled her with awe and usually had snubbed her (after all, she was a "kept woman"). In the meantime, her common sense, her piquancy, and her wit astonished and amused Etienne.

Twenty years old and an outsider, she was discovering the Great World, upon which she gazed first with curiosity and then with disdain. What did she see? A society in which the destiny of

---

*Elizabeth, the daughter of Agenor de Gramont, Duke de Guiche, and Isabelle de Beauveau, was the granddaughter of the Duke de Gramont, minister of foreign affairs for Napoleon III, and half-sister of the Duke Armand de Guiche, a great friend of Marcel Proust. After the death of his wife, Agenor married a daughter of the Baron Charles de Rothschild of Frankfurt. His third wife was an Italian, Maria Ruspoli, whose second husband, François Victor Hugo (whom she divorced), became a great friend of Coco Chanel around 1930. Her memoirs are entitled: *Souvenirs der Minde, 1890–1940.*

young, well-bred girls was absolutely predetermined: a smatter-
ing of education *(belles lettres,* music, sewing), followed by a
period of waiting around for marriage, and eventual passage
from their fathers' to their husbands' domination. The wait,
which was sometimes long, was punctuated almost solely by
those celebrated balls, where, as the Duchess de Gramont wrote:

". . . Ugly, skinny, young men who did not know how to
dance were in store for us. They dirtied our satin dancing shoes,
rumpled our dresses, and breathed in our faces the stale odor of
what they had just eaten at the buffet. The best of them cast a
contemptuous glance at our crowd and went *elsewhere."*

"Elsewhere" meant the "cocottes," such as the "Belle" Otero,
Liane de Pougy, and Emilienne d'Alençon, through whose slim
hands fortunes slipped, or the "little women for five gold louis,'
whom the head waiters at Maxim's disdainfully called "today's
special." With them, whether they were aristocratic cocottes or
plebian whores, the men were sure to find what was rarely available at home: delicious meals, low lights, witty and relaxed conversation.

Although on the eve of their decline, the great courtesans were
still the recognized queens of fashionable Paris; they *set* the fashions. The gossip columnists credited them with witty remarks.
Gaston Calmette, editor-in-chief of *Le Figaro,* was infinitely indulgent toward them, and their clothes were described in detail
in the columns of that staid and serious daily paper. It was the
day of plumed toques, hats decorated with birds of paradise
feathers, and chinchilla stoles. The sons of the wealthy and the
influential fought for the honor of ruining themselves for these
ladies, and even the sons of royal families did not turn up their
noses at lolling in monumental and costly beds in the overheated
luxury of the small private houses on the Plaine Monceau.

Around 1910, a young poet and writer, Jean Cocteau, caught
a glimpse of these lionesses dining in the Bois de Boulogne:

". . . Chokers, corsets, whalebones, braided epaulets, leggings,
high boots, gauntlets, corselets, pearl halters, shields made of
feathers, belts of satin, velvet, and precious stones, coats of mail;
those chevaliers bristling with tulle, those sacred beetles armed
with asparagus tongs, those samurais of sable and ermine, those
cuirassiers of pleasure harnessed and caparisoned from daybreak
on by robust ladies' maids, stiff and unyielding, appeared
capable only of finding the pearl in an oyster. The idea of

undressing one of them seemed costly and difficult, an enterprise better to foresee in advance as comparable to moving house."

The young Coco was able, then, to muse on the feminine state and dress while contemplating one of the aging lionesses, Emilienne d'Alençon, when the latter visited the owner of Royallieu, for whom she entertained a disinterested and sincere "weakness."

The cocottes were hardly simpering ninnies. As François Balsan told us:

"Can you imagine that after my uncle Etienne had fallen off his horse during an obstacle race, Emilienne dared to go for news of him to the family home at 8 rue de la Baume, where he had been transported. . . ."

The daughter of a concierge in the rue des Martyrs in Montmartre, Emilienne had made her debut at the Cirque d'Eté in 1889. Dressed as a clown, in a costume reduced to a minimum, she presented a tamed rabbit act. Not much later, preceded by a magnificent basket of flowers, one of the greatest names in France, the young Duke d'Uzès, entered her dressing room. Emilienne passed without pause from her unheated attic to a small private house, to jeweled necklaces, servants, a horse and carriage. She was launched.

"I am going to Scotland to hunt grouse. Come with us. You will call yourself the Countess de Songeon and I shall introduce you to my cousin Edouard," wrote King Leopold II of Belgium. The "cousin" was King Edward VII of England.

"I was soon to know all the kings," d'Alençon wrote in her memoirs. Indeed, one day a disrespectful columnist called her "an international morganatic queen."

In short, the woman Coco contemplated stood at the head of the fashionable world, and with the benefit of hindsight, we should not be surprised that the two liked each other. They were two of a kind.

"I liked Emilienne d'Alençon a lot. She smelled good," Coco said later. It seems that the successful courtesan also felt a liking for the young provincial girl, or perhaps she was merely curious to see what this thin young girl, whom a celebrated Don Juan had made his mistress, was all about. Emilienne must have asked herself what this saucy little girl had to capture Etienne's fancy, especially in a day when full-blown women were preferred. Coco

Chanel seemed to have nothing—except her youth, her simplicity, and a certain caustic verve.

To d'Alençon, those were few enough assets, and even Coco had moments of concern. She was not "well born" and had no money. Her only "dowry" was the freshness of her twenty years. Only in the ambience of Royallieu was this not necessarily scanty capital. The friends of Etienne Balsan were the kind of men who kept mistresses. Sometimes they even married them.*

Moreover, Etienne and Coco were bound together by ties of profound friendship rather than of true love. Coco was his horseback riding partner, his accomplice at the race track, and the companion of his pranks and distractions. What held them together was something outside the usual relations: Coco was neither his fiancée nor his kept mistress. She was his pal, the girl who didn't stamp her foot in annoyance when he slipped away at the race track to discuss among men the qualities and defects of a horse.

"What was Coco like at that time?" we asked an old friend of Etienne Balsan, M Valery Ollivier, a marvelous horseman in his youth, a gentleman rider who today lives in retirement in the Pays Basque in southwest France. He remembers having met Coco at luncheons at Royallieu.

"She was a tiny little thing with a pretty, very expressive, roguish face and a strong personality. She amazed us because of her nerve on horseback, but aside from that there was nothing extraordinary about her. Her figure was good, but not outstanding.

"We certainly could not foresee what she would later become. We looked at her merely as Etienne Balsan's little girl friend. She wasn't the Coco Chanel of fashion; she was the Coco Chanel of nothing at all, a pretty slip of a girl."

Although he lived the life of the rich young gentlemen of his day, Etienne Balsan was different from his peers. Thus he was able to give Coco what no other man could have or would have wanted to offer: the possibility of preserving her independence. Thanks to Balsan, she had the time to choose, to reflect, to understand, and to judge. His offhand manner guaranteed Coco's

---

*This happened to Adrienne Chanel, Coco's young aunt, who became the Baroness Edouard de Nexon on April 29, 1930.

independence. He was her first stroke of luck. She had waited a long time for it.

But freedom is valuable only if it can be enjoyed. There was a less attractive side to the coin. Material difficulties should not really have been a problem. After all, there was no reason there shouldn't be another man after Etienne to take care of her. But *that* precisely was the problem for a money-poor free spirit—free before her time. What she didn't want at any price was to become "another" mistress, another woman who all her life was dependent on men—their desires, their whims, their money. Yet to a poor, beautiful, and ambitious young girl living in the first decade of the twentieth century the only alternatives were to be either a wife or a courtesan.

It was only after considerable thought that Coco hit upon a third way: work. And given her criticism of contemporary fashion, as well as her experience with Mlles Guerrier, Boyer, and Cusson, it is hardly surprising that Coco chose to work in the field of fashion.

At first, of course, there was no question of full-time work. Etienne did not approve. He could or would not understand that simply being Balsan's girl friend was no longer enough for Coco. When she asked him to buy her a milliner's shop, he replied: "But why do you want to work? Aren't you happy here?"

In fact, she was becoming bored at Royallieu. Her only distraction besides horseback riding was playing with the many different kinds of animals that were kept caged or allowed to roam about the grounds. She adored a little monkey, which, as it happened, hated the majordomo Michaux intensely and sometimes bombarded him with flower pots!

Characteristically, Coco persisted in her demands, and finally Balsan gave in. Soon, under his amused gaze, she began to make hats for friends, and she was so successful that she quickly outstripped Compiègne. Coco then installed her hat blocks in Balsan's Parisian bachelor quarters on the Boulevard Malesherbes, quarters that he shared with the Marquis de Saint-Sauveur.

Hers was still not a "business." It was simply a matter of three women's working together: Coco; a friend, Paulette, who was to become the greatest milliner of the Belle Epoque; and Coco's youngest sister, Antoinette. Yet limited as the business was, success was instantaneous. Coco proved she had the knack of pleasing her customers, who soon became her friends. Her hats possessed an unparalleled chic. While they were simple boaters—she bought the blocks at the Galeries Lafayette—she adjusted them, touched them up, trimmed them with taste and discretion, and made them stunning.

At the race tracks, where there was an abundance of bonnets plumed with feathers and bird's nests, Coco herself was a sensation, with her boater crammed straight down on her heavy hair. She wore simple navy blue suits that had jackets cut like a jockey's. The first was made for her by a small artisan tailor in Compiègne, and later Coco was to say: "It is he who inspired all my models."

Coco opened a breach in the bastion that was Paris fashion by attacking with hats, but her success in the area, combined with her personal success at the race track and elsewhere, soon had her most audacious customers asking her to copy her own dresses for them. One of her first customers was the Countess de Gontaut-Biron, daughter of the U.S. ambassador to Germany. The countess remembers having bought a hat and a little unlined cotton coat. Coco, her mouth full of pins, did the fittings.

Thus, around 1905, Coco's debut in fashion began in earnest. Her boaters and cloche hats were being worn by several society ladies, all of whom became avid propagandists for Coco Chanel. Perhaps the most enthusiastic was Baroness Henri de Rothschild, mother of the present-day Baron Philippe, who gave Coco's address to friends and encouraged all to patronize the daring young designer of Boulevard Malesherbes. Another client, and one who immediately brought success to Coco, was Gabrielle Dorziat, a leading actress. When Mlle Dorziat wore a Chanel hat on stage in *Bel Ami,* demand for Chanel hats mushroomed. Later she was to wear one of Chanel's first jersey dresses.

Did Coco have more definite ambitions or expectations in 1905? She was twenty-two years old. Certainly she was ambitious; her opinions of contemporary fashion were well formed. She saw how women dressed; she frequented the fashion houses and looked and studied in silence; she was ready whether she knew it or not.

Meanwhile, another comet was already blazing. While Chanel was trying her hand at placing her first pins, a revolution was shaking the world of established designers such as Worth and Doucet, the two fashion dictators to the women of the world. A new designer, Paul Poiret, the Magnificent, had begun what was to be an invincible ascension.

In 1850, at the age of twenty-four, a young Englishman, Charles Frederick Worth, abandoned London. His silhouette was celebrated in Hyde Park, where, dressed à la Sherlock Holmes, he walked his dogs every morning.

With a considerable reputation for tasteful dresses and hats, in 1858 Worth installed himself in his own establishment at 7 rue de la Paix and, using his wife as a model, undertook to show his first creations to the Princess de Metternich, who launched him.

Worth arrived at exactly the right moment. The Second Empire was marked by the desire to show off: buildings, avenues, clothes, whatever—but especially clothes. Aristocrats and bourgeois alike went to the showrooms of the rue de la Paix to look at the fabrics, to chat, to drink a cup of tea, and to order clothes from Worth. Thus high fashion was born in Paris—thanks to an · Englishman.

In 1900, Worth was still the dressmaker of the courts. He sent his fitters with the dresses by special trains to the duchesses and archduchesses of central Europe. But his fame soon brought competitors who were fated to make his star shine less brightly. Among them was Jacques Doucet. Elegant, refined, an expert collector of furniture and engravings, Doucet was one of the first to recognize the talent of a new school of painters—the impressionists. While at Worth's the clothes were made only of brocade —the dresses designed with trains bordered in ermine— Jacques Doucet dressed mostly modern young women—society girls and demimondaines. He was the regular dressmaker of the cocottes, who shared with royalty an immoderate taste for corsets and frills and furbelows.

Doucet was the first dressmaker to hire a designer, a ruined Spanish grandee named de la Pena, whom the seamstresses familiarly called "Pépé."

By 1905, however, everybody was speaking not of Doucet but of the newcomer, Paul Poiret, who had just made a sensational entrance into the silky protected world of high fashion.

Several years later, Jean Cocteau wrote:

"A distinctive stamp has just marked the city's frivolous soul. It is Poiret's stamp. The corsets are being unlaced. The gold of the theater loges no longer frames cocottes encased in armor and dog collars. The duchesses are ready to be dressed, undressed, costumed by Paul Poiret. It means being transformed into Egyptian dancing girls, silk and fur furniture covers, lampshades, an à la mode sultan's harem cushions."

The press covered Poiret with praise. *Le Matin* was the most enthusiastic of the dailies. Misia Edwards, one of the reigning queens of Paris, the wife of the owner, was Poiret's most ardent supporter.

The son of a small fabric dealer whose store, called, optimistically, L'Espérance, was located in the Paris market district, rue des Deux Ecus, Poiret had begun as a shop assistant for an umbrella merchant. But he could not bear the humiliation, the role of petty clerk and workhand. His ambition and his plans for the future went far beyond that.

Thus he set about satisfying his hunger for fame. He called on all the fashion houses—Paquin, Worth, Doucet—to present the models that he designed at home in the evening.

Finally, Doucet noticed the assiduous young man who kept returning with his designs and called him in. Doucet was completely fascinated by the revolutionary sketches Poiret showed him and immediately worked out an arrangement whereby Poiret would work exclusively for him.

Poiret did not stay with Doucet for very long since he was impatient and soon quarreled with his boss. Yet certain aspects of his first employer were not lost on the young Poiret: an extreme sense of refinement, beauty, elegance, and good taste. These qualities made an impression that stayed with Poiret throughout his life.

Poiret next went to work for Worth, where his designs were enthusiastically admired, largely because Poiret sought to adapt a style to the demands of the day (in 1905 that meant, among other things, designing clothes that could be worn either in a car or on a bicycle).

Then, after his stint with Worth, Poiret decided to set up his own house, and, after the failure of two successive installations that taught him the fundamental rules of commerce, he chose finally to move into an eighteenth-century private house on the rue d'Antin, next to the Opéra. He was an immediate and dazzling success.

Poiret was bursting with ideas and projects. When dress

designing was not enough for him, he launched perfumes. The heady scent of his Nuit de Chine and Lucrece Borgia pervaded all the salons. Then he decided to open a school of decorative arts. An innovator, he invented the bar for individual apartments, a feature that became wildly popular and was adopted all over the United States, and the sunken bathtub, often encrusted with precious materials on its sides and bottom (his own bathtub was adorned with gold coins).

A wildly extravagant man, Poiret, for whom nothing could be too luxurious, also had simple tastes and unpretentious friendships. He was a close friend of the painters Derain and Vlaminck, at that time damned and scandalous, and often visited their little cottage on the banks of the Seine at Chatou. He also recognized the talent of Raoul Dufy, the painter with the light and gracious touch in clear, gay colors and hired Dufy to create patterns for fabrics. Poiret was so pleased with what Dufy produced that he set up a factory on the Avenue de Clichy simply to launch Dufy into silk printing Their research into the techniques of painting and chemical acids resulted in the discovery of processes that still are used today.

Within a few years the influence of Poiret was so widespread that he was able to treat the great ladies of the day with supreme arrogance—an attitude demonstrated when the Countess Greffulhe, one of the queens of Parisian elegance and a close friend of King Edward VII of England, came to him for the first time. She chose from the collection a gold-colored sheath edged with sable. Surrounded by a respectful court of fitters and seamstresses, she contemplated herself in the mirror, then, satisfied, said haughtily:

"Poiret, I thought that you knew only how to dress working girls. I didn't know that you were also capable of dressing great ladies!"

"Madame," replied Poiret, "a great Belgian lady [the countess was Belgian] always has something to learn about good taste from the working girls of Paris."

For all the revolution that he was responsible for, Poiret had limitations. Though he began to liberate women from collars and corsets—and thus prepared the way for greater simplification in fashion design—the clothes he designed were a riot of feathers, brilliant fabrics, vertiginous swinging drapings. Rebelling against a sense of economy and discretion, he launched audacity in all its forms: bouffant Turkish trousers, "tiered" dresses, and flow-ery, plumed hats.

Indeed, he is better described as a man of *arrested* revolution. He launched a movement that he was later incapable of control-ling and carrying through to a successful end. In 1906 he aban-doned the corset, in 1908 he cut his mannequins' hair, but some-one else was needed to liberate women more completely from their clothes of yesteryear. Coco Chanel waited in the wings.

As Poiret's popularity soared, Coco, dressed in short skirts and tailored jackets, continued to cut a few dresses for her friends. She read the fashion magazines. She kept her hand in.

While helping out financially so as to balance the budget of her shop, Etienne Balsan, complaining, "My horses cost me enough in themselves," was still skeptical of Coco's plans. But at Royallieu, one man began to take her seriously, one of Etienne's best friends, Arthur Capel, who entered Coco's life in 1904 or 1905. Well-known in Paris, cultivated, distinguished, rich, En-glish, Boy, as Capel was called, had holdings in coal in England. He was an accomplished sportsman, an experienced polo player, and, unlike Etienne, a true playboy. Among other things, Boy was passionate about automobiles, and he drove racing cars that reached the then-breakneck speed of nearly forty miles an hour.

As Boy became more and more seriously involved with Coco, the two friends began to argue about her.

"But you're courting her!" exclaimed Etienne.

"What do you expect when you neglect her so!" answered Boy.

One evening, probably in 1906, the conversation became more serious. In the drawing room at Royallieu, after three glasses of port, Coco announced her desire to open a luxurious fashion boutique where she could reach a more elegant clientele. But she couldn't do it alone. She needed financial help.

"Oh," replied Etienne, offhandedly, "be content with making hats with Paulette and Antoinette!"

Embarrassed, Boy intervened: "Come on, Etienne," he exclaimed in his inimitable English accent. "Coco has brilliant ideas, talent enough and to spare. You mustn't discourage her!"

It was no longer possible to hide the change in affections. Coco and Boy were too close to each other. Etienne, who liked Boy very much (although he railed against the marks that his pomaded hair left on the leather armchairs), understood and was not offended by Boy's love for Coco. He did not try to fight with Boy over her—on the contrary. The transition came about quite naturally around 1907, after Etienne had won a race at Le Tremblay riding his horse Falot and another of his horses had won in Milan, Italy.

Boy and Etienne, celebrating with a bottle of champagne, came to a simple understanding.

"I'm madly in love with Coco," said Capel.

"If she loves you, she's yours," answered Etienne simply.

Coco admitted that she loved Boy. So it goes.

With Etienne Balsan, Chanel had made her first step into the world, the great world. Love did not last long; friendship did. Much later, when Coco was famous, Etienne Balsan never failed to come to see her when he visited Paris. He was like an older brother to her, perhaps the only person who never was overawed by Coco's success.

With Boy Capel, two hearts were on fire together. It was Coco's first taste of love, passionate, lucid, and tender. The tall young man with the tan complexion, who played polo energetically and negotiated business nonchalantly, was the most attentive of lovers. They settled in an apartment facing rue du Faubourg St.-Honoré on one side, Avenue Gabriel on the other side.

A period of intense happiness began for Coco. Boy took her to the Opéra, to Maxim's, or to the Café de Paris every evening. In summer he rented the handsomest suite at the Hotel Normandy in Deauville. The slender little woman, wearing a tiny round hat, always dressed in a navy blue suit with an immaculate white blouse, intrigued the full-blown feathered women of the day. She was often the center of attraction, but never more so than for Boy Capel.

With Boy, Coco became one of the queens of Paris and of all the places where people had fun: Deauville on the Normandy coast and Biarritz on the Basque coast.

A carefree Paris did not dream that a war was in the offing. It remained a pleasure capital where the princes of the western world, English lords, and Russian grand dukes—among them the handsome Dimitri, cousin of the czar—amused themselves. To Coco the frivolity and gaiety were fascinating for a time, but she recognized its lack of substance and never turned her back on her work projects. Social life and horse races were not enough to keep her busy.

Thus it was that, to humor her, Boy Capel eventually offered her a small shop at 21 rue Cambon, two steps from the Ritz, around 1910. It is highly ironic that the lease specified that Coco did not have the right to make dresses there because there was a dressmaker in the building already.

In any case, Coco stuck to hats, and she remained bored, all the more so since the shop did not have much success at the outset.

In her *Memoirs,* Elizabeth de Gramont writes of having been told, in confidence, by Boy, a childhood friend:

" 'I have been very much attached for several years now to Coco Chanel and I am looking for a job for her. I am very busy, and not free in the afternoons. She is alone, she is bored, and that worries me.'

" 'What?' I replied, 'She can't keep busy during the afternoons?'

" 'No. You don't understand how much idleness can weigh on some women, especially when they are intelligent. And Coco is intelligent. You have family, friends, social obligations, charitable works. She has nothing. When she has finished polishing her nails, she has nothing left to do from two to eight; naturally, I don't like the idea of her sitting around with nothing to do. It's incredible how important a role people's daily schedules play in a love affair. One always speaks about the heart; it isn't difficult to make hearts beat in unison, but the hands on two different watches is another problem. I've set her up in a small millinery business, but it hasn't worked out very well. Nevertheless, she is active, she has the qualities necessary for a businesswoman. She's from Auvergne, after all.'

" 'Like Barres,' I replied politely.

" 'She would like to open a sweater and jersey store. We must see about it.' "

In 1912 sweaters and several dresses were added to Coco's hat collection. A second shop, in Deauville, was opened.

Mme Henri Bernstein, widow of the famous playwright whose plays filled the theaters of the Paris boulevards for half a century, recalled several incidents for us:

"I met Chanel before the 1914–1918 war. I don't remember

the exact year—1912 or 1913. In any case, she was a very young woman, perhaps thirty, physically really charming. Deauville was having a renewed success. Chanel had opened a shop where she sold hats on the rue Gontaut-Biron.

"My mother and I often went to Deauville; that is how I met Chanel. It amused me to look at what she had in her shop. Then in Paris I went to see her. In the beginning our relations were purely professional and commercial. It is only after the war that we became fond of each other."

Mme Montezin, who began with Chanel when she was a slip of a girl and who today, a distinguished lady with white hair and very blue eyes, makes the cloaks for the Chanel fashion house, gives us some idea of what life at the House of Chanel was like in the beginning:

"Everything I know, I learned from Mademoiselle. I was almost a child when I went to work for her in 1912. After a period of training at Charlotte Enard's, rue Vignon [the most famous milliner of the day: Chanel first met her when she bought hats at Charlotte Enard's shop], Chanel set up on her own on the first floor of 21 rue Cambon. She hired a forewoman, Lucienne, who later made the worldwide reputation of Caroline Reboux. Mademoiselle already knew how to choose her collaborators, and if she didn't know how or didn't want to use a needle, she possessed the art of giving orders and directing an establishment.

"Always the first to arrive and the last to leave, she ruled over the salon and the two large workshops in which she employed forty or so people. Difficult but just, Mademoiselle was horrified by mediocrity.

"Her sister, Antoinette, who had at least as much charm as Coco, was responsible for the showroom and received the customers. She was very gay and loved to sing."

During this period, Coco's relations with Boy Capel, which remained as passionate as ever, evolved in another direction: Boy became Coco's silent business partner, doing justice to his criticism of Balsan. It was partly thanks to his money that Coco became successful so rapidly. But that is not the full explanation for her success. Coco's hats appeared at the right moment. Their conception derived from a general reaction against the hats that the elegant women of the day were rigged out in: "Grotesque hats decorated with all the fruits of the horn of plenty and weighing more than half a pound." She was resolved to "rid women of their frills from head to toe, for each frill discarded makes her look younger."

Her first collection, presented in Deauville in the late summer of 1914, was a success, a revolution. But it did not cause much ado, despite the fact that it was attended by such social figures as the Rothschilds and Cécile Sorel, because the roar of the cannons captured almost everyone's attention.

July 1914. Europe was going up in flames. Boy was mobilized.

In her shop in Deauville, Coco waited. She liberated women's heads, but their bodies remained enclosed in corsets or bundled up stiffly in Poiret's Turkish creations.

At the outbreak of the war, Coco was a rather famous *modiste,* highly thought of in social circles, but not cited by name in the fashion magazines, *Minerva* and *Femina.* That last matter would soon change.

After Etienne Balsan and Boy Capel, Coco was to have her third stroke of luck: the war.

3.
The Opportunity of War

P<small>ARIS</small> in six weeks!" The streets of Berlin echoed with the cry as flower-bedecked soldiers left for the front.

"To Berlin!" shouted newly mobilized young Frenchmen saying goodbye to their families at the Gare de l'Est in Paris.

Both capitals were filled with a holiday air, for all were unanimous in their forecast of the days to come: the war would be short, three months at the most. But the war was not destined to be short. A world was about to founder, and almost no one seemed to realize it.

Women, eager to help, rushed to the Red Cross centers. They donned nurses' smocks over their shortened, frilly dresses, always managing to look hurried and busy. The first wounded were looked after with devotion; soon every charitable organization had gone "military." The cream of the Bottin Mondain, the French Social Register, devoted every afternoon to rolling bandages.

France's entry into the war in early August 1914 put an end to all theatrical activity in Paris. The theaters had presented a brilliant season that had included Paul Claudel's *L'Otage* at l'Oeuvre, *La Pèlerine Ecossaise* by Sacha Guitry at the Bouffes Parisiens, and *La Belle Aventure* by de Flers and Caillavet at the Vaudeville. The Opéra-Comique had presented *Mârouf* by Rabaud, and the Ballets Russes Rimski-Korsakov's *Le Coq d'or*.

Paul Bourget had just published *Le Démon de Midi* and Anatole France *Le Révolte des Anges*. Things to come would be different.

In Deauville, where she had moved, Coco's latest creations in hats—supremely original in their simplicity—were admired by the elegant ladies of Paris who deserted the soon-threatened capital. Her attention to detail always hit the mark.

But there was a war on. French couture could do no less than any other: it, too, did its duty and contributed to the war effort. Coco, like many other women, became a volunteer nurse, and the back of her shop became a meeting hall. Poiret set an example. He converted his delivery trucks into ambulances, one of which was driven by his designer, the painter Paul Iribe, always accompanied by Misia Edwards, swathed in a magnificent nurse's uniform especially designed for her by the illustrious couturier.

Misia, as the war began, was queen of the Paris literary and artistic world and empress of the Ballets Russes, which in 1913 had scandalized France with Stravinsky's *The Rite of Spring*. In her wake followed a young protégé who was soon to be very much talked about in the worlds of art and literature. Writer, painter, decorator, composer, discoverer of unknowns, and destroyer of the famous, Jean Cocteau was to orchestrate an era rich in talents.

Old enough to be mobilized, yet declared unfit for military service, Cocteau finagled his way into the medical corps. At the front lines he picked up the wounded, accompanied by an aristocrat well known to Paris society, of which he had already become an indefatigable leader: Count Etienne de Beaumont, later put in charge of this strange fleet of ambulances.

One evening after an exhausting day, Cocteau and Beaumont found rooms in an inn where the British staff and its commanding officer, Sir Douglas Haig, had installed themselves. That night a group of grave-looking British officers were sitting in the drawing room when suddenly shells were heard exploding nearby. This startling occurrence was soon followed by a tremendous crash on the staircase. In stupefaction, the officers watched two terrified men come tumbling down the stairs: Cocteau, dressed in a pink nightgown, and Etienne de Beaumont in sumptuous black pajamas. Both were wearing gold ankle bracelets.

Misia, Jean Cocteau, Iribe, Beaumont—such people would soon become part of Coco's world. She stood on the verge of achieving complete success.

1915. Along the front lines, the belligerents buried themselves in trenches.

In the world of fashion, tired of sewing on buttons in one of the commissariat's warehouses, Paul Poiret, whose superiors had forbidden him to wear the uniform he had designed for himself —a blue suit, blue silk shirt, and a tie displaying a nude woman —decided to devote his services to the defense of the nation. His new design for a military overcoat saved four hours of labor and nearly a yard of fabric. He became the chief of wartime France's military tailors.

In Paris social life resumed, under the cover of charity galas. Theaters reopened; devotion to good causes flagged. While the war raged along the battle lines, the home front began to enjoy itself again.

Coco, tired of rolling bandages, often left Deauville to join Boy Capel in Paris. Upon occasion she left with him for Biarritz, where, far from the front, society took refuge.

Having first been a liaison officer for the British army on the Ardennes front, Boy Capel was now on detached service, not coincidentally making a fortune by supplying France with coal. The Duchess of Gramont met him at the time:

"During the war I ran into one of my old childhood friends in the home of a famous hostess. After dinner, the guests, all important persons, conversed about the belligerent armies, the supply services, transportation, and freight. Arthur Capel, known as Boy, owned coal mines in England and had contracts with several French companies. The war brought out his abilities as a businessman. By 1916 coal was so scarce that it had become an overriding preoccupation. Capel, for whom Clemenceau had developed a great affection, became the man on whom the coal supply depended. He always managed to assure the timely arrival of boats loaded with coal. Sitting at one end of the sofa, we had a friendly chat.

" 'Are you happy?' he asked me. This sort of question is

usually a prelude to intimate conversation. I answered that it was impossible to be happy during a war but that if the war didn't exist, I would have no reason to complain."

The war went on monotonously even for those engaged in battle. In the cities, Paris, Deauville, and Biarritz, a slow evolution could be felt in women's manner of dress. Left to themselves, women adopted simpler clothes. They had to work, to get around easily. None of the couturiers, many of whom had gone off to the war, were able to grasp this new trend—except for Coco.

Now in her early thirties, she had never stopped observing everything around her, her strangely serious eyes glancing at the frivolity of the world that surrounded her.

"Those who anticipate the future," wrote Elizabeth de Gramont, again in her *Memoirs,* "succeed. Our discerning Auvergnate foresaw that women were about to become more sporty. Her little hat shop may not have been very profitable, but the back room, where society ladies came to chat between social engagements, was always busy. In her conversations with these ladies Coco realized that they would be needing knitted wool or silk outfits."

Coco, who had begun to tire of hats, discovered jersey, out of which she had already made sweaters. Next she made skirts, not by accident, but by vocation.

In 1915 Coco officially went into couture. Her medium was jersey—a dressmaking material that she could work with at 21 rue Cambon. Her lease forbade her making dresses, but jersey was not considered a fabric.

Coco also opened a shop in Biarritz that year. An old lady, retired in Anglet in the Basque country, remembers. It was July 1, 1915. Mme Deray was twenty-one years old:

"My family lived in Bordeaux, and at the time I was on holiday in Bayonne. I was looking for work in couture, which is not always very easy to come by in the provinces. My parents did not want me to go too far away from them. In those days"—Mme Deray's smile erased the wrinkles on her face—"a young girl did not 'go up' to Paris. I heard that a Parisian was opening a boutique in Biarritz, so I went there.

"Mademoiselle Chanel was not there. There was her sister, Antoinette Chanel, and another lady. I was hired and I became one of the mainstays of the firm.

"We immediately enjoyed a great success. Soon I had about sixty workwomen under me. I worked for very famous women who were often friends of Chanel, such as Marthe Davelli, an opera singer of the time. All these ladies gave her a lot of publicity.

"In the beginning we worked only in jersey. No one before her had ever dared make dresses out of this type of wool fabric. An important manufacturer, Jean Rodier, proposed to her that she use his materials. She accepted.

"For us it represented a real *tour de force,* for jerseys were badly woven in those days. The 'diagonals' went any which way, and work had to be started over several times—especially since Mademoiselle demanded perfection! When a fitting did not go well, she flew into terrible rages. She loved to enrage people. Believe me, I often cried in those days. She was hard, even ruthless, with her employees.

"But what she made was sensational, of unparalleled simplicity and chic, and so different from Poiret and Madeleine Vionnet.*

"To be sure, she was given a great deal of help—industrialists from Tours,** a man who used to come often to Biarritz to see her [Boy Capel] and Baroness Henri de Rothschild, who brought her most of her customers.

"Mademoiselle Chanel had audacity and incredible nerve, especially since she was more of a milliner and knew very little about dressmaking. But she had innate taste and knew how to explain things to others.

"She chose everything: laces, ornaments, colors. She always chose the most beautiful tones among all the different pastel shades that the Lyon and Scottish dyers could produce in silk and wool. Our workrooms were like fairyland, a veritable rainbow.

"We sold a great deal in Spain—San Sebastian, Bilbao, Madrid—wherever there were elegant women and money.

"Soon she sent me to Paris. She had just moved into 31 rue

---

*A famous dress designer of the beginning of the century, Madeleine Vionnet, who had prodigious technical ability (she was known as the "Sorceress"), revolutionized work methods by inventing a way to sew fabrics on the bias. She celebrated her ninetieth birthday in 1971.

**Most probably Etienne Balsan and his brothers, who, we should not forget, were in the textile industry.

Cambon. I was in charge of a workshop where sixty people worked on clothes for Spain alone. The entire court ordered from me. These ladies bought dresses by the dozen—in Paris it was wartime and one did not always have enough to eat. Soon I was one of five forewomen."

Five forewomen meant five workrooms. By 1917 Coco headed a prosperous business—an astounding success, prodigious if one remembers that in 1914 she had only two very modest hat shops, logical if one remembers the exceptional conditions and how cleverly she managed to take advantage of them.

In choosing Biarritz she knew she would be able to annex Spain, where much of society was taking refuge, as a market.

"Oh! she was intelligent," continued Mme Deray. "And ambitious! She had gotten the most out of the people who were around her. She never gave a compliment but held on to us through our devotion to our work . . . or through our sense of duty.

"I remember, it was in 1917. Paris was being bombarded by German long-range guns or by zeppelins. My family, very worried, wanted me to come back to Bordeaux. I went to see Chanel.

" 'Mademoiselle, I am terribly sorry, but I must leave you. My family wants me to come home.'

"She let me talk, then took me into the large showroom full of saleswomen and said to me:

" 'Marie-Louise, you are patriotic. You have no right to leave Paris. What would become of your coworkers?'

"She was leaning against the mantelpiece in a very theatrical stance. For the first time her tone of voice was gentle, almost angelic. It was the tone she reserved for her best customers. Her eyes, usually so hard, were like velvet. She sensed that I was weakening. Her voice suddenly became much harder:

" 'You will go and see your family and tell them that your place is here.'

"I had been 'had' by her. I came back.

"Yet she had never shown me the least kindness. Indeed, she took a certain pleasure in torturing those who worked for her.

"I remember . . . a few days after settling in Paris . . . I did not know the city at all. One evening, late, around nine o'clock, I had just finished a dress for Marthe Davelli. It was a beautiful chiffon dress that Mlle Davelli was to wear that night. She had insisted to Mademoiselle that the dress be delivered to her by me, as she wanted me to help her get into it. When the dress was ready, Mademoiselle, instead of telling me to take a taxi or having me accompanied by one of the errand boys who sat around the hall twiddling their thumbs, simply snapped: 'That girl has to learn to fend for herself. Show her the subway entrance.'

"I got lost and arrived very late. Marthe Davelli was furious. Fortunately the dress was beautiful. That calmed her down.

"Mademoiselle never set foot in the workrooms. She would call us together to tell us what she wanted after she had chosen the fabrics. Though very imperious, she had trouble expressing her wishes, for she lacked the necessary craftsmanship; this hampered her when she talked, despite her authoritative tone.

"So naturally she did not always obtain the results she wanted. Scenes and unpleasant remarks ensued. In fact, she wanted to prove that she was the boss. In spite of her innate taste and flair, she did not have much technique.

"Yet her method must have had something good to it, since we made such admirable things—in jersey, of course, but also in cotton fabrics. Partly through her influence, the straight tunic with a large satin belt worn below the hip began to be in fashion.

"During the war she herself wore large jersey coats, quite long and of a school-girl simplicity. She was extraordinarily chic.

"You should have seen her, getting out of her Rolls-Royce in front of the firm on the stroke of noon—for she had quickly acquired a Rolls with a chauffeur and footman. She was a queen! She would stay until two or three o'clock, even later if she had famous customers. Then she retired to her drawing room, where she entertained a great deal.

"In spite of the war . . ." Mme Deray added.

Mme Deray, Coco's early associate, would have nothing of the legend that Chanel had gone into couture by chance, inspired by a sudden whim. Although anecdotes alone cannot explain Coco's fantastic success, no matter how good they are, this story, characteristic of Coco, was told by Mme Deray:

"One afternoon in Deauville when a freezing wind was blowing from the Channel, she put on a polo player's sweater. Since it was too big for her, she tightened her belt around it and pushed up the sleeves. Back at the hotel, looking at herself in a mirror, she realized that such a sweater made to her measurements would be very becoming. She had some made and put several of them on sale in her shop. They were snapped up immediately, which proved to her that she was perfectly capable of doing something else besides hats."

The story had variations: the polo player sometimes became a jockey, the sweater a sailor's coat. Or Coco would claim she had simply adapted the English blazer of her nephew André Palasse, whom she had adopted after her sister Julia's death, and whom she had put in a boarding school in England, the Beaumont College, run by Jesuits.

No matter, Coco's rapid success cannot be explained merely by the chance occurrence of a puff of wind. Her entrance into couture was a deliberate, well-thought-out enterprise. Rich friends ready to help her, jersey, the war: all these circumstances Coco exploited to the utmost, following a plan conceived by someone intelligent enough to perceive the tendencies of an epoch and the underlying trends of the present.

The ten years of "hats," during which she observed women and assimilated the futile but complex mechanism of that fleeting phenomenon called fashion, were followed in just two years by the establishment of a couture house. Her fashion house became successful—and Coco's success permanently assured—because she realized that the one final and necessary ingredient, one she set out deliberately to acquire, was status as a celebrity. She had to acquire the social position without which a fashionable couturière cannot exist. She did it in her own way, preferring future glories to those of the present.

And the key to such status was a more than passing acquaintance with such society figures as Misia Edwards, Jean Cocteau, the Count de Beaumont, and Serge Diaghilev, the producer of the Ballets Russes.

One cannot fully understand the reasons behind Coco's success—nor why she was more than just a couturière—without knowing something about the celebrities who occupied such an important place in her life.

Misia Edwards was preeminent.

Throughout the history of French literature and art there appears, from time to time, a woman—Mme de Rambouillet in the seventeenth century, Mlle de Lespinasse in the eighteenth—who, without writing or painting, and with nothing more than her powers of seduction and conversation, inspires revolutions. Marvelous hostesses, often rich, these women possess access to the worlds of creativity and beauty. The talented flock to meet each other in these women's drawing rooms and theater boxes, and from these encounters schools and new art forms are born. These women are more than patronesses of the arts; they themselves are prodigious sources of inspiration.

Such was Misia, and no major artist or writer at the beginning of the twentieth century failed to be touched by her influence.

In museums and private collections are found several portraits of a ravishing blonde woman with a lovely pink complexion; sometimes the portrait is that of Mme Thaddée Natanson, sometimes Mme Edwards, Mme Sert. They bear the signatures of Toulouse-Lautrec, Renoir, who did several portraits of her, Bonnard, Vuillard, Sert, Picasso, Dali. They are all portraits of the same women: Misia Godbeska, born in St. Petersburg to a family of Polish origin for whom the most important thing was the development of cultural taste.

Misia loved money and was not embarrassed about her love. She married successively two fat, bearded, rich men.

First she married the banker Thaddée Natanson, who founded the *Revue Blanche,* the magazine of the Belle Epoque. Thus Misia came into contact with all the important people of the epoch: Stéphane Mallarmé, her friend, wrote poetry for her. The poet Saint-John Perse wrote her a love letter, which she received a year later, the letter having gone around the world. She was one of the first to recognize the genius of Vincent van Gogh. Grieg, Debussy, and Stravinsky played for her; Ibsen corresponded with her.

Then, under rather mysterious circumstances, she married the wealthy M Edwards, director of the newspaper *Le Matin.* While cruising on the Rhine on his yacht with Edwards and his wife, the actress Lanthelme, the latter disappeared. She was found drowned a few days later. Later, when Misia and Edwards got married, people gossiped about the incident.

Paul Morand, the diplomat and author, in his *Venises*, has drawn an amazingly apt portrait of Misia:

"Misia was all of these: bubbling with joy or fury, original, given to borrowing, harvester of geniuses, all of them in love with her—Vuillard, Bonnard, Renoir, Stravinsky, Picasso—

collector of hearts and of pink quartz Ming trees, she indulged her whims, which were promptly . . . exploited by the decorators, talked about in the newspapers, and copied by empty-headed society ladies. Misia, queen of modern baroque . . . Misia, artful and pouting, gathering around her friends who do not know each other, in order, as Proust said, 'all the better to incite them to quarrels later on.'

"Brilliant in perfidy, refined in cruelty, Misia, of whom Philippe Berthelot said it was best not to entrust to her what one loves. 'Here comes the cat, hide your birds,' he used to admonish whenever she rang his doorbell.

"She inspired genius, as some kings know how to produce conquerors, with the vibrancy of her being, with an almost invisible tap of her wand. Misia, strong as the life she breathed, avaricious, generous, devourer of millions, cajoler, scamp, subtle, businesslike, appraising and scorning people at a glance. Misia of symbolist Paris, of fauve Paris, of wartime Paris, of Versailles Peace Treaty Paris, of Paris in Venice. Misia, as comfortable as a sofa, but if you craved rest, that sofa would land you in hell. Unsatisfied Misia, whose piercing eyes were still laughing while her mouth was already drawn into a pout.

"With this oversated glutton, disgust followed rapture, no followed yes as thunder comes after lightning; with Misia you had to make it quick."

When Misia spread her protective wings over Coco, who had known nothing but the superficial side of the bourgeois and aristocratic worlds, a new dimension opened up: that of intelligence and sensibility, of art and culture. Before Misia took her under her wing, all of Coco's energy had been sacrificed to her ambition: to get to the top. She had almost succeeded; better still, she had acquired a certain polish. But if her education permitted her to perform honorably in a drawing room, she was still a poorly cultivated woman without great competence in the arts. Thus she willingly put herself in Misia's hands and accepted—for a while —her spiritual and moral guidance.

The two women met around 1917 and entered into a very complex friendship: passionate, not without jealousy and violent quarrels, yet deeply intimate and marked by great loyalty.

Misia, it seems, was the only person to whom the proud Coco ever gave in, the only one whose criticisms she ever accepted to the point of behaving like an obedient little girl. Coco accepted everything without a word and with lowered head, allowing Misia—some say she was ferocious when she wanted to be—to humiliate her in front of others whenever Coco clearly got out of her depth in the intellectual circles Misia frequented and felt at home in.

Misia had a strange power over her, and Coco endured what in others she found intolerable because Misia fascinated her and because she *needed* Misia, her connections, her influence. Misia could promote the reputation of any courturier; she had done as much for Poiret. Misia opened up the worlds of music, art, letters.

1917. The war dragged on. On the front, the new French command launched a carefully planned offensive in the face of opposition from some quarters. Three weeks later the French army had lost a hundred thousand men.

In the rear Mistinguett sang in English for the recently arrived American troops waiting to be thrown into the battle. In all the music halls the girls kicked their legs high, vowing death to the *sales boches* and promising to be true to their *poi-poi,* the glorious poilus.

French society ladies' ardor for caring for the wounded cooled somewhat, but they were replaced by American women, who came in ever greater numbers to France.

On May 18 Coco, practically invisible in the wake of a radiant Misia, attended the première at the Châtelet of a "cubist ballet," *Parade.* The tickets had been sold out two weeks before. Paris yearned to have fun, to see Diaghilev's Ballets Russes once again.

Before the war Paris had been assaulted by this fantastic company, which completely overthrew the esthetics of choreography and ushered in the era of modern ballet. Before Serge Diaghilev, ballet music was left in the hands of paid composers, decor and costume to workmen without talent; with him ballet became an artistic spectacle. Great poets, painters, and composers of genius gathered around him: Cocteau, Stravinsky, Ravel, Poulenc, Auric, Milhaud, Picasso, Matisse, Utrillo, Braque, Derain. He discovered great choreographers such as Massine, Balanchine, and Lifar.

In 1913 the Ballets had caused a scandal with the première of *The Rite of Spring.* In spite of the support and enthusiasm of

Countess Greffulhe, Countess de Chevigné, Henri de Rothschild, and the Aga Khan—madly in love at the time with star ballerina Tamara Karsavina—in spite of the prodigious leaps of Nijinski and the magnificence of Stravinsky's music, the Ballets Russes went too much against the grain of habit and were accepted only by worldly esthetes.

At the head of this group was the incomparable Misia. A tiara on her head, Misia always presided over the company's premières, joking with and greeting the artists. At *Parade,* an intimidated Coco hovered by her side; at thirty-four Chanel looked like a debutante.

Parade had a dazzling playbill. Decor: Picasso, already at the height of his glory; argument: Cocteau, who threw himself into ballet, as he did with everything else, in a frenzied way; music: Erik Satie, the future leader of *Les Six*—Darius Milhaud, Georges Auric, Germaine Tailleferre, Francis Poulenc, Arthur Honegger, and Louis Durey—who were to revolutionize music.

Scanning the audience through his monocle, disdainful of staring eyes, the real animator of the Ballet waited for the curtain to rise: Serge Diaghilev, the focus of Coco's major artistic patrons.

Paul Morand described him thus:

"His secret lay in the fact that he thought only of pleasing himself, seeking approval from scarcely a dozen friends, Picasso, Stravinsky, Misia. . . . He was totally indifferent to the tastes of the times, always in the forefront and never saving a penny. Only sleepwalking could explain his boldness, his way of ignoring obstacles, his mad improvisations.

"I look back on Serge and his destiny, revolutionary and classic; he was a master of monsters, descending on Paris to scatter his Muscovite seed—painting, music, then song and dance.

"Diaghilev wanders through my past like a stag in a forest. I knew him in triumph and met him again in Spain living in misery; I never knew him rich. He was undaunted by catcalls, full of an old-world courtesy that was occasionally marred by tantrums when some drama occurred in the seraglio. Beneath the Russian a Chinese always dozed . . . triumphs, ruin, debts . . . cosmopolitan in appearance, but Russian in his soul . . . playing Nijinski against Fokine, Lifar against Massine, in a tempest of champagne, delirious telegrams, gastronomic feasts or dried bread, with promises of happiness and threats of suicide, and to cap it all, suffering from a mortal case of diabetes, which he treated with forbidden dishes . . . such was Serge, the tormented torturer. . . .

"I saw Diaghilev when he resettled in Paris. He had already found time to look over the new painters, choosing the best without ever making a mistake, never allowing a source to run dry."

In Misia's loge, Diaghilev smiled and talked only to Misia herself, his savior of the Ballets, that bottomless pit into which patrons sank fortunes. Misia, who loved money, was open-hearted in her support of artists and writers. A few years earlier, on the night of a dress rehearsal, the door of her loge had opened to reveal Diaghilev, pale with anxiety. He rushed over to her:

"Quickly, Misia, do you have four thousand francs?" he asked.

"Not here, but at home, yes. Why?"

"The costumer refuses to leave the costumes until he's paid. It's awful! He says that he is not going to be had again and that he will leave with all his stuff if he isn't paid immediately!"

Misia sped home. Ten minutes later, the costumer was paid and the curtain rose, after an adventure that typified the life, on a daily basis, of the Ballets Russes.

Later Coco said of the première of *Parade*: "That night he gave me a glacial stare and barely greeted me. And I had right to this honor only because I was with Misia." For Diaghilev, Coco was still just another slightly snobbish young society woman. But for her it was a start.

Indeed, an indication of how far Coco had come was that later that night, she dined at Weber, the restaurant where all faithful fans of the Ballets Russes gathered after the show. She sat with Misia, Picasso, Stravinsky, and Jean Cocteau, who got up from time to time to dance on the tables.

She kept quiet and listened, fascinated, to these men who, in contrast to Coco's other friends, evoked in their conversations things other than women, horses, and money. Did she foresee that they were already part of her future? That soon they were to beat a path to her drawing room?

Misia pointed out to her a man whom the gay company had greeted on entering. He apologized for not being able to join them and sat apart, shaken from time to time by coughing fits. A pale and sickly man—his neck snuggly wrapped in a white scarf, his cheeks looking blue through a badly shaven stubble—he sat and wrote as he ate a chocolate Bavarian cream.

"Take a good look at that man," Misia said to Coco. "He is very ill. He is only waiting to finish his work before dying. Then everyone will realize that he has been the greatest writer France has produced in a long time. His name is Marcel Proust, and he had to pay for his first book to be published. André Gide, that pharisee of vice, turned it down."

The next day Proust visited Cocteau and had him describe for him the première of *Parade*. He had his friends tell him every little detail, including how the women were dressed. Perhaps a few of these details helped enrich one of the silhouettes that haunt the thousands of pages of *Remembrance of Things Past*.

Much later Coco said: "I often used to see Proust at the Ritz, where he came after having telephoned to ask that the maître d'hôtel close all doors and windows before his arrival, for he despised drafts. He would greet me from afar. I never dared to invite him to join me for fear of being refused. After drinking his chocolate, he would disappear up the staircase. It was a long time after his death* that I found out that he used to go up to the garret room of one of the servants whom he paid to note down, hour after hour, the names of all clients, what they ate, how they were dressed."

When Proust became famous, shortly after the war, everyone played the game of portraits. Who was this or that hero? Proust still came to the Ritz, more distant and absentminded than ever, or so it seemed. As soon as he sat down, a very curious phenomenon occurred: everyone shifted attitudes, sat up straighter, as though each wished to be seen at his very best by the ashen-faced author, both fearing and hoping to be taken as a model for one of his characters.

"As for me," Coco added, laughing, "I read and reread *Remembrance of Things Past*, and I am very vexed that my presence near him at the Ritz or at Larue's never inspired him."

If she didn't know Proust well, she was still moving up—an ascent measured, perhaps, by the fact that in 1922 it was she,

---

*Marcel Proust died in 1922, a few days after putting the final touches to his *Remembrance of Things Past*. The Prix Goncourt, France's major literary prize, awarded him in 1919, made him widely known.

and not Misia, to whom Diaghilev was, as usual, appealing and who secretly bailed out the Ballets Russes.

1918. For Coco, the last year of the war had a festive air. In Paris, everyone felt the armistice to be close at hand. Victory was assured, despite the collapse of the Russian front; American strength increased daily. American officers took the place of the aviators in the hearts of women.

In Paris, bread rations decreased to three hundred grams, but at Maxim's and Larue's champagne continued to flow.

An ambulance driver was gravely wounded on the Italian front; his name was Hemingway. Joyce published *Ulysses*, Charlie Chaplin made *A Dog's Life*, and Igor Stravinsky composed *Story of a Soldier*. Le Casino de Paris put on *Pa-Ri-Ki-Ri*, starring Mistinguett and Maurice Chevalier.

Coco watched her couture house grow. By the end of the war she had eight workrooms. Completely wrapped up in her new friends, Misia, Cocteau, and Picasso, she slowly drifted apart from Boy Capel, who sometimes spent his leaves away from Coco's apartment on the Quai de Billy.

Mme Bernstein visited Coco's apartment at the time:

"It was quite small and unpretentious, but there was a room that served as a dressing room. The walls were entirely covered with mirrors, and there was a sofa bed in the room. One day my curiosity got the better of me and I asked Coco what she used the bed for.

" 'When I am tired and depressed I stretch out on it. Since I can see myself in all the mirrors and since I can't stand my face when I'm depressed, I immediately cheer up.' "

For Boy, as for Coco, the war had not been disadvantageous. He had increased his fortune considerably. He was still alive, which he had never doubted would be the case. A member of a theosophical society, he had once predicted to Coco: "I know my destiny. I shall die a violent death; it will not be in war. . . ." But in Coco's eyes Boy had lost a great deal of his charm. This rich industrialist, sporting and distinguished, belonged to a world that had begun to seem rather insipid to Coco.

And then there were the other people hovering around Coco.

Stravinsky fell in love with her. He gave her an old Russian icon, which followed Coco throughout her life. She kept it on her bedside table. Was theirs a shared passion? Neither one ever told anyone. At times Picasso's jet-black glance fell on her. But Picasso married one of the ballerinas of the Ballets Russes, the very distinguished and middle-class Olga Khoklova, daughter of a general of the czar. He gave up his bohemian life, his pipes, his cycling shoes, his pullovers with holes in the sleeves, and bought a dinner jacket. In short, he entered upon his bourgeois period.

Coco felt the time had come to break with Boy, and the latter prepared to marry a young Englishwoman, Diana Lister, then twenty-five years old.

Mme Bernstein recounted to us:

"Boy was an extremely attractive young man and had many women in his life. Chanel knew it, and she also knew, for she was an intelligent woman, that he probably would never marry her. And this, by some sort of devious logic, gave her the idea of pushing Boy into marrying a little English girl, with whom he was rather unhappy. Chanel knew how insignificant the girl was and doubtless thought she would be able to keep a certain hold on Boy. It did not happen quite that way; Boy did indeed come regularly to see Chanel, but only to tell her his troubles. This bored Chanel to the nth degree and she did not know how to get rid of him."

As the war came to an end, the Russian Revolution thrilled some and frightened others. It also caused a certain disorder in the Ballets Russes, which split up into "reds" and "whites." For Coco a page turned; with the war coming to an end, fashion would again be excusable. Another battle was about to begin. Already, on the haute couture front, she was feverishly preparing her models. The other houses were about to reopen. Poiret was thinking about his next collection.

On November 11, an anonymous bugler at the front blew a call that was soon taken up by thousands of others. An uncanny and unaccustomed silence spread across the regions where for four years, day after day, the sounds of the cannon had thundered into a sky devoid of birds, tolling off every second of the long ordeal. A tremendous noise arose from the trenches. Millions of men were able to view their surroundings from their full height for the first time in four years.

In Paris all was joy and happiness—except for Coco's friends. One of them had died in his bed of a simple case of grippe, one of the greatest, the poet Guillaume Appollinaire.

On November 13, his funeral was held at the Church of Saint Thomas d'Aquin, and Coco followed the cortege to the Père Lachaise cemetery, passing the garlands and lanterns of the victory celebrations on the way. She walked along only a few steps away from one of Appollinaire's great friends, the yet unrecognized poet Pierre Reverdy. It was an omen of things to come.

4.

The Crazy Years

T HE pulse of the world was beating perceptibly in Paris," said Maurice Sachs about the post-World War I years. It was an incredible era, one that would not be seen again, a sudden explosion of all the forces that had survived the massacre. There was a hunger for glory, pleasure, creation in the rediscovered joy of being alive.

Amid the drama of empires giving way and of triumphant revolutions, France and the West had learned from Paul Valéry that "civilizations are mortal." Almost without regret, humanity allowed the old universe to slide into its tomb. A new world was needed to replace that which had died in the war.

In the East, still lyrically capable of nursing extravagant hopes, the Soviet revolution fired poets and artists with enthusiasm. Meyerhold invented the modern theater; Eisenstein turned films into a true art form; and Maiakovsky brought a new vigor to poetry. Before Stalinism, with its grayish realism and repressive attitudes, buried these wild illusions, there was joy and wild passion.

Paris, too, recovered its position as the center of the world of mind and spirit. Paris, capital of a France victorious—at the cost of over a million dead—became a mecca for all those who wrote, painted, composed, sculpted. They came together in Paris and delighted in participating in the festivities of a new-found peace and in the birth of a new world. Never before had there been so wonderfully amusing an era; never had there been so much artistic creation; never had life been so free, so gay, so optimistic. They met in artists' studios and in new cafés; the most famous stars enlivened evening parties, and, in a sparkling whirl-wind of brilliant conversation, music, and light, Parisian society forgot the black years.

New tendencies began to surface as an aftermath of the war. The need for something else, for something new and original in painting, literature, music, and fashion, which had heretofore been felt only by a few rare prophets, now became the essential craving of a majority of the creators who were forming the substance of a new era. Buried under the debris of past turmoil and torment, the old customs and habits were no longer obstacles to the spread of new ideas and forces. Everything began to change: the way of thinking, the way of looking, the way of writing, painting, listening. Life suddenly became transformed so that even the most everyday acts, loving, speaking, and dressing, were affected. The new forms created in Paris spread throughout the world, and the twentieth century was born.

The painters were Picasso, Modigliani, Foujita, Soutine, Derain, Vlaminck, Dufy, Braque, Marcoussis, Laurencin, Dali. The dancers had Diaghilev and his ballet stars—Nijinski, Balanchine, Massine, and, later, Serge Lifar. The writers and poets included Gide, Cocteau, Desnos, Proust, Radiguet, as well as dadaist and surrealist poets such as Tristan Tsara, Louis Aragon, and André Breton. The musicians were Maurice Ravel, Georges Auric, Erik Satie, Igor Stravinsky, and Arthur Honegger. In architecture Le Corbusier appeared. All of these people, in varying degrees and in different domains, gave face and form to the new world that was just beginning to blossom.

On the surface, all this new-found creativity might seem far removed from Coco's world, but that was not the way it was. In order to understand her special kind of genius, one must see her in the context of the world over which she sought to extend her empire. Among the innovators, she had her place and her role—to change the way people dressed, to give people a new silhou-ette. She came to know closely practically all of the artists of her time, and she was one of those who were busy creating a new world in the face of lingering and tenacious past values. She un-derstood the words of the new creators, the friendships that united them, the hates that tore them apart, the signs by which they recognized each other as belonging to the same tribe.

Possessing no other culture than her own, no other fortune than that of her friends and lovers (her personal fortune was still small, practically nonexistent), Coco possessed true wealth: the genius necessary to acquire access to the world stammering into existence.

Like actresses, fashion designers generally leave only a fleeting memory, unless they become a symbol and their influence goes beyond the sophisticated and futile little world of fashion. Coco's influence went even further.

"Chanel created a feminine personage whose example had never been seen in Paris before her," wrote the strange Maurice Sachs, one of the most brilliant chroniclers of this epoch, whose work *The Decade of Illusions* remains the best description of this period. A self-opinionated parasite, always on the lookout for an invitation, striving to worm his way into "society" (he succeeded at Coco's), never balking at having to wheel and deal to force open the doors of elegant salons, Maurice Sachs devoted twenty or so pages of his book to Coco Chanel. He gives the following portrait of Coco:

"I had the pleasure of knowing her at the moment when her fame was best established, when nothing stood in the way of the superb workings of her will, when she was bursting with temporal and spiritual power, when it seemed as though Paris obeyed her least desire.

"When she appeared, her small size was surprising. She was very thin. Her hair was black and thick, her eyebrows met, she had a smiling mouth and hard, sparkling eyes. She was almost always dressed in the same way, very simply, usually in black. She put her hands in her pockets and began to talk. Her delivery was extraordinarily rapid and stacatto. But her mind developed its logical conclusion. Unlike so many other women, she was not full of fantasy and illogicality in her reasoning and so her conversation was clear and concise. She did not give the impression of wool-gathering, nor was she deflected from her main theme onto incidental subjects which would keep her idea from arriving anywhere.

"Two different qualities came to light in her—one due to her peasant extraction, the other to her femininity. The first caused her to be attentive when listening to brilliant men, as though, trained in the fields of her childhood, she were waiting until the winds brought her the familiar sounds by which she could get her bearings. The second caused her to be imitative (which is an important sign of femininity) and to make use of what she found pleasing in others. . . ."

Mme Henri Bernstein had known a more relaxed Coco: "We became real friends immediately after the 1914 war. Chanel had bought a small house at Garches, behind the St. Cloud golf course, and as my husband and I also had a small place there, we were neighbors.

"Chanel had baptized her house Noix de Coco ["Coconut"], I remember. She had it painted completely in beige, her favorite color.

"And then we spent a season at Uriage together. Many people at that time 'took the waters,' as it was called."

It is indicative that, like society, Coco visited spas: it was fashionable to do so. At this time Coco's liaison with Boy Capel had shaded off into an amorous friendship, warm if no longer passionate, and as their affair waned in intensity, Coco was seen a great deal in the company of a handsome and very rich Argentinian, Eduardo Martinez de Hoz, who lived in Paris.

Yet if she was adhering to a new life style and drifting away from friends such as Boy, whom her new circle did not really appreciate, she had not gone so far that she was not greatly affected when suddenly, fulfilling his own premonition, Boy Capel was killed in an automobile accident on December 22, 1919. He was thirty-eight years old. His car blew a tire, careened off the road, and caught fire. On December 29, the Paris correspondent of the London *Times* wrote:

"Captain Arthur Edward Capel, mortally wounded during the accident while enroute to Cannes, has been buried with full military honours. The death of Captain Capel has profoundly shocked his many French friends. He was undoubtedly one of the best-known and best-beloved of the English living in France."

Coco was deeply shocked, crushed. She immediately raced south and insisted on being conducted to the site of the accident. She would never forget him, for he was the first person to believe in her when, as a wild young girl at Royallieu with Etienne Balsan, she had expressed the desire to work. She owed him her first shop and, even more important, her entrance into society and her knowledge of its customs. He had been the only person to whom she had been able to confide her doubts and fears.

Returning to Paris, partly in reaction to Boy's death she threw herself completely into her work. Her objective was to revolutionize the female costume. And it did not take her long. As early as 1920, the two high fashion magazines of Paris, *Femina* and *Minerva*, were filled with Chanel models:

> Chanel launches this ravishing dark-green jersey sports suit . . . Chanel launches a dress made of long black silk fringes . . . Lady Fellowes* wore a raw silk mousseline dress labeled Chanel to the Ritz . . . Chanel continues her theme of skirt and jumper for daytime wear . . . Chanel launches the black tulle dress . . . For evening, she has created a red chenille dress . . . Chanel has created furs and married the monkey with white breitschwanz . . . Another Chanel creation for evening—a white satin sheath covered over with an embroidered and beaded cloak . . .

In two years she became the foremost designer of her day, and she did it in the simplest way possible—by setting out to battle against her competitiors, Poiret and his Turkish-style concoctions, Madeleine Vionnet and her draperies, and by challenging the stupid designs that victimized modern women, the requirement that, in order to ensure the proper trimness of the silhouette, a woman burden herself with several pounds of paraphernalia and apparatus. She came out instead with clothes that permitted a woman to feel free to move, to have fun, to love. And she brought them out just when the modern woman was ready for them.

"The corset," said Chanel, "is nothing more than a survival of the Middle Ages chastity belt. It guaranteed to the husband that his wife would not be unfaithful. Once the corset was off, she had only two desires—to stretch out and to breathe. The lover had only to put his clothes on again sadly."

At Deauville, at Biarritz, or at the race tracks, surrounded by women who were wearing curls, laces, petticoats, and enormous straw hats to protect themselves from the sun, Coco appeared in a little Shetland sweater with her marvelous pearls, pushing ele-

---

*Daisy Fellowes, daughter of Duke Decazes, first married Prince de Broglie, then the Hon. Reginald Fellowes, who was related to the Churchills.

gance to the extreme, wearing jewels as though they were fake. The women looked at her out of the corners of their eyes—and then immediately wanted to imitate her.

She imposed short hair on women, making a cut of the scissors give birth to several thousand hairdressers, of whom the most celebrated, Antoine, installed himself on the rue Cambon, several steps away from what was fast becoming the sanctuary of Parisian fashion.

Although probably apocryphal, the following story is nonetheless wonderfully characteristic and worth recounting if only because, as Coco herself said, "Legend is the consecration of celebrity."

One evening as she was preparing to go to the Opéra, Coco's water heater exploded and burned part of her hair. Another elegant woman would have shut herself up for several months until it had grown back in again, but Coco seized a pair of nail scissors and in a few seconds had cut off the rest of her hair. At the Opéra, where she appeared wearing a short dress—its waistline below her hips—her "hairdress" gave rise to a very long silence. That evening the lorgnettes of·the Parisian ladies were focused on Coco's box more often than on the stage.

The next day, Misia Edwards, Madame Letellier, a famous beauty of the time and wife of Henri Letellier, owner of a well-known newspaper, and Cécile Sorel, the great actress who played Molière's Celimene at the Comédie française, the national theater, and became the Egeria of the Third Republic, had Coco cut their hair with her nail scissors!

Coco, cutting a lock here, a frill or a flounce there, manipulating her scissors firmly and precisely, destroyed the woman of yesterday by teaching women to have a more natural bearing. Chanel liberated women; it is as simple as that. She launched the modern woman with her famous aphorism (the first of many): "A fashion that does not reach the streets is not a fashion." Thanks to her, fashion did reach the streets. Conversely, the friendly smile of the street, its alert way of walking and breathing, erupted into the boudoirs of the marquises. She brought the saucy style of the working girl to the great society ladies, and to the petite bourgeoise she lent the bearing of a duchess. Her innovations continued without interruption. She suppressed epaulets, launched the twin-set (skirt with matching sweater and cardigan), leather belts that held in the waist and embellished it. She brought out sports dresses in knitted lace, short evening dresses, sailor pants, practical jersey outfits that allowed women to be elegant from morning to evening.

All her clothes were rational. The traveling coats were comfortable, the pockets placed so the wearer could put her hands in them, the hats small enough to pack away in a suitcase, the buttons, for the first time, no longer simply decorative. Belts slid down to almost nonexistent hips and stopped there, as though by a miracle. Hair was short, and usually flattened down under a cloche hat. The dresses, cut out of jersey or black wool, were so simple and so strict that there was no room for variation: grandmothers dressed like their granddaughters and were mistaken for them!

The newly rich, who enjoyed showing off their fabulous pearl necklaces or their diamond rivières, had their money's worth. "Coco had invented a style: the deluxe 'poor look,'" said Poiret. She had understood that in a period when elegant women took the bus, the subway, and taxis, the future lay in the simple dress.

At the Opéra, within the sumptuous and baroque frame of the Garnier Palace with the impressive Republican Guard standing at attention, Coco had another new idea. During the Opéra gala's intermission, as she contemplated the motley crowd in the orchestra section below her box, the women, dressed by Poiret in all the colors of the rainbow, seemed to her to resemble the palette of an insane painter. She leaned over the scarlet velvet of the balustrade and suddenly said to herself: "This can't go on any longer. I'm going to stick them all into black dresses."

The next morning she closed herself up in her salon, chased away the seamstresses, and set to work with pins and paper and several yards of black fabric. Several hours later the little black dress appeared, a creation that will signify for eternity the Chanel mystique. Coco only had to go out once dressed in this fashion for the gaudy delirium and the "Turkish" creations of the great Poiret to become passé immediately.

Poiret and Coco were adversaries worthy of each other, and characteristically Poiret did not give up his crown without a fight, without a last glorious flourish. In an effort to survive, he exaggerated the audacity of his inventions, making them increasingly bizarre and unbelievable. Thus he created evening dresses lit from the inside by tiny electric bulbs and equally tiny batteries! Commenting on this stupifying invention, the newspapers proposed that the electricity be furnished by power produced from the simple dancing movement of the wearer—instead of water power or wind power.

Poiret's extravagances certainly got him talked about—in his designing and his life. As prince of society's merrymaking, he organized even more fabulous fêtes and galas. In his private house on the rue d'Antin, The Oasis, he constructed a theater where parodies of successful modern plays were performed.

Poiret continued to give his costume parties and masked balls, which had heretofore been extremely successful: "the marketplace of Paris"—dukes and ambassadors dressed as market porters or butchers; "the nouveaux riches"—everyone obligated to wear costumes of gold and silver, finding real pearls in their oysters at supper; the ball of "the bottom of the sea"— branches of coral growing in the gardens, dolphins and sirens kidnapping delighted sailors, Boniface ("Boni") de Castellane (he had married Anna Gould, daughter of the American railroad king) sitting in a diving suit reading a paper in the light of an illuminated sea sponge!

But all this was in vain; the battle was already lost. While friends came in great numbers to his theater, the public held itself aloof. The latter preferred the cabarets and afternoon tea dances that were opening up all over Paris. And more and more, the fashionable world turned from his extravagances.

The shift in tastes had no effect on Poiret. The great commoner who had held his own with authentic aristocrats, who could permit himself every foible, always sure of imposing his imagination's last invention, allowed himself to be lured into a frantic pursuit of glory in defiance of any sort of common sense. The spectacle of this titan defiantly forging his ruin was mad but noble.

. The Exposition of Decorative Arts in the twenties was Poiret's last opportunity to dominate Paris in his customary manner.

Poiret's name shone at the Arts Deco almost as brightly as that of another spendthrift, André Citroen, who had just splashed his name in lights the length of the Eiffel Tower. Poiret designed a large illuminated fountain and his three barges— *Amours, Delices,* and *Orgues*—decorated with Dufy canvases, glistened at night on the Seine on the fringes of the exposition. Draped in a superb cape, Poiret personally greeted his supper guests as they came up the gangway.

It was a magnificent exit. But it marked the end of the Poiret period. Coty offered to buy his perfumes. He turned down the offer. An English firm offered him fourteen million gold francs for his fashion house. Poiret laughed at them.

Poiret accepted nothing for as long as he could. He was far too proud. But as his financial difficulties turned into embarrassments, the bankers converged. They laid down strict rules of conduct: no more extravagances and sumptuous parties, no more generous gifts, especially to pretty girls who wanted to launch their careers. They wished to impose logic, moderation, fashion designs that, with universal appeal, could be mass produced. Poiret chose to leave his establishment.

Later, a large department store offered him employment; he lasted barely three months.

He had one last chance in 1928 when he was invited to conduct a lecture tour in the United States. From New York to Chicago, Indianapolis to San Diego, he spoke to several thousand persons at women's clubs.

He explained to them his philosophy of elegance and personality; he answered their questions; and, as all the American ladies filed past him, he suggested to each what color would best suit their individual coloring.

"Why do you dress as though you were all in uniform?" he asked one day. "You all have a corsage of flowers pinned to your furs. Were it a personal idiosyncrasy it might have a certain charm, but it becomes terrifying when done en masse."

After that particular lecture, more than eight hundred corsages littered the ground.

He was supposed to receive a thousand dollars for each lecture, but when the time came for him to be paid, Poiret's manager had disappeared. He was found dead in the wreckage of his private plane. Poiret's money went with him, and though his name still had an important commercial value in the United States and he received many other offers, he never knew how or never wanted to use it.

A manufacturer of boots for Texas ranchers asked Poiret for permission to use his name, in return for about sixteen thousand dollars a year.

"Let me have one of your cigars," Poiret answered. "You owe me at least that for I have just saved you a fair sum. By using my name on your shoes you would be harming my reputation without adding anything to your own."

His publicity agent who had made the deal and prepared the contract did not see it that way. Poiret was forced by a court decision to pay the man 25 percent of the contract he had just turned down.

In everything Poiret was a far cry from Chanel, the shrewd businesswoman from the Auvergne who, when she launched the cloche hat, used to go to the Galeries Lafayette to buy hats that she sold, without compunction, with but a few added touches, for four or five times the price she paid for them to the elegant ladies who "had to have" the Chanel label.

Poiret could have exploited his vogue in the United States and found backers. Instead, he complained loudly during his lectures that the models offered for a mass market in America were simply pale and distorted versions of the real Parisian creations.

Yet he was the first fashion designer to understand, no matter how confusedly, that high fashion could not survive unless it extended its influence to the United States.

As it turned out, he was never able to capitalize on his intuition, and it was to be Coco Chanel and Christian Dior who would be the chosen ones; only they would find their fortunes along the trail that Poiret had blazed.

In other ways, also, Chanel copied and enlarged upon Poiret's example. Although perhaps less spectacular than that of her rivals, Coco's social life was no less brilliant. Misia, divorced from Edwards and now accompanied everywhere by the magnificent José María Sert, the painter, was invaluable to Coco as her initiator into the mysteries of society. Soon Coco was receiving Picasso, Cocteau, and Stravinsky, as well as the pale and enigmatic Raymond Radiguet, the brilliant nearsighted child whose first work, *The Devil in the Body* (1923), caused a scandal. At twenty, Radiguet made his way in life by pushing away the crowds with his "third hand": his cane. He was the most talented of the French novelists of his day, the successor to Marcel Proust who, his work almost completed, was soon to die.

Coco was as at home in this world of artists as she was in the social world that she received in her residence at 29 rue du Faubourg St.-Honoré. Not far from the Elysée Palace, the house was a vast place with gardens stretching to avenue Gabriel, separated only by a few trees from the Champs Elysées, and it became one of the centers of Parisian cultural life. At home Coco mixed together artists, aristocrats, and the wealthy upper-class bourgeois.

Cleverly counseled by Misia, Coco made her home one of the most luxurious in Paris. Starting at the entrance hall, marvelous lacquered Coromandel screens surrounded the visitor with a very special atmosphere (at the same time they hid the green painted walls she had not been allowed to touch because they were classified as "historical monuments"). In the salons, decorated in three colors—beige, white, and chocolate brown—there were vast Louis XIV chairs in antique wood covered with white velvet. From the window, there was a lovely view of the terrace, the stone steps, the fountain in the middle of the lawn, and the several hundred-year-old trees. There were white flower bouquets placed in enormous vases in all the rooms.

Coco was the first fashion designer to be "received" in society. One columnist known as le Tigre (The Tiger) noted that if by chance a Worth and a Doucet came upon a society woman, a client of his house, at the Opéra or the races, he pretended not to recognize her so that she would not be forced to greet him. Coco, in contrast, had innumerable friendships in the social, artistic, and literary worlds; the prejudices against "tradespeople" were beginning to falter, and she knew how to surround herself on the rue Cambon and the Faubourg St.-Honoré with brilliant fallen aristocrats. For example, her fashion house became the refuge of the Russian aristocracy, and the Grand Duchess Marie, sister of the Grand Duke Dimitri and cousin of the czar, ran its embroidery atelier. Though most of these women she hired did not furnish very useful work—far from it—they did bring an important cosmopolitan clientele into the house, not to mention a cachet all its own.

A dress presented from time to time to a young lady "temporarily" financially embarrassed made for such excellent publicity that soon, going further in her exploitation of the vanity of certain of her contemporaries, Coco did not hesitate to use young aristocratic ladies as mannequins. Several years later, that great lord of elegance Count Etienne de Beaumont was himself making jewelry for Coco.

By 1920 the little girl from Auvergne had shown her mettle,

and Paris lay at her feet as it danced and made merry. Dancing parties were improvised in the great hotels and the clubs. The new rich danced the tango in the arms of "Argentine" men-about-town, who pocketed the money due for their services with a blasé air. Exiled Russian princesses began to sell their jewels. American women in their seventies, dieted to extraordinary limits, found their youth again in Paris. Thus Lady Elsie Mendl, her hair tinted green or blue, threw balls at her sumptuous home in Versailles of a luxury equal to those of Etienne de Beaumont and served food even more delicious and copious than his.

"Surprise parties" began to be fashionable. Anyone could come to an apartment, a bottle under his or her arm, and half an hour later an "orgy" would be going full force. In the social world, it became the custom to go from an afternoon tea dance to a surprise party, then on to a chic cabaret, and finally to finish up, the women in lamé dresses, drinking cheap red wine or coffee with cream in a bistro amid gay and boisterous rag-pickers and bums who had great difficulty in preserving their distinctness from café society on a spree.

The operetta *Dedé* triumphed thanks to a young artist named Maurice Chevalier. His salary rose at one fell swoop from six hundred to one thousand francs a day. Mistinguett, first his mistress and then his box-office rival, with whom several crowned heads of Europe were in love, was the star of the Casino de Paris, and everyone went to see her because of her famous white teeth and lovely legs.

It was also the Negro era, the jazz era, with Josephine Baker and Sidney Bechet arriving from New Orleans to bring the blues to the Old World. They danced the Charleston and the shimmy. The most "in" place to go was the Boeuf sur le Toit, a bar that opened on the rue Boissy d'Anglas in 1921. The Boeuf was launched by Moyses, an admirer of Arthur Rimbaud, with the help of his friend Jean Cocteau, who reigned there surrounded by beautiful young men.

Jean Oberlé, the cartoonist and humorist, remembers: "One saw the prettiest women in Paris there, accompanied by gentlemen dressed in tails sitting next to Picasso in a sweater or Derain smoking his pipe. . . ." René Clair, Tristan Tsara, the Count de Beaumont, Maurice Sachs, Diaghilev, Prince Youssoupov, King Ferdinand of Rumania all went there. Toward morning, night workers and painters from Montparnasse, the other center of Parisian life, joined up with the night's carousers.

One of the most admired of the Parisian ladies, Daisy Fellowes, would arrive at the Boeuf with her "stable" of dancers, usually wearing a spangled jacket cut like a man's smoking jacket. Very rich, with some literary ambitions, Daisy Fellowes was, along with Lady la Abdy, one of the most beautiful women in Paris. Following in her wake were a young anarcho-surrealist wearing a black tie, Louis Aragon, who had not yet met Elsa Triolet's eyes, nor love, nor communism, and Nancy Cunard, heiress to the most celebrated maritime company in the world, in revolt against her family and society.

Everyone in this world, including Salvador Dali, who was soon to make a sensational entry into it, drank at the Boeuf sur le Toit, dined at Coco Chanel's, and danced at the Count de Beaumont's or Mrs. Corrigan's (a Russian married to an American oil king). Love affairs between writers and artists (real or fake) and millionaires started and ended during these evenings. They drank, danced, and loved.

In the midst of all this was Coco, one of the animators of these celebrations, always in control. Journalists gave dozens of definitions of her: "The woman stronger than her desires"; "The woman who places ambition above love"; "The woman who forces her heart to remain silent." She loved men, wanted to be loved by them—she could not tolerate not being loved—but she did not want to be their slave or their prey at any price. If the presence of someone pleased her, she would do without it, although it might cause her unhappiness, as soon as the elected of her heart became a handicap. When work and passion became incompatible, she relegated passion to a back seat.

Few penetrated Coco's defenses, especially after the death of Boy Capel. But some still did. One, a Russian, an extravagant, gambling butterfly, was to enchant Coco. Full of anecdotes and wit, Grand Duke Dimitri Pavlovich, first cousin of Czar Nicholas II, eluded the ambitious contradictions of Coco. He did not preoccupy her nor bother her; in fact, he even flattered her. The spoiled, grown-up-child behavior that Pavlovich inspired in Coco provided a delightful change from the image of a "little black bull" that Colette once used to describe Coco.

"Empresses love clowns," affirmed Cocteau. The eccentricities of her new companion (a hero who came straight out of Dostoevski's novels) amused Coco, especially since he was often pathetic, with his nostalgia for his childhood and the Russia of the Czars.

Elegant and full of charm, Dimitri had been the Czarina's favorite because his stories and youthful pranks amused her. His best friend was Prince Felix Youssoupov, three years his senior, heir to one of the greatest fortunes in Russia and after World War I, one of the leaders of Parisian society, with hostesses of all kinds fighting for the privilege of his presence at their suppers.

Youssoupov was, along with Dimitri, the hero of the extraordinary drama that was the prelude in 1916 to the collapse of the Czar's empire—the execution of Rasputin, the lewd and debauched monk who won the confidence of the Czarina by pretending to be able to cure her son Alexis of hemophilia. Because of his disastrous influence, Rasputin did more for the Russian revolution than a thousand hardened Bolsheviks, and it was Dimitri, Youssoupov, and an influential member of the Russian Douma, Vladimir Parishkevitch, who decided to eliminate the man who, by his excesses, was compromising the future of Holy Russia.

It was a Dostoevskian drama. In the Moïka Palace, where the three conspirators had lured the monk under pretext of offering him the chance to participate in an orgy, the poison that Dimitri had put into the cakes had no effect. Rasputin sang. Youssoupov, borrowing a revolver from Dimitri, had to shoot Rasputin twice, and even then he was strong enough to flee into the garden, where Parishkevitch finished him off. The news of Rasputin's death was greeted with joy and relief in all of Russia, though the Czar and Czarina were crushed by this crime committed by members of the Imperial family, and Dimitri was exiled to Persia to serve with General Baratov and his Russian troops (thus escaping the massacres of the 1917 revolution).

In Paris after the revolution, Grand Duke Dimitri was for some time the chief pretender to the throne, finally abdicating in favor of his cousin, Cyril Vladimirovitch. It is then that he became an intimate friend of Chanel, though he had known her casually before the war, in Biarritz.

The affair lasted several years. They were seen everywhere together, and Chanel the dressmaker was received by everyone as though she were of the Grand Duke's rank. Many of their friends believed that in the end Chanel would marry the Grand Duke. But marriage would have meant wiping out her business and losing her independence. Slowly, Chanel, who had obtained from the Grand Duke all she could expect—prestige among the aristocracy and in society, wealthy customers for her "maison de couture"—lost interest.

Eventually, in 1924, Chanel met the Duke of Westminster, and her affair with the Grand Duke was over. Dimitri married a rich American, Audrey Emery, whom he divorced in 1937.

During the twenties, Coco's supremacy was total. She launched a new type of emancipated woman, a certain style, to which a literary scandal soon gave unparalleled publicity—the Bachelor Girl. A spicy novel entitled *La Garçonne,* by Victor Margueritte, recounting the peregrinations of a young woman of good family through the byways of vice, was taken to be the portrait of a certain type of free woman liberated from prejudices, not disdaining homosexual adventures. And her physical type— short hair and small, if not quite nonexistent, breasts—was actually launched by Coco. Within several months, the sale of the book had reached the fantastic figure of seven hundred thousand copies.

In fact, the style of elegance advocated by Coco did lead to confusion between the sexes. Did she foresee the influence that homosexuals would exercise on the culture (and the high fashion) of the twenties? Perhaps. It is difficult to tell. But like many women of her time, she liked to be surrounded by pederasts. The war of 1914–1918 over, the duchesses and upper-class bourgeois had had enough of heroes. As for the husbands, busy at their offices, they scarcely minded their wives being in the company of such inoffensive males.

In any case, Chanel's style of costly simplicity and expensive cheapness, which in a sense took away women's mystery, eliminated both the fashion designers concerned with sophisticated seductiveness and the conventional notion of femininity.

Here, as in many other domains, Coco owed her success as much to the time as to her talent. To know how to feel out and divine the right moment to strike during an evolution, and how to prejudice tastes in a certain direction, were the trump cards in her fabulous and rapid triumph.

5.
Chanel No. 5

As the demand for Chanel jersey dresses and hats increased, business mushroomed in the rue Cambon, where the original workrooms, opened in 1919 at number 25, spread out, annexing successively numbers 27, 29, and 31. Business also was brisk in the shop on the rue Gontaut-Biron in Deauville, where, even more than before the war, Paris society thronged the boardwalk to launch summer fashions, and in Biarritz, somewhat in decline since the end of the war because vacationers no longer felt the need to put the greatest distance possible between the blue line of the Vosges mountains and the blue horizon of their seaside resort.

Of the cocottes' furbelows, corsets, and full dresses, nothing remained. Coco had remodeled the silhouette, shattering the formula that equated the beauty of a jewel with its price. She had brought the utilitarian spirit into the choice of accessories.

Of the pre-1914 society woman, haughty, straitlaced, proudly exhibited by her husband—a doll and a pompous ornament, a silent and submissive mother—the war, the Roaring Twenties, and Coco Chanel had made a free woman. Pleasure, independence, and freedom of choice, no longer the exclusive privilege of demimondaines, forced their way even into the hallowed residences of the Faubourg St.-Germain. At last, it became permissible for men to admire, and pamper, women. Furthermore, the privilege of arousing men's passions was no longer reserved for cocottes, for love and the taste of freedom were offered to women of the world of the Faubourg as well as of the Champs-Elysées. Indeed, from 1920 on, the two worlds increasingly coincided.

By cutting their hair, throwing away the laces and pantalets of their grandmothers, and wearing jersey sport dresses, which assured elegance from morning to evening, the women of 1920 not only affirmed their desire for a new fashion but also for a new way of life.

Every vestige of the past was soon swept away—except for the almost overpowering vapors of turn-of-the-century perfumes, the heavy scent of flowers, mixtures of iris, chypre, gardenia, and rose with ridiculous and pretentious pseudo-oriental names such as popular opinion and bad literature identified with the "woman's world" and with sensual pleasures. Words crowded and intermingled on the multicolored labels as if fascinated by the same bad taste: Orient, Suave, Sortilège, Virginité.

Women used these perfumes lavishly, in increasing doses, as they became inured to them and to combat their own body odors. Hygiene was still rather primitive and haphazard at the beginning of the century. Daily baths were reserved for cocottes and for the sick. We have already seen how, as early as 1903, Coco's impression of Emilienne d'Alençon had involved smell: "She smelled so good. She washed." As for other women, it wasn't until after the war that they forced themselves to take a daily bath or shower. In the meantime, perfume flowed in torrents.

Considering the circumstances, it is hardly surprising that Chanel became interested in perfume. With her impeccable good taste and her overall approach to dress—to life itself—it was inevitable that sooner or later she would pay a tribute to perfume. Her encounter with d'Alençon serves only to underline her sense of awareness of the matter.

In fact, we know when and how Coco was inspired to create her own perfume, crowning her fashion masterpieces by developing a perfume of true elegance and thus opening a new field of activity to the fashion world. She later recounted the story to one of her best friends, Robert Chaillet, her tax adviser for many years, who recalls:

"How did she hit upon the idea of creating a perfume, she, a fashion designer, and at a time when perfumes belonged to the exclusive domain of perfumers? She had already liberated women from what she disdainfully labeled baubles.

"Since she dressed them from head to toe, she decided to dress them entirely, and for her the feminine scent was an integral part of clothes. Just as artificial flowers were stuck on the hats of women in those days, so their clothing was drenched in perfume. In other words, everything became flowers.

" 'A woman must smell of woman and not like a rose,' cried Coco in a crude parody of a barracks-room song. And she added:

" 'In those days, a woman was put into corsets, her hats covered with roses, and on top of all this she was drenched in perfume so she would smell even more like a rose. But a woman shouldn't smell like a rose. Why? She smelled awful!'

"She stressed this with vigor, aware that she was pronouncing shocking truths. Ah, yes! Those women dressed in ball gowns, whose photographs we contemplate not without a touch of nostalgia, were dirty. The Duchess of Guermantes—dirty; Albertine and the young girls in flower of Cabourg so dear to Marcel Proust's heart—careless. Listening to Mademoiselle Chanel, fifty years later, as she sent the Faubourg St.-Germain out to wash its hands, one has a greater understanding of the pernicious charm that the cocottes exercised on the rich bourgeois and aristocrats of the turn of the century. They smelled good—perhaps of nothing but soap.

"And Coco, the Coco of this period, her first days in Paris, still redolent of the rough yellow soap of her childhood and the orphanage, timid, often humiliated by the scornful smiles distantly accorded her by great ladies, remembered:

" 'They were dirty. Are you surprised? But that's the way it was.'

"What secret pleasure did she take in doing away with our admiration for such women? For how many humiliations was she seeking revenge?

"Mademoiselle added: 'I who love woman wanted to give her clothes in which she would be comfortable, in which she could drive a car, yet at the same time clothes that emphasized her femininity, clothes that flowed with her body. A woman is closest to being naked when she is well dressed. I wanted to give her a perfume, but an artificial perfume. I insist on artificiality, just as a dress is artificial, fabricated. I am a fashion artisan. I don't want rose or lily of the valley; I want a perfume that is a compound.' "

Coco hit upon a brilliant and startling paradox. If a perfume is to exude a *natural* odor, she realized, it must be created *artificially*. In total contrast, the heavy perfumes of the day had a "natural" scent that rang quite hollow. A natural perfume is the result of elaborate work and imagination. This much all perfume makers know today, and it is to Chanel that they owe their knowledge.

From the beginning of her work in fashions, Coco had her own doctrines. As to perfumery, we know she was aware of what was needed long before she did anything active about her ideas. She had to wait for the right moment before launching the venture of making a perfume different from all others, until, that is, she was so well established in her fashion business that she had financial security and a loyal clientele who would support her new venture.

In the years following the death of Boy Capel, she worked harder than ever. One new idea followed another. "What she sells is less what she likes than what she has got tired of, which happens to her very quickly. What has been done must not be done again, that is the absolute principle from which springs all her genius," wrote the Princess Bibesco,* for whom Coco "invented" a costume for air travel.

Never before had there been such a designer. A volcano of originality on the rue Cambon, Chanel also was at the center of Parisian social life. The chandeliers in the drawing rooms of 29 rue du Faubourg St.-Honoré, her home at the time, never went out. Coco entertained elaborately every evening. Paris society thronged around her, especially when she was taken up by Count Etienne de Beaumont, master of the art of elegant distraction and a member of the highest French aristocracy. Misia had presented Beaumont to Coco, who, knowing of his talent for jewelry design, a pursuit he followed as a dilettante, immediately engaged him to create jewelry for the Chanel firm. Characteristically, Coco seldom hesitated to offer employment to those

---

*Princess Bibesco, a Hungarian married to a Rumanian prince, wrote books about European society.

who traditionally were "above" work. Coco saw nothing demeaning in labor and felt no one else should have such irrational delusions, either. (It was a tribute to her forthright approach to life that Beaumont, in return, demanded pay for the work he did.)

"Count Etienne was one of the most brilliant and distinguished gentlemen of the period between the two wars," Mme Gripoix, herself a designer of costume jewelry, told us. "In the early twenties, the count used to come to my house to design jewelry, which he would later give away for name-days and birthdays. In their town house, on the corner of rue Duroc and rue Masseran [today the property of Baron Elie de Rothschild], the Count and Countess de Beaumont lavishly received the world of the aristocracy and of the arts. Marie Laurencin [the well-known painter] was his great friend and protégée. Mademoiselle Chanel knew that by employing the count she had gained access to a world that till then had ignored her.

" 'All those fancy little aristocrats,' she often said to me, 'they've turned up their noses at me, but I'll have them kissing my feet!' Then she would start doing funny imitations of society ladies, their airs and graces, making fun of them all and envying them at the same time!"

In many ways, Chanel was the true parvenu. For all her taste and natural elegance, she sought desperately to impress. While nonvintage champagne was served in the drawing rooms of most of her competitors—for that is how she saw them— Mademoiselle's tables groaned under caviar and champagne of the best years. Artists and writers, who were invited because Coco genuinely appreciated them and their talents, imbued these gatherings with a veneer of brilliance that was a revelation to the aristocracy, largely uncultivated and often frozen in its pomp and prejudices.

But there was a price tag on all this. The strain was enormous, especially since Coco had far from fully recovered from the shock of Boy's death. The combination of effects was irresistible. Chanel's house became the center of social life for Paris. Even though she went to bed late, Coco could not sleep. When the guests left, the memory of Boy haunted her in the dark. She could not forget his tragic death, and though she pretended to be gay and amusing with her guests, once alone she wept. By eight o'clock in the morning she was at the rue Cambon. Feverish, silent, dead tired, she wandered through her workrooms like a sleepwalker.

It was Misia, whose liaison with José María Sert had become official, resulting later in marriage, who saved her. Around 1922, Coco left on a trip with the couple. They went first to Italy, where, with Sert acting as her professor, she discovered the churches and the masterpieces that awaited curious eyes to bring them to light. Friends met on the way joined the Serts, forming a gay band that permitted itself every fantasy and extravagance this side of vulgarity. Among them was a young aristocrat whose name alone evoked the splendors of the Italian Renaissance— Lucchino Visconti, descendant of the Dukes of Milan. At twenty Visconti was already interested in films and was soon to leave for Paris, where, introduced by Coco to Jean Renoir, he became Renoir's assistant before spreading his wings to become one of the great directors of our time.

Under Misia's and José María's careful guidance, Coco learned to love art and to choose and discover it. Of Sert, that truculent giant whose ferocious appetites concealed unexpected tenderness (his frescoes cover the walls of one of the reception rooms of the Waldorf Astoria in New York), Coco spoke with affection, a rare gesture for a woman who in later years so easily demolished Picasso and Dali, both friends of hers.

Sert hated museums because in them, he said, "Works of art fought each other." He admired paintings, preferably anonymous, come upon by chance down long corridors. "I love the silences of chiaroscuros disturbed only by footfalls on the tiled floors." There he could stand motionless before an angel's smile and salute it ceremoniously, taking off his huge hat.

Was it because posterity proved to be so cruel to Sert—"They go flat," said Degas of Sert's immense frescoes—celebrated though he was during his lifetime, that Coco always spoke tenderly of him and defended his work? If so, it was like her to choose to champion Sert. Later, she sang the praises of the poet Pierre Reverdy, whom she loved and who never knew success. Though we find it easy enough to remember Coco's ferocious criticisms of successful writers and artists, too often we forget her stubborn defense of those such as Sert whom glory had deserted or those who had been ignored, such as Reverdy.

The Italian trip ended with summer. Sert and Misia returned to Paris to be married. They left behind a woman who, satiated with months of sunshine, art, laughter, and extravagant flights of fancy, had again found an equilibrium that, if tenuous, was nonetheless real.

Instead of returning to Paris, Chanel directed her steps to the south of France, to the Côte d'Azur. There she sunbathed, an unheard-of practice at the time.

St. Tropez was a small fishing port where only a few artists and painters came to stay. There were only two nightclubs (where Coco danced the Charleston), Chez Melanie and Chez Palmyre. Alice Halincka, who designed settings for a massive ballet and was married to the artist Marcoussis, remembers seeing a strict notice forbidding dancing "between the sexes." This did not prevent young sailors from keeping up with the times, and dramas between the sexes abounded. There were many threats of suicide.

It was all very gay and charming, a far cry from today's monstrous arena. "I loved St. Tropez," Coco later said. "How could they have turned such a charming little village into what it is today? It's disgraceful. People destroy everything."

For her, the port, so simple, so virginal, exactly matched her mood, her style, and it is hardly surprising that she rejected out of hand the symbol of modern life that St. Tropez later became. Garish nonconformity is in every way opposed to the elegance of simplicity that Chanel always propounded.

In a television interview shortly before her death, she held forth about modernity in fashion:

"You see women without modesty and it's revolting. I think that what one guesses at is more exciting. . . . Because of all this, it's all very pretentious. Ours is an era of pretention. You can be as dirty and disgusting as you like; you don't need to dress. St. Tropez produces nothing but filth." She pronounced the word with incomparable clearness. "Last year it was considered chic there to be dirty. Do you call that fashion?"

The scorn of the old lady was formidable; it is always difficult —perhaps impossible—to remain *au courant*. We invest too much of ourselves in what we make our own.

The rare women on vacation in St. Tropez were elegant, dressed in the Chanel style. Among them was Colette, ten years

older than Coco and about to be divorced from Henri de
Jouvenel, spending her holidays at Beauvallon with her future
husband, Maurice Goudeket.

Coco met Colette and her husband at that time and related:
"They ate the most incredible amount of melon." And she, too,
developed a taste for melon (iced for dessert and accompanied
with frappé'd Riesling wine). Colette was writing one of her masterpieces, *Le Blé en herbe*, and it was natural for the two women
to be drawn to each other, for their destinies had much in
common. Both had encountered similar problems and had escaped from the same type of rich men. Both had fought hard for
and gained their independence, one through fashion and the
other through literature, but in the same way—by being finicky
about details.

"Sleeves, everything depends on the art of putting them
together," Coco mumbled through the pins in her mouth, having
just pulled a sleeve down for the twentieth time.

"Ah, those adjectives," sighed Colette, rolling her dark eyes
expressively below her brown curls.

The two women saw each other often throughout the years,
especially during the somber hours of World War II, and when
Coco built her villa near Roquebrune, Colette was often a guest.

In 1922, accompanied by her new friend, Coco made long
trips into the interior of Provence. There, in shaded villages—
red-tiled roofs reaching toward the sky—artisans fashioned all
kinds of graceful and picturesque artifacts for everyday use—
pottery, wickerwork, and olivewood sculptures.

Coco found visits to these workshops an unending delight, and
she would idly cast about for a new idea, a brilliant find. With a
mysterious sense of belonging to the same guild as these obscure
artisans, she never grew tired of watching their timeless gestures.

Next, Coco, with her interest in perfume never far from her
thoughts, headed toward Grasse, where lavender- and jasmine-
covered terraces spread luxuriously over the heights that dominate Cannes. In Grasse, the world capital of perfumes, inside
small factories and laboratories, men gifted with an exceptional
sense of smell combined mysterious ingredients and sniffed their
test tubes, performing wonders. Perfumes are concocted with
many ingredients, some of which, separately, smell quite vile.
The art of the perfumer, really a chemist, lies in the ability to

distinguish, to discriminate, to combine to the ultimate degree of sensitivity.

Among those working in Grasse in 1922 was a chemist of genius, Ernest Beaux, who had spent part of his youth in Russia at the court of the Czars, where his father had been employed.

Certain of his perfumes were already famous. But Beaux, though he bowed to the taste of the times and produced heavy floral scents, was not content to stand still. Thus he was one of the first to speculate on the role synthetic perfumes were to play. Though synthetics could not replace the essential oils from animal matter (such as amber, which comes from the stomach of the sperm whale; musk, which is extracted from a glandular sac under the skin of the abdomen of the male musk deer; and castor, which is secreted by glands in the groin of the beaver) or the essential oils of vegetable matter (all the plant extracts), Beaux guessed that synthetics could be combined with natural oils to prevent them from undergoing the changes that often resulted from exposure to air or perspiration, increasing their aromatic strength and making them "vibrate."

In the privacy of his laboratory, Beaux ceaselessly experimented with new mixtures, tirelessly combining the rarest essences. Calling on all the resources of organic chemistry, he carefully examined compounds such as benzyl acetate, which simulates jasmine. One of Beaux's first brilliant successes was the discovery of how exactly to blend the natural and synthetic in such a way that the synthetic essence reinforced and enhanced the natural and assured its stability.

Most important, Beaux was one of the first perfume chemists to discover the importance of the aldehydes in perfume manufacture. Their use completely revolutionized the fabrication of luxury perfumes and was instrumental in the creation of the famous, irreplaceable Chanel No. 5, the first of the modern perfumes.

And No. 5 did spell revolution.

Somehow, Coco got wind of Beaux's experiments—in that day, the world of fashion and the world of perfumes were never far apart. She made a point of meeting him during her stay in Grasse. She immediately felt at home in his laboratory, with its often suffocating vapors, but at first she observed in silence. Then, little by little, she began to ask questions, to suggest unexpected experiments.

"How I annoyed him," she recalled.

Beaux, at first rather skeptical of this dress designer and her interest in perfumes, gradually came to realize that Coco was willing to try anything to break with the perfumes of yesteryear. With her, Beaux understood, he could make his dream perfume a reality.

Coco learned fast. She soon was able to differentiate between essences—bringing her already strongly developed sense of smell under disciplined control—and to tell Beaux exactly what she wanted and what she expected of him. For his part he knew that he was dealing with a woman who knew her own mind and who followed his experiments closely, constantly, always intervening, sniffing a certain test tube, putting it down with "That's not quite it yet."

She wanted "her" perfume to be unalterable, subject, at worst, to only slight fading.

"There, that's good. You've got something. Maybe just a bit more of this." It was a constant process of selection and elimination. Finally, Beaux gave her about ten samples. She tried them one after the other, compared, hesitated. Her quivering nostrils lingered over the fifth.

"Yes, that's what I wanted, a perfume such as has never before been made. A woman's perfume with a woman's scent."

Beaux, though delighted, was a bit worried.

"There are more than eighty ingredients in that sample," he said. "It will be very expensive. It contains a great deal of jasmine, and nothing costs as much as jasmine."

Imperiously Coco interrupted: "In that case add more of it. I want to create the most expensive perfume in the world."*

As for a name, there was no problem. The chosen fragrance was the fifth sample bottle.

"Number five—five, my lucky number. It will be Chanel No. 5."

The best perfume in the world, the most expensive, it was to sell more than any other, for Coco had two inspired ideas: the name No. 5, so different from the complex and tasteless names of rival perfumes; and the style of the bottle.

"She designed something supremely simple and therefore su-

---

*Patou's Joy is the most expensive today; Chanel No. 5 is in second place, but it is the perfume that sells most widely throughout the world.

premely sophisticated," Robert Chaillet told us. "The bottle has never changed. There is total recognition. We can run full-page ads in the most fashionable magazines simply by photographing the bottle. We need no explanatory text."

Coco designed the bottle in Beaux's laboratory in Grasse as soon as she felt she had finally found her perfume, and that evening, delighted, she dined with Beaux and a few friends in the largest restaurant in Cannes. She placed an atomizer of her perfume on the table and sprayed everyone who went by.

"The effect was amazing. All the women who passed our table stopped, sniffing the air. We pretended not to notice," she later said. When the perfume made its debut in her Deauville, Biarritz, and Paris shops, it created the same sensation.

Thus, with perfumes as with everything else—whatever project Coco undertook—when she was finished, nothing was ever the same again. Coco and the times were so in tune that almost instantaneously artificial perfumes became *the* perfumes, and all the other perfume makers rushed to bring out their own.

Forty-five years later, during a television program that represented a lesson in elegance for millions of televiewers, Coco defined her philosophy of perfume. Nothing had changed:

"Perfume? It is the most important thing. You live with your sense of smell. Of all the senses, it is the sense we lose when we live with dirty people, the one we must have when living among respectable people. Really, then, perfume is a luxury. It can be very light, a mild little perfume, but it must resemble the person wearing it. Paul Valéry used to say: 'A badly perfumed woman has no future.' Well, he was quite right. A badly perfumed woman is a woman who doesn't use any perfume at all, who is so pretentious that she believes her personal odor is quite enough. I say: No! A tiny bit of 'smell-good,' as I used to call it when I was a little girl, is an excellent thing. A well-perfumed woman is very agreeable."

Coco was not the first designer to sell perfumes. Before her, Poiret had used the medium of fashions to sell perfumes. But while Poiret, the man of almost-revolutions, first had the brilliant idea, he lacked the audacity and sense of the times to carry it through. His products were old-fashioned perfumes, not only in odor but also in name (Nuit de Chine, Lucrece Borgia) and packaging. He called his line of perfumes after one of his daughters, Rosine—a great mistake because few realized that Rosine was a Poiret, a name with great glamour. Because of these factors, Poiret's perfume was a total failure.

No. 5 was quickly followed by Bois des Iles, "the life and soul of tropical forests," Gardenia, "the coolness of a spring morning," Cuir de Russie, "dear to the hearts of perfumers but which only Chanel wears to perfection," and No. 22.

Although sales figures of the new models were favorable, none of the perfumes attained the success of No. 5, about which a fashion reporter of the time said: "Chanel launched black in fashions and black and white in perfumes. She was the first to bring together the woman, the dress, and the perfume under a single spell. No. 5 is at once a prelude and a symphony."

Chanel's sales promotion for No. 5 was, as usual, inspired. Having chosen the formula, found a name, and designed the packaging, she returned to Paris—finally taking up residence at the Ritz—at the beginning of summer. She was triumphant, her calm restored by success. She brought back in her bags several hundred bottles of No. 5, which she graciously presented to her best customers. The reasoning behind her action was most astute:

"The perfume? What perfume? Oh, yes, the little bottle I gave you the day before yesterday. You want to buy some? You mustn't think of it. Anyway, I don't have any. I don't sell perfumes, my dear. I just happened to stumble on it in Grasse, in a little perfume shop whose name I don't even remember. I just thought it would make an original gift for my friends."

Almost embarrassed, the friend and customer departed. This scene was replayed many times, for in the fitting rooms the salesgirls sprayed and sprayed. Coco, who was flooding Beaux with telegrams urging him to accelerate production, increased the pressure.

"Really? You think I should have some made and sell it? You like *my* perfume that much?"

She knew that her perfume was being widely talked about, especially since she continued to give it to a few privileged customers, preferably those most often seen in society.

"Maybe you're right."

And when Beaux announced to her that mass production could begin, she said to her customers: "Yes, I took your advice.

Tomorrow I am receiving a shipment of that perfume you liked so much."

Success came immediately and spectacularly. A success due above all to Coco's energy, as one of her friends, Lady Abdy, told us:

"Her egocentricity was extreme, her energy fierce. When she decided on something, she followed her idea to the end. In order to bring it off and succeed she brought everything into play. Once she became interested in perfumes she wanted to learn everything about them—their formula, fabrication, and so forth. Naturally, she sought the advice of this and that person. She managed to steal the best chemist from one of the largest perfumers in Grasse, and yet when all was said and done she was the one who decided."

She was interviewed by a fashion reporter at the time on the use of perfume:

"Spray yourself wherever you might be kissed. A woman who overdoes it with perfume has no future, for she will only offend her friends and admirers."

Forty years later, during her triumphant trip to the United States (after her comeback) she gave the same answer to an American journalist.

But when she read her words in the headlines the next morning, she confided, in characteristic concern for sales, to one of the mannequins accompanying her:

"I was wrong to say that. The little old ladies, those who are no longer kissed, won't buy any."

She needn't have worried.

6.

Mademoiselle

THE success of her perfumes did not induce Coco to turn her back on fashion, for she was well aware that therein lay the real source of her influence and power. While perfumes may be paralleled if not copied, design always must be original. Then, too, her clientele was rapidly expanding. When the grand duchesses, busy selling their remaining jewels in order to survive, made fewer appearances in her salons, and as her ardor for the Grand Duke Dimitri cooled, Coco acquired a South American clientele brought along by such Argentine millionaires as Raoul Sanchez Elia and his friend Eduardo Martinez de Hoz. Elia had a long-standing weakness for Coco, and she a great, though perhaps not entirely disinterested (he brought her a lot of customers), friendship for him.

Coco reigned as queen at the rue Cambon. There she received her friends—painters, artists, writers, and other artisans. Sometimes Etienne Balsan dropped by with his young aristocratic friends. Now married, he had become an old pal with whom she could reminisce about Boy Capel. Balsan was sophisticated enough—and close enough to Coco—not to be shocked by her statements. Then, too, while he took Coco's talent seriously, unlike so many others he was not intimidated by her. To him she was still the same wild girl who had galloped bareback through the forest of Compiègne. With Balsan, Coco was able to laugh.

M Valery-Ollivier, a rich playboy and former husband of one

of the Singers (of the sewing machine family), who was a close friend of Balsan and a gentleman-rider himself, described the Coco of this period, whom he had known at Royallieu, thus: "With Etienne and one or two other friends we often went around noon to have a drink at the Ritz bar. And then we crossed the street to go up to Chanel.

"Of course we saw Coco, and also Pauline de Saint-Sauveur who was in charge of the perfumes, trinkets, and scarves. Actually, we came mostly to look at the mannequins. We sat at the top of the staircase until lunch time.

"Coco was lively and full of vitality, but she did not seem to be very interested in us. She was indifferent to what we did or said. She was interested only in her work."

The rue Cambon, the center of her professional life, was also the place where Chanel liked to receive people such as her constant friend Misia, José María Sert, Jean Cocteau, José Iturbi, the pianist, and others, as well as Maurice Sachs, the incorrigible sponger, from whom we borrow the following lines:

"She was alert, authoritarian, just, and good. The employees called her simply 'Mademoiselle,' just as Paris said 'Chanel.' She was always one or the other, never both at the same time. . . . She gave her orders with extraordinary moderation and surehandedness. . . .

"Like a soldier, she became timid again as soon as she left her battlefield. She preferred to hide from the public and felt more at ease in the rue Cambon. When a season's work was finished and the new collection was to be shown for the first time, she attended the opening, seated at the top of her staircase. The beautiful girls wearing the models paraded before the flight of stairs and bowed gently before their master before going through their paces for the buyers of two continents. They did this with a grace that came from the heart, and on their faces they wore the ingenuous expression of a conscript saying: 'You see me here in all my youthful beauty, but I am leaving to go through fire for you.'

"All these women loved her and were devoted to her."

In these last lines, Maurice Sachs slightly misrepresented the facts: if Mademoiselle was charming with visitors, she was implacable with her staff. She tyrannized and humiliated them, and she paid starvation wages.

Lady Abdy, although full of indulgence for her friend Coco, told us: "This woman resembled nothing so much as a gypsy.

She could suddenly become a veritable monster of egotism and unkindness. Her outbursts of anger were dreadful. Her staff, her mannequins, her best friends know something of this. She became angry with everybody. Luckily, she quickly forgot her anger, and the person she had treated like a dog one day would be the most adorable creature in the world the next."

The staff had to put up with a great deal of abuse, and many left. In 1925, after ten years of employment with the House of Chanel, Mme Deray, the head of the workroom, quit. She told us:

"I worked like a galley slave, as one did in those days. I was probably not an exception, but I worked without respite. Hours had no meaning. I arrived at nine in the morning and left for lunch at one thirty, more often at two o'clock, because the Parisian ladies who usually went to bed late only came in at noon. I had to be available. I only had time to grab a bite at a corner bistro and run back to my workroom, where I often remained until eight or nine in the evening.

"I had sixty-five girls working under me and earned only five hundred francs [less than one hundred dollars] a month.

"Mademoiselle had no personal attachment to her staff. She parted with them easily. When something displeased her, no sentiment! One day I said to Monsieur de Fontenoy: 'Sir, it is impossible for me to approach Mademoiselle; would you please ask her to give me a raise of fifty francs. I can't live in Paris on so little money.'

"That was true, I had just enough to eat and pay for my hotel room. So Monsieur de Fontenoy asked for my raise of fifty francs. Mademoiselle answered him curtly: 'If she isn't content, let her leave. She will never have more than five hundred francs here in my house.'

"That was categorical; it was useless to insist. When I left, my girls wept."

Mme Deray was silent for a moment, then picked up the thread of her recollections:

"I don't bear her any ill will. When she died, I was sorry. I am still moved today.

"In retrospect, I think that that era was, still and all, a happy one, the most wonderful time of my life. I would do it again if I had the opportunity, because Mademoiselle was an exceptional woman who loved only what was beautiful.

"But when I left her it was final. She was too hard, royally egotistical. Only she existed. No human weakness showed. She was made of iron in every aspect of her character—especially when it came to money.

"In 1918, Coco paid her mannequins one hundred francs a month, about a tenth of the price of one of her dresses. And when Madame Fred, who was in charge of the mannequins—a charming and sweet woman who had known Mademoiselle Chanel from the earliest days—took advantage of their intimacy to say: 'Coco, you must raise the salaries of your mannequins; they are the most beautiful in Paris,' Coco laughed scornfully and replied: 'Raise their salaries? You can't be serious. They're beautiful girls. Let them take lovers; they can be kept by the wealthiest and most elegant men in Paris!'

"I heard that with my own ears," confirms Mme Deray, still shocked fifty years later.

Mademoiselle's retort was without doubt harsh and offensive. And while one cannot excuse its unfeeling cynicism, it is nevertheless characteristic of Chanel's personality and requires an understanding of the milieu within which she worked.

First, Mademoiselle's policies were not unusual in the fashion world. The salaries everywhere were very low, the working conditions difficult, the hours insane. As the eighteenth-century moralist Chamfort said: "Fashion is the most natural form of taxation that the industriousness of the poor can apply to the vanity of the rich." Things were no different in the twentieth century.

Above the vast showrooms with their gilt chairs and sparkling chandeliers, the workrooms were small and often badly lit. The seamstresses were crowded elbow to elbow along the length of long tables. Fashion thrived on presenting a fine face to the public, but behind the scenes, where the clients never penetrated, the spectacle was miserable.

Second, fashion, an art of representation, always made concessions to appearances. In the twenties, the world of fashion was the privileged place where parasites assembled, and so those who could dispensed favors to all those who were thought to have it in their power to make reputations: actresses were dressed for nothing, great ladies did not pay their bills, leaders of society and gay Parisian night life had to be "paid off." The dress designers had a showy style of life either because they believed that it resulted in good publicity or because, aware of

the fragility of their success, they were mysteriously frenetic in
enjoying their success to the full. Jean Patou, for example, who
maintained that each million lost at the gambling tables helped
him to win at least two in business, was not exceptional in his attitude.*

It required the Popular Front and the fear of the "haves"
when confronted with the "have-nots," the social laws passed
after World War II, the competition with ready-to-wear designers, especially when they started to snatch away the staffs of the
fashion houses, before the situation of the seamstresses was to
improve, at least in those houses that survived. And these were
few. Haute couture, a prodigious devourer of work hours and entertainment budgets, weathered with difficulty the new regime of
paid vacations and decent salaries.

Despite this, Chanel was generous with artists, writers, and
many ordinary unknowns.

The forewoman of the workroom today, Mme Manon, who
went to work for Chanel in 1929, recalls:

"She took care of certain cases in bad straits that were brought
to her attention. I knew an apprentice in the House who became
blind. Mademoiselle paid for the girl to be sent to a reeducation
home. Later, she sent one of the youngest seamstresses on vacation [paid vacations did not yet exist] to a château in Mimizan.
. . . She returned at the end of the month and received her entire
pay."

However, instances of generosity were few and unexpected; in
the commercial world the climate remained tough, even merciless, and Coco responded accordingly. Even though she softened
her attitude somewhat later on, she always remained ferociously
paternalistic, contemptuous of young assistants and anonymous
seamstresses alike.

"Social evolution bypassed her," confirmed Marcel F.,
director of the House since 1969, who was responsible, among
other things, for the difficult mission of reconciling Mademoiselle's caprices with the requirements of the law or even of simple
humanity.

"Her sudden changes of mood were frequent. One day she
said to me: 'Monsieur F., you are too good, too nice. Me, I see

---

*This calculation proved to be false, alas, because Patou, who had done
business worth more than fifty million francs between 1923 and 1925, died
a poor man.

what goes on, I hear them. Those girls aren't working! Tomorrow, you will fire half of them.'

"She was sure that everything went badly as soon as she turned her back."

The fact that there was only one staircase at the rue Cambon posed unbelievable problems! From her office at this crossroads of the internal communications of the House, Mademoiselle heard everything, saw everything. Frequently, she became aggravated at normal everyday activities; a harridan who interfered everywhere, she treated her workers abominably.

When leaving for lunch, the latter were obliged to come out from "behind the scenes" and to pass through the showrooms, where their modest clothes looked out-of-place. Chanel often commented on their appearance. She frequently accused one or another employee of theft.

"Be careful. I see them. They are taking packages; they're stealing," she'd say.

"Mademoiselle, the staircase is there. You can see them go up and down. How could they take anything away?" was the reply. But it made no difference.

Perhaps because of her upbringing, certainly plagued by a guilty conscience, Coco Chanel stepped up her persecution of the workers.

While it is impossible to explain her morbid mistrust, it is somewhat easier to understand her toughness and her cynicism. She would take revenge on her employees for past and even present humiliations. Coco would use them as scapegoats for times when Misia fiercely and condescendingly told her (still a "novice in the world of arts and letters" but determined to plunge into any conversation) to shut up: "You don't know what you're talking about."

Mme Henri Bernstein told us:

"Before 1914, Coco was already leading a rather brilliant life, but though she was seen in the company of elegant young men of excellent family, she was not 'accepted' by good society. They greeted her in her shop, but the women of high social position did not speak to her—at the races, for example. And this kind of behavior certainly caused her to suffer; she was marked by it for the rest of her life. Later on, she contrived to take a brilliant revenge on this humiliation, and God knows she succeeded."

After the war, when her success was spectacular, Coco, who

had not forgotten her treatment at the hands of the titled aristocracy, hired the young ladies of the Faubourg St.-Germain to
work for her.

Mme Hélène de Leusse, who worked for Chanel for eighteen
months as head of the Chanel boutique and who for many years
was a writer for the fashion magazine *Marie-Claire*, recalls:

"What do you expect? She came from an exceedingly—*exceedingly*—simple milieu. She had received no education to
speak of. Balsan put her foot in the stirrup, but at the outset she
had no culture at all. She became cultivated little by little
because she surrounded herself with intelligent people and
because she herself was basically intelligent, supremely intelligent.

"I saw her treat people appallingly. In my opinion, she was
rather snobbish, and snobbery helped her a great deal. She liked
to belittle people, above all when they belonged to a milieu like
the aristocracy. She chose the people whom she wished to humiliate from that milieu to which she did not belong by birth. She
also liked to have women bearing great names as her employees.
Though this was due in part to snobbery, it was also deliberate.
Those women usually brought her a wide clientele. She had a
Machiavellian side, if you like. She was very proud and wanted
neither to obey anybody nor to depend on anybody, prince or
duke."

Coco was always contemptuous of the aristocracy and its off-
spring, whom she had seen from afar in her youth.

"Those women don't know how to do anything," she would
say.

She had more sympathy for the colossally rich, the
Rothschilds, say, and above all for those who, like herself, had
made their own fortunes—provided that, of course, they were
not vulgar. It is typical of the woman that she dismissed a great
reception given in honor of a new fortune with: "All this
hullabaloo and these borrowed jewels, with policemen to protect
them, what a bore!"

When she had definitely "arrived" and no longer needed anything from anyone, Coco became even more aloof:

"In society, it is not the privileged women nor the wealthy as
such who interest me. People with money can afford to go to any
of the fashion houses. They have decided to wear priest's shoes;
they want to carry stationmaster's bags. I don't call that fashion.

I call that a nouveau-riche fad. There is that and then there is fashion."

But she never forgot the indissoluable link between fashion and money: "I prefer rich people to poor people because they can afford the time for beautiful things."

Another key to her aloofness, which she never admitted, was her fear of poor people. Coco the orphan had quickly left poverty and a low income behind her. She forced herself to forget her childhood, erased it from her memory, pretended that it had never existed. She would never even go into the workrooms. Her only contact with her workers was by way of their supervisors, and she contented herself throughout her life with a few easy truisms about the "lower echelons."

After all, she reasoned, the world was not such an unjust place since she herself, a poor, simple working girl, had been able to become what she was. And how about the men who kept her? And what if a young working girl was ugly? Coco maintained that her success had little to do with looks and patrons. It was a matter of talent and tenacity. All this is no doubt true, but one is always left with a "but." And it was these "buts" that Coco refused to recognize.

Chanel's political and social creeds were ferociously conservative. She was an advocate of "order" and discipline, without which, she said, wealth is not possible. "The poor must content themselves with work well done and find their happiness in the satisfaction of work accomplished," she said.

In 1936, with the rise of the Popular Front, her workers went on strike. She never forgave them. On this matter, she clashed violently with her staff. The first day of the strike she arrived— with some magnificence, it must be admitted—covered with her most beautiful jewels. "Ah, she had nerve," recalls Mme Gripoix. "She had been advised not to wear them for it was very dangerous to do so; she did as she pleased. Nobody dared move. The next day, however, she could not enter her fashion house. The picket line refused to let her pass.

"Some time later, she took revenge on the employees who had been the most intransigent. Mademoiselle heard the girl whisper to one of her fellow workers: 'This evening, I am going to rush out of here because I'm going to the theater.' A bit later, Mademoiselle called her into her office and, in the most natural way possible, said: 'Tonight, you will stay with me until nine o'clock to choose the materials.' " In such matters, Mademoiselle found nothing too petty: for her, business involved war to the death.

In May 1968, when the uproar and the tear-gas fumes invaded the streets in a delirium of liberated imagination, Coco confided her "impressions" about these events to her great friend André-Louis Dubois: "The poor security police! Why don't we support them more? This is allowed in the streets now? Since when? What times these are!"

Hers was a simple moral standard perhaps, one characteristic of the turn of the century, an era not famous for its kindness to the anonymous and the humble. The boss enjoyed divine right and was responsible only to God for the welfare of his employees, and what better way to help fulfill this responsibility than to earn money, lots of money? Starting with nothing, Mademoiselle very soon provided work for over three thousand workers crammed into the buildings on the rue Cambon. She fulfilled her "social contract," according to her standards.

More words from Maurice Sachs:

"She was a general: one of those young generals of the Empire in whom the spirit of conquest dominates. Yes, that's what it was: her creative rapidity, the sure-handedness of her orders, her attention to detail, and, most particularly, her devotion to her army of workers."

Forty years later, in the flood of newspaper articles acclaiming Mademoiselle Chanel for the last time, these few lines of the editor-in-chief of *L'Express*, Françoise Giroud, are like a distant echo, almost a confirmation, of what Sachs wrote:

"In her work, she behaved like the captains of industry of the nineteenth century, unrelenting about shortcomings which she overlooked when they were her own, both feared and adored, never admitting that one could have other worries, other interests, other passions than those concerning the fashion house that bore her name. As for profits, naturally they were for her, what could be more normal?

"She said: 'Everything here has been done by me, everything.'

"Chanel a dress designer? Come now! A captain of industry, one of the last great industrial barons and creators of this country. When they are all dead, and they soon will be, they will be spoken of like the dinosaurs. The species will be extinct."

Coco was as clever in managing her other business affairs as she was in running her fashion house, especially in her dealings with her suppliers and her other business associates. She was like honey to a fly; if some admired her because of her charm, others, more businesslike, crowded around her for different reasons, attracted by the prestigious name of Chanel and hoping that by working with Chanel their own futures would improve. Among this group was Théophile Bader, owner of the Galeries Lafayette, who furnished Coco with raw materials such as hat blocks and fabrics, but there were others, some less scrupulous. Businesswomen were rare enough to be thought easy game, especially a young woman in her mid-thirties with such a seemingly unbusinesslike occupation. Many suppliers thus offered her trick propositions, "miraculous" deals, but Mademoiselle outwitted them all.

Tax expert Robert Chaillet and international lawyer Claude L., her advisers for much of her life and at times advisers for her adversaries when Chanel launched into "big business" with the worldwide commercialization of her perfumes, summed up Coco's attitudes toward money.

"Coco knew nothing about figures," said Chaillet. "Rather, she possessed the cunning of a crafty horse dealer. Money? She did not count it, but she liked to make it. Why? She told me that she devoted so much energy to the task because she liked perfect work but she expected that her efforts be remunerated accordingly."

Claude L.'s impression is slightly different: "I am not sure she was sincere when she said that. Actually, she had two other more deep-seated motivations. First, I believe that she really loved money for its own sake. Second, having dealt with financiers, aware of what vast sums they made, she always had the impression that she was being cheated.

"She said: 'All those people are making fortunes with my name, but the Chanel label wouldn't exist without my talent, without my work. I am exploited and the only way to avoid being cheated by those horrible characters is to make them fork over the maximum. Then they'll have some respect for me.'

"She also said: 'It's not money for its own sake that interests me, but since it *is* the symbol of success, I must make as much of it as possible!' But I believe those were false reasons. She was eternally haunted by the fear of not being equal to her task and of not being capable of defending herself in a man's world."

In answer to a question about how skillful she was, how well she negotiated, L. replied: "She was very tough." A shadow passed over his face as he recalled some difficult moments.

"Mademoiselle Chanel had a series of eminent 'advisers,' but really they were her instruments rather than her advisers, pawns that she moved around with an astonishing intuitive understanding of psychology and an unfaltering capacity to estimate the value of the friends or adversaries facing her.

"And we all fell into the trap, even when we knew we were being manipulated. Her grasp of detail and ability to execute ideas were remarkable. But she allowed none of this to show.

"At seventy she was still very feminine and her company a singular pleasure. You can see what she must have been like at thirty-five! It was obvious that when, having monopolized the conversation for a good hour, she granted you a quarter of an hour to say your piece, she did not hear 90 percent of what you said! Of the 10 percent that remained, she only retained one-fifth —what she could use later against you or against the people you had spoken about.

"It was a painful feeling; one would have liked so much to be her friend. She managed to make you feel that she sympathized with you, that she understood you, divining, for example, the small disappointments that you might have had as a lawyer with clients opposed to her. Sometimes, I let myself be taken in. Each time, six months, nine months, one year later, what I had imprudently confided to her came back to me either as a cannonball or as grapeshot.

"I ended by quarreling with her. Then she spoke of me to mutual friends and asked what had happened to me, why I didn't come to see her. I did return to see her once or twice.

"And," concluded Claude L., "in spite of all that I knew about her, she had such charm that I would hate to think that she had felt no friendship for me. I want to believe that on some evenings when I took her to dinner and she said to me, 'Claude, I am tired . . . ,' that she was being sincere. It would be very painful for me to know that she had bamboozled me, that she had made a complete fool of me."

Crafty, Machiavellian, still prone to play-act and to get away with murder because of her charm (at seventy), imagine what the young Coco must have been like!

According to Robert Chaillet: "She feigned impatience, anger, but with a definite aim in view. I was her closest adviser during her last years and, at the same time, adviser to those who were her friends, associates, or adversaries, depending on the moment. She often jumped up and down with rage. 'You are going to kill me,' she would scream. When she felt that I had had enough, she would stop, smile, and say, 'Take a little whisky. We're going to talk of more amusing things.' She did this on purpose with a definite aim in view; she manipulated all of us."

That was Mademoiselle, tough on herself and on others, sometimes generous, sometimes tightfisted. However, in contrast to most professional philanthropists, her acts of generosity were done strictly in private.

"Everybody is going to take me for a Sister of Charity," she yelled at Jean Cocteau, who at the Boeuf sur le Toit and elsewhere chattered all about Chanel's generosity to the Ballet Russes. She never forgave him but nevertheless continued to pay his hotel bills and to have him dried out from his frequent bouts with drug addiction.

She also helped many others: Al Brown, the world-champion boxer, ravaged by drugs, whose cure she also paid for so that he could regain his crown; the poet Pierre Reverdy; Serge Lifar, the celebrated ballet dancer; and Raymond Radiguet, the novelist, the author of *Devil in the Flesh.*

She felt a real maternal affection for Radiguet. He once had said to Coco: "What I would like to know is at what age one has the right to say: I have lived."

In December 1923 he fell ill from having lived too much, loved too much, wanted too much. Coco accompanied a grief-stricken Cocteau to visit Radiguet. A doctor diagnosed typhoid and Raymond died three days later in the arms of his last love, his Polish mistress Bronia.

Even in her generosity, Mademoiselle refused to let anybody *ask* her for money, whatever the reason.

Serge Lifar, who willingly bears witness to the good turns that Coco did for him, had this experience:

"Only once in my life did I ask her for money. It was in 1939. The curtains by Picasso for the sets of *Parade* were going to be put on sale. It made me ill to think that they might be bought by just any old person. They cost 100,000 francs at that time. I asked Coco to lend me the money. She refused to listen. I was not able to buy the curtains. That, too, was Chanel."

If Mademoiselle accepted that extraordinary artists should not be treated according to ordinary rules—that it was normal to help them—still, she felt, they should behave according to certain common rules. And, vis-à-vis a woman such as herself, she expected them to behave decently, with dignity.

"Chanel, who was a very rich woman, never paid," continued Lifar, "at a restaurant or anywhere else, even when she was with a man like myself who was not always rolling in money. For example, when she needed to see me and I was at the other end of France, she would telephone and ask me to come immediately. I would jump into a train and that would cost me a lot of money. She often said: 'I hate men who ask for money.' "

Occasionally she was generous to the poor. Mademoiselle adopted a certain aristocratic conception of charity, of noblesse oblige, which meant that if the wealthy could dispose of their fortune as they saw fit, without a bad conscience, it was their duty to answer the demands of the needy, to have "their" poor.

Those who wrote to Mademoiselle, wealthy and celebrated as she was, were legion. They wrote her naïve and artful letters, and though rarely moved, she always answered petitions for help.

Sometimes she became furious, as she did with a woman living in the Marais who, claiming to be paralyzed, asked for a raincoat, a suit, and perfume. Coco dictated a letter full of insults. She did not receive an answer.

Later she was to soften up, to have secret charities that she hid like private playthings. She said: "I am too old to improve my legend."

She had strange concerns. "I want something to be done for people who have had their hands burned, because there is nothing worse for an artisan like *me*—after all I am only an artisan —than not to be able to use her hands anymore," she said one day to Robert Chaillet, at a time when her hand was paralyzed, following, it was said, a particularly violent fit of anger.

Perhaps one can sum up this captain of industry with the words of one of her friends with whom she was no longer on the best of terms:

"Nothing in the world could have made me marry you to take you to bed, but as a businessman, I would marry you instantly."

7.

The Dressmaker and the Duke

1924. Coco was forty-one years old. A photograph shows her lying on a couch, over which hang leafy scrolls of sculptured wood. According to Maurice Goudeket, her husband, Colette once described Coco's eyes, which seem lost in reverie, as having "the color of flaked granite, the color of a mountain pool nestling among sun-kissed rocks." She is dressed in black. Is she wearing a dress or a skirt and blouse? We can distinguish nothing except the extraordinary suppleness of the material from which her head emerges, resting against the back of the sofa.

"Her slender body hardly dents the fawn-colored suede cushions. She rests in the indolent pose of Madame Récamier as she was painted by Baron Gérard. But don't be deceived: her back is as taut as a steel rod; her slender fingers brush the cushions in a restless caress, her piercing eyes come to rest here and there, their gaze so intense that everyone thinks of them as black," wrote Gilbert Guilleminault, journalist and historian.

In the last years, things had changed rapidly for Coco. She was the undisputed queen of Paris fashions. At 29 rue du Faubourg St.-Honoré and at 31 rue Cambon, Coco, entertaining lavishly and throwing fabulous balls, was more and more the queen of the three worlds of a Paris in which the Roaring Twenties were beginning to run out of steam: the Faubourg St.-Germain and its titled aristocracy; the Boulevard Haussmann and the Champs Elysées, where the nouveaux riches displayed their wealth; and the domain of the inspired bohemians, centered first in Montmartre and later in Montparnasse.

Misia Sert remained her great friend, but they were on equal footing by 1924. Misia dared far less often to say to her: "Shut up, you idiot. . . ." By the mid-twenties Coco had asserted her independence; she required no introduction into the worlds of art Misia had dominated, and she was now richer, in her own right, than Misia. Not that their artist friends were interested in money; they appreciated Coco's wit, culture, and spirit more than what Bernard Grasset called "the Great Mademoiselle's pensions." Only three years before she had asked Diaghilev: "But who are Picasso, Satie, and Stravinsky?" Now she received them in her salon. Coco quickly learned who her new circle of associates were and what they did. And, by this time, her advice was sometimes taken as a command; since she was usually right, her counsels were followed.

Much later, Coco was to confide to one of her intimate friends: "Misia? She lasted only a moment. I used her." And one must wonder, though one cannot tell—Coco was far too careful to let on about such matters—if this was a sincere admission or posthumous vengeance against a woman who had dominated her. Or, it may have been simply a desire to make people forget that she had ever cared about someone and a determination to preserve her image as a tough woman.

With Coco truth was dependent on the circumstances of the moment; it was merely a word. She admired herself in the mirror of pleasant recollections but saw herself differently in the glass of humiliating memory.

As it was, circumstances in the mid-twenties all conspired to make Coco forget her humiliations and provided a far more solid basis for Coco's success. Indeed, as we have seen, some of the elegant young ladies of the prewar era (those who had been dressed by her but who had refused to greet her at the race track) were now employees of the Chanel firm.

It is tempting (and untrue) to say that Chanel "bought" everything: a Grand Duke as a lover, the Ballets Russes for social climbing, the Faubourg St.-Germain as employees. Even if it were true, it would be unfair to both Coco and her friends to see all those names from the worlds of art, literature, and dance simply as parasites attracted by Mademoiselle's generosity. Certainly, Coco benefited financially from her reputation as a patron of the arts, but financial success was not her only aim in life. She used money and influence in the arts to help compensate for her modest origins (sometimes she used it for vengeance) and her poor education.

Yet what made her such an extraordinary personality cannot be explained so simply. Her astonishing self-confidence, her inordinate pride, with which she overcame her morbid timidity, her innate ability to discern real talent, her tremendous gift for understanding and foreseeing the evolution of her times—all these remain part of the mystery of Chanel.

Some of her so-called friends, whose only claim to fame lies in the futility of their existence, to this day ridicule her "lack of culture." But the small-minded are always jealous. Those who knew her well, and with whose opinion no one will quarrel, knew better. Of Coco, Jean Cocteau said: "No history of French literature would be complete without citing the name of Coco Chanel"; André Gide, "I have never understood the connection between fashion and literature, but Chanel explains it"; Georges Auric, "She was also one of the most intelligent women I have had the privilege of meeting"; Maurice Sachs, "There are friendships that mark a lifetime. They bring greatness if one is prepared to receive it. Chanel's was."

Many others could be quoted—Hemingway, Picasso, Dali, Colette, and Stravinsky, among them. Clearly, no fashion entrepreneur could develop this sort of reputation as a mere adjunct to her business activities. Coco was never a couturière who cultivated the friendship of others just to better her fashion career.

To accentuate these characteristics, Coco was paradoxical about money. Although she was painted as ambitious and greedy, no woman ever gave so much without counting the cost. "Money was freedom. I loved it for that," she often said when talking about that period in her life. "Rich, therefore free." Happy?

Was she happy? No one can tell. Coco probably had no real liaison in the middle twenties—her affair with the Grand Duke Dimitri, never white-hot, cooled severely before she met Westminster—perhaps because she didn't need one. She had never been so beautiful, so fascinating, so well regarded. Lady Abdy, her friend off and on over a period of forty years, describes her for us:

"Her charm was incomparable. It was like magic. I watched

her charm an American businessman, from whom she hoped to get a great deal. She made use of every artful device—moving close to him, looking into his eyes, speaking in a low voice, and playing with one of her marvelous pearl necklaces which she kept brushing against her lips. By flattering him in this almost contemptible manner, she got what she wanted.

"She had a Florentine sense of the art of intrigue. She knew better than anyone how to arouse people one against the other. In the end the decision was always hers, and she did what pleased her."

Georges Auric also remembers:

"Paris in 1925 was a perpetual party. And Coco Chanel was the living symbol of every luxury and every extravagance of the period.

"First of all, she was beautiful. More than beautiful—glorious, glorious, with infinite charm. She was extremely sure of her own importance in fashions; she knew she was right and said so without modesty. But this did not bother us, for in fact she was right. She was never mistaken.

"I remember a soirée given by the Princess Eugénie Murat, where I was particularly struck by Coco's grace and vitality. It must have been around 1925. Stravinsky, José María Sert, and Misia were there. Chanel was wearing a pearl necklace at least two yards long. She was wearing a fortune around her neck.

"Everyone was very gay. We had all had quite a bit to drink. Chanel suddenly started dancing the Charleston to a frenzied rhythm. Her fabulous necklace swirling about her, she had abandoned herself to the dance, when suddenly—crack! The necklace broke. There was a moment of silence; everything stopped; then everyone rushed about looking for Coco's pearls. In those days, tails, not tuxedos, were worn, and it was an extraordinary sight to behold all those elegant gentlemen crawling on their hands and knees, looking under furniture and rugs. In fact, I've always wondered if one or two pearls didn't end up in someone's pocket. Only Coco remained serene and calm, as if what was going on was of no concern to her at all."

Her love life?

"She never wanted to get married. She was much too jealous of her independence. She couldn't imagine herself becoming a man's companion."

Lady Abdy's judgment is much harsher, without nuance:

"She really only had one real love—herself and everything she stood for, that is to say, her fashion house. Everything else was merely passion, weaknesses, adventures without a future, calculated liaisons."

Perhaps Lady Abdy is not far from the truth. Chanel left Etienne Balsan and refused to marry Boy Capel; she discarded Grand Duke Dimitri. It was she who chose to act, or not to act, not her sponsors. The first two helped her financially; Dimitri helped launch her. To that extent, her liaisons were calculated, but not on the usual level. With Coco the motivation was original: her determination, her need to owe *nothing* to anyone. In calculation, for Coco, lay the route both to her success and her independence. Unfortunately, independence became such a passion that it also resulted in loneliness, cruel solitude.

A spendthrift, she could not stand anyone she suspected of being a parasite, and she alienated almost everyone sooner or later. It was just such a suspicion, probably not entirely unfair, that put an end to her friendship with Maurice Sachs, whom she had paid handsomely to assemble a library for her. "At first I was nothing more than a supplier," Sachs wrote in *Witches' Sabbath*. "Gradually I became an habitué of the house and a friend."

Here is how he described their final breakup:

"Soon Mademoiselle Chanel, whose shelves I had filled in a few months, was no longer my customer, but since she was one of those people whose hearts are a little spoiled by money and who forget that one could love them for themselves, while perhaps detesting their wealth, she began to take me for a typical hanger-on. This lasted until the day when one of our dear mutual friends obliged us by stirring up trouble between us."*

The episode illustrates the heart of Coco's tragedy. Surrounded by people, animated by a desire to dominate and to possess them in her dread of solitude, she became overly suspicious whenever she began to imagine that perhaps people preferred her possession of money to her as a person.

By 1925 her obsessive suspicion had already become the principal thread of her existence. A queen and conquering heroine, Coco was, after the death of Boy Capel, a free woman in search of true love, but in spite of many impassioned episodes she never

---

*Probably Cocteau, who was not spared Sachs's vicious gossip.

found it. When she thought she had, it always turned out to be an impossible love.

The great achievement of her life was fashion designing, but one can also see in her single-minded attitude to her career, in the time she accorded her business, a way to distract herself from and compensate for her heartbreaks.

Or was it the other way around? Did she sacrifice the impulses of her heart to relentless work? Did she put her work ahead of her private life?

It would be vain to try to answer. But it is quite evident that beneath that brilliant wrapping, that lavishness and that imposing worldliness, lay hidden the tragedy of an emotionally unstable life.

Serge Lifar underlines this facet of Coco:

"In 1929, Diaghilev presented his last spectacle on the stage of the Sarah Bernhardt Theater. Stravinsky's *Apollo,* Prokofiev's *Prodigal Son,* Stravinksy's *Renard,* which was my first choreography, were on the program. It proved to be a fantastic evening! After the show, Coco entertained in her home on 29 rue du Faubourg St.-Honoré. We drank rivers of champagne and vodka. I can assure you that Coco drank as much as anyone else. As always, she flirted with the men. She was very kittenish, even purring, pretending she was completely captivated, when suddenly, pfft! Nobody there! She was a little like Cinderella. She disappeared around two in the morning so as not to miss her beauty sleep. She allowed men to think that everything was possible, but she never gave anything. That is Chanel's tragedy. She searched for happiness, for love. She found it only once, with Boy Capel, who had everything, money, charm. . . . Her revenge [for his tragic death] was celebrity and success."

Admired, supported by friends, honored, rich, she had come a long way from the orphanage. But the obsessions of the little girl who had invented a father gone to seek his fortune in the United States and who had conversed with the dead in the cemetery were still the same—solitude and fear of poverty. Her wealth inexorably made her a prisoner.

Whom, then, *could* she love? Coco herself was silent on the subject. Even at moments when her relations with her friends were excellent, as they were in those years, the minute the subject of love came up she lowered a veil and the inquirer soon lost his way.

Then on September 29, 1924, readers of the gossip columns of the London *Daily Express* read the following item:

"The second marriage of the Duke of Westminster is already quite compromised; the Duchess of Westminster, after spending a short holiday in the United States, arrived here yesterday in the White Star liner *Homeric*. 'I have come back,' she told me, 'but where I am going to stay I do not know, because I have no home and no friends. I cannot say what I shall do until I go to London. The only thing certain is that I am homeless. My position is really unthinkable, and unfortunately I cannot forget it.' An injunction sought by the duchess to restrain the duke from ejecting her from Bourdon House, Daires Street, Berkeley Square, was recently refused by the Court. It was stated during the hearing that the duchess filed a divorce petition in June."

This was not the first time that the love life of Hugh Richard Arthur Grosvenor, Duke of Westminster, cousin of the king, had become the talk of the town. Immensely rich, heir to what was said to be one of the largest fortunes in England, Westminster, who was known to his friends as Bend-or, after his grandfather's famous horse, which had won the Derby in 1880, fought boredom throughout his life. Very tall, slightly corpulent, with immense blue eyes, blond hair, and a complexion weathered by sun and sea, he frequented fashionable places, indulging an unparalleled taste for luxury.

The duke was not handsome in the conventional sense, but he had a superb presence, irresistible charm, and two passions, both in keeping with his great name: horses and women. He abandoned himself to these passions vigorously and lavishly. In his castle, Eton Hall, the stable boys were organized in brigades; inside his huge greenhouses several hundred gardeners cultivated lilies, carnations, and orchids, which were dispatched to his innumerable conquests in the four corners of Europe by way of diligent messengers. When the duke took a fancy to a lady, he, lovesick as a schoolboy, would rush out at dawn to pick wildflowers in his park for her.

Loelia Mary Ponsonby, who became his third wife, has left a colorful and vivid portrait of Bend-or, *Grace and Favour*, which helps us to understand his exceptional and passionate nature:

"He was a sixteenth-century buccaneer searching for adventure, and the enemy he struck against was not the Spaniard but the Establishment—long before the word had been invented.

"He was a formidable and capricious autocrat, a czar, a sultan, Jupiter hurling bolts of thunder, a god whom it was impossible to treat as an equal.

"His smallest desire had to be obeyed as though it were a divine command. The good fairies had given him everything: a great name, immense properties, a magnificent bearing, a brilliant mind, a great heart.

"On top of everything else, he had charm. His charm was not always innocent but it was irresistible. At times I observed him, trying to analyze him, and I think that the miracle was that he could, when he wanted to, become a child. His blue eyes became innocent, and the autocratic duke disappeared, to make room for Peter Pan.

"Living with him, one realized that he was a giant among men. His virtues were gigantic, as were his vices, and I never saw him do or heard him say a petty or mediocre thing. He thought big. His generosity was colossal. And don't think that this is the common rule among rich people! In general, it is quite the reverse."

His way of counting or not counting was rather confusing, or was it a matter of mood? The duchess adds:

"He distributed generous tips, but rarely wore a hat, for he claimed that it would cost him three hundred pounds per year for the cloakroom! Servants recognized his panache and adored him.

"On the other hand, he could be without mercy if he thought someone was trying to thwart him or play a dirty trick on him. But he lived surrounded by parasites, profiteers, intriguers, buffoons."

The same contradictions, the same inability to reduce things to a simple formula, were present in the domain of his intellect:

"Here he was a real puzzle, at times displaying ignorance and narrow-mindedness, at others astonishing everyone with his acute powers of judgment."

The duke loved France. The graceful silhouette of his yacht, the *Flying Cloud,* appeared in the ports of the Côte d'Azur, lighting up as night fell for the duke's lavish parties. Often at dawn, the yacht, emptied of its guests, would raise its anchor, taking the duke and his favorite of the moment off on a cruise that would last until the next port of call, the next encounter.

Covered with jewels, drying her tears, the castoff favorite would leave the ship and for years to come would receive weekly a superb spray of orchids.

The unhappy duchess who had confided so sincerely, if indiscreetly, her distress to the *Daily Express* was the duke's second wife, Violet Mary Nelson, formerly divorced from George Rowley. Westminster had married her on November 26, 1920, and their divorce was decreed in 1925. The duke had been surprised in the company of a certain Mrs. Crosby at the Hôtel de Paris in Monte Carlo.

His first marriage had lasted longer. Celebrated on February 16, 1901, at St. Paul's, Knightsbridge, London, it was the wedding of the year. Indeed, the marriage was juicy newspaper copy from the start. The very ostentatiousness of the marriage was scandalous, for the Court was still in mourning for Queen Victoria, who had just died. Still, the Boer War had ended and under the aegis of King Edward VII, the new reign promised to be gay, especially if the new king continued in the manner he had conducted himself as Prince of Wales.

Among the guests at the wedding was a great friend of Bend-or, a twenty-six-year-old member of Parliament, Winston Churchill, whom Great Britain had hailed as a hero two years before after his spectacular escape while a prisoner of the Boers.

The duke was very proud of his young bride, Constance Edwina Cornwallis-West, nicknamed Shelag. She was beautiful; she danced and skated superbly, rode horseback to perfection. For three years, in all the festivities for which England rediscovered its taste, they were considered the ideal couple. They were handsome, young, and rich; they adored each other.

Alas, happiness was fleeting. Though Bend-or loved his wife, above all he loved to *love*. More and more frequently he left on long cruises, and Shelag, abandoned, became bored.

Family difficulties did not help matters. The duke grew tired of his in-laws' game of using their daughter to extract vast sums of money from him. Their castle of Ruthin was almost in ruins, and though Bend-or was not constitutionally opposed to family obligations—the upbringing of the English aristocracy presupposed fidelity to certain traditions—he was forced to face the fact that he had married not only the pretty Shelag but the entire Cornwallis-West clan. And he found that a bit too much.

For all these reasons, while relations between the duke and Shelag remained courteous, they became progressively more distant. Then on June 18, 1919, Shelag sued for divorce.

On October 13, 1924, a few days after the item published in the *Daily Express*, there appeared in the *Star* the following unattributed lines, in which, beneath a vagueness marked by a certain elegant humor, the rumor became more definite:

"Rumor is busy with the future of a duke whose matrimonial affairs have recently been much discussed. A few months ago, when trouble between the duke and his duchess first began, it was said that the next duchess would be a very good-looking girl whose parents have become prominent quite lately. Now gossip has it that she will be a clever and charming Frenchwoman who presides over a very exclusive dressmaking establishment in Paris."

A few months later, the duke was photographed in the company of his friend Galloper Smith, Earl of Birkenhead, and of Mademoiselle Chanel at Aintree race track near Liverpool. At their last meeting in Paris, the duke had promised Chanel that he would take her to the Grand National, the great steeplechase that is run at Aintree each spring: thus the visit to Liverpool. But if this seemingly sudden liaison came as a surprise to London, Paris society had been noticing for some time the off-and-on presence of the duke at Mademoiselle Chanel's side at Opéra premières.

In May and June 1924, he had been seen several times in Coco's wake, at the theater of the Champs Elysées during rehearsals of *Train Bleu*, for which she had designed the costumes, Cocteau had written the story, Darius Milhaud had composed the music, and Henri Laurens and Pablo Picasso had designed the sets.

Indeed, it was in Coco's company that a hitherto unimagined world, that of avant-garde art, was revealed to the silent and intrigued duke. He watched in astonished amusement, already captivated and soon very much at ease. Diaghilev with his monocle stuck in his drooping eyelid, Picasso dressed haphazardly as usual—usually in a workman's blue denims—Cocteau full of lively energy, forever jumping from idea to idea.

Later, in the magnificent villa near Roquebrune on the Côte d'Azur that he was to give Coco, the duke and his friends were to get along beautifully with all these artists, each discovering the other, surprised to find a quite different reality from that which he had imagined. It was not the least of Coco's strengths that in her presence, nobility of blood and nobility of spirit hit it off perfectly.

True enough, the plot of *Train Bleu* had everything to amuse the duke. The scenario was simple, almost trite: the departure of the train for the Côte d'Azur, the seaside romances between gigolos and their girls, carefully dressed by Coco in little beach costumes, which transformed them into boyish-looking creatures in perfect contrast to the enormous women, flaunting exuberant bosoms, that Picasso had painted on the backdrops.

Misia was often there, talking, teasing, suggesting. Coco kept quiet, rarely speaking except about *professional* things; no longer did she have to prove herself, to gain acceptance. She had taken her place in the ranks of ballet creators through her costumes and enjoyed equal footing with these fabulous artists, in an achievement that seemed casual enough. Misia, despite the fact that she had been an "angel" of the ballet long before Coco, was never to attain this kind of acceptance. She never achieved as much power as her friend and rival, for whom Diaghilev hid his respect behind a mask of haughty silence.

Of all the artists, only the dancers still reacted to Coco with some diffidence. Although Coco had made costumes for the theater, she had never before designed for the ballet. Serge Lifar told us: "You could tell. We, the dancers, felt it. They were not costumes conceived for dancing. When we performed certain movements, they became either too long or too short."

Coco studied the gestures of the dancers. At the last moment, as usual, the afternoon of the première, she took apart and sewed back together sleeves and trouser legs. When the curtain went up, the costumes were perfectly adjusted.

How things had changed! Once Coco had trailed after Misia. Now she was mistress of all in her own right. As Lifar says:

"Ever since the famous check [when Chanel had bailed out Diaghilev financially], Coco had not done much to help Diaghilev financially. Still, what she did was very important: her name was linked to the ballet, she designed costumes, and she brought a great many people with her."

Train Bleu not only brought Westminster and Coco together; it also saw the beginning of Serge Lifar's friendship with Coco. She met him at the time of her idyl with the duke, and their friendship was to last the span of her lifetime, a life in which Westminster lasted but a moment. What is more, she *made* Serge Lifar.

Serge Lifar has given us a touching account:

"Coco came to rehearsals. She was always there. We, the dancers, didn't know too well who she was and why she was always there. We used to say to each other: 'What an odd one that Coco!'

"Diaghilev was looking for a star dancer from the troupe for *Train Bleu*. He had not yet decided who would dance the role. I remember that Chanel was seated in the orchestra between Picasso and Diaghilev. Suddenly she fixed her eyes on mine and leaned toward Diaghilev.

" 'There's your dancer!' she said.

"I heard her and I began making faces in the hope of being noticed," Serge Lifar ingenuously confessed.

"Then Picasso insisted: 'She's right; that's your dancer. His body has the ideal proportions.'

" 'So you think that your protege dances well enough?' answered Diaghilev with feigned indifference.

"And," concluded Lifar, "that's how I became a star dancer. From that moment on, Chanel and Picasso became my godparents in the arts."

Coco took great pleasure in putting up a smoke screen about her first meeting with Westminster—the truth was their meeting was inevitable, given the circles in which they traveled.

She saw him for the first time at Christmas in 1923, in Monte Carlo, where she was staying with a friend, Vera Bates Lombardi, an Englishwoman married to an American. Vera, who knew everyone in London society, loved to ride horseback, and this was what drew her to Coco.

Vera Bates, who later married Signor Lombardi, an Italian, before World War II and lived in Rome, presented the duke to Coco in the Hôtel de Paris. That evening Coco dined on the *Flying Cloud*, lulled by the strains of the violins of a gypsy orchestra that the duke had hired for the occasion. Later, they went dancing in a nightclub. Three months later they saw each other again in Paris. In the meantime, Coco's town house was filled with flowers as never before. When Westminster wooed a woman, he took no half-measures.

Yet Coco hesitated. "The duke frightened me," she confessed later to Lady Abdy. The presence of Westminster in her life reversed a certain "order of things." She could not forget Moulins: men who kept women were not so far away. With the ruined Grand Duke Dimitri she had "cleansed" herself and perhaps enjoyed an innocent revenge. Now she was rich, a patron of arts and letters, and *independent*. She no longer had the youth or the heart for sudden passions. Would not a lasting liaison with the duke cause her to lose everything she had acquired in the past few years, especially her prized independence? Besides, Bend-or's escapades were famous. With a disarming ease, made possible by his fortune, rank, and nobility, he went from adventure to adventure, unconsciously making the women he loved into cocottes.

Coco hesitated for three months: if she was to love the duke, it could only be as an equal. Her complete disinterest had to be practically shouted from the rooftops. She had to be unique, to remain what she had become only in these last few years: Mademoiselle Chanel.

The duke was in Paris during Holy Week of 1924 with the Prince of Wales. Later, Coco recounted that they both came one evening to the rue du Faubourg St.-Honoré. It seems that the heir to the throne sat in an armchair, his back to the fabulous screens, and with a charming smile said to Coco: "Call me David."

Two days later, Coco joined Westminster in Bayonne, and they left on a cruise.

Bend-or took Coco to England. There she discovered the duke's castle: Eton Hall, in Cheshire, an immense pile in Victorian Gothic style. On the walls hung one of the most fabulous collections of paintings in the world—Goya, Velasquez, but very few modern works.

"He detested modern painting, sculpture, and music," his third wife, Loelia, noted.

Suits of armor lined the dining room walls, alternating with the footmen, who stood with the same immobility.

In the midst of this sumptuous setting, where the heraldic inscription of the royal family and of the Order of the Garter, *Honni soit qui mal y pense*, was woven into the silk upholstery of the seats, Westminster lived, surrounded by his court. His old school companions were there, holding almost honorary positions. One supervised the stables, another the greenhouses; a third filled in as secretary.

Coco was to have pleasant memories of this decor and the kind of life she led there. She especially appreciated the liberty accorded to guests: "I enjoyed it greatly, except for the rain. The hosts left you alone. In France, when you're invited by friends for the weekend, they ask you at what time you want to play tennis, walk in the park, have tea, make love."

She read a great deal, took long rides on horseback in the park, and—sacrilege!—cut whatever flowers she wanted in the greenhouses. The duke's servants had never before thought of setting bouquets around. Thanks to Coco, the drawing rooms and halls were decorated with flowers, which were changed daily.

"I hoped to make the ghosts and the suits of armor more friendly to me," she said.

Often Coco was bored. It seemed that "everyone [was] forever doing needlepoint, looking at rose gardens, changing their clothes, boiling in front of a fire, and freezing away from it!"

Sometimes Misia came to visit her friend. She joined them on cruises and on salmon-fishing trips to Scotland, but open-air life did not suit her style: she rode badly, and the wind carried her witty remarks away from the hearing of those for whom she intended them.

Once she told Coco: "When the English are really in love, they give everything. Since the duke treats you like a greedy empress, he must be madly in love with you."

But the comment annoyed Coco, who characteristically avenged herself cruelly. "Take a horse," she said, when Misia asked to make a trip to a place some fifty miles away.

Coco came to know the duke's high and low moods: Jupiter and Peter Pan, his rages and his rejoinders, his cruelty at times with subordinates, which he later would try to make up for with infinite delicacy, his childish jokes.

"He adored good wine, cognac, green Chartreuse; he often amused himself by filling empty bottles with the best labels with bad cognac, just to watch his friends go into ecstasy, claiming that they could tell the year with their eyes shut," Loelia noted.

His was a refined elegance—old tweed jacket impeccably pressed, brightly polished shoes with holes in the soles but ironed laces. Westminster liked to be comfortable even while he kept up his appearance; thus his old shoes always looked new—a lesson Coco never forgot.*

In London the Roaring Twenties were at their height, and, as usual, the English were much more audacious than the French, their cabarets more daring and less "intellectual" than the Paris nightclubs. Mrs. Meyrick, a woman of incredible energy, opened a series of nightclubs where the most beautiful girls showed up in outfits that defied the period's rules of decorum. The police regularly shut down the club most recently opened—only to find it opened up again under a new name at a new address.

Mademoiselle Chanel and Westminster frequented the Embassy, the smartest of the restaurant-nightclubs, where the celebrated Ambrose orchestra played and where the maître d'hôtel, Luigi, made a reputation in high society for his faultless mastery of protocol, knowing how to place guests at just the right table in accordance with their social position, age, fortune, status, and, in the case of women, beauty. Its decor was simple and neutral: a balcony and wooden staircase, which suddenly became famous throughout the world when an American dancer, Leonora Hughes, used it to perform the shimmy-shake, which consisted in shaking from the neck down to the ankles in a very sexy manner.

Just as in Paris, London society whirled from drawing room to drawing room. An American, Emerald Cunard, had a gift for entertaining akin to genius. She didn't care about her guests' social positions, imposing on them a single draconian rule—they had to be attractive. Coco charmed her.

Another fabulously rich American woman, Mrs. Corrigan, attempted the conquest of London society by giving receptions for which she brought orchestras from the United States. She organized lotteries, and the prizes consisted of jewelry from Cartier. As "luck" would have it, only duchesses won. As for Mrs. Corrigan, she won the right to a stool in their drawing rooms.

Coco, herself, preferred being entertained by the extraordinary Mrs. Richard Guinness, who had married into the

---

*When we inquired about Mademoiselle's wardrobe from her last personal maid and the only one present when she died, we were told she had: "A few tweed suits, which Mademoiselle wore for a long time. When they became too shiny with age, she'd have them dyed, for she hated to get rid of them.

" 'I really feel at ease in an old suit,' she would say. 'But not rough, heavy stuff. They didn't know how to make lightweight tweeds in Scotland until I insisted.' Her eyes twinkled at the memory of that battle."

Guinness brewery family. She was a heavily built woman with the nickname of "somber Beatrice" because of her deep voice. Mrs. Guinness had a most disconcerting sense of humor. When buying a hat, she would announce to the salesgirl in the gravest tone possible (and she could be quite terrifying): "What I want is a hat for an old and ugly woman, whose husband hates her."

This amazing woman had an exceptional flair for detecting talent, and in her house on Great Cumberland Place she received many still-unknown artists. Coco adored the atmosphere, which was comparable to that she had created in her Parisian salon. Seen with Mrs. Guinness at the beginning of their careers were Noel Coward, Oliver Messel, and Cecil Beaton, who painted at that time one of the few existing portraits of Coco.

Another famous hostess was an American, Maxine Elliot, who entertained at Hartsbourne Manor outside London. During her receptions, which the Prince of Wales frequently attended, there was much laughter and high-stake gambling. Once Lord Beaverbrook and Galloper Smith, Earl of Birkenhead, made a bet of one hundred pounds (an enormous sum in those days) during a tennis match. Birkenhead, wildly encouraged by his friends, including the Duke of Westminster and Coco, barely managed to win.

As in Paris, everyone loved costumes; masquerade balls were the rage. The most grandiose balls were given by the Duchess of Sutherland in her Green Street town house, Hampden House. There Duff Cooper was seen coxing an eight-oared shell, brought down from Eton, with society ladies at the oars. The Duke of Marlborough disguised himself as a lady swimmer about to attempt the crossing of the Channel. One evening the Duchess of Sutherland appeared in a frilly dress trimmed with feathers and ended the evening dressed up as a wooden soldier. Lord Ednam arrived in a nanny costume, pushing a pram containing Lady Ednam. The Prince of Wales and the Duke of Kent dressed up as little boys in short pants, while fourteen members of White's, one of London's most select clubs, arrived as monks.

Once again, putting to good use her remarkable entrée into elegant London high society, Coco, with the help of Vera Bates (it was she who had introduced Coco to tweeds), gained quite a large clientele. She established showrooms, where she dressed, among others, the Duchess of York, wife of the future King George VI, and Daisy Fellowes. Half-French and half-American,

Daisy reigned in London as well as Paris. Slender, with dark hair, she had the silhouette of a young boy and the Chanel style was enchantingly becoming to her. It is hardly surprising that she had been one of Coco's first customers in Deauville when Coco began selling hats and sweaters.

Though Coco, on the arm of the duke, was received everywhere and though she acted as hostess at Eton Castle, her position caused a great deal of gossip. A grand seigneur who delighted in shocking the Establishment, the duke wasn't in the least worried about the situation. Coco never mentioned it, but just as in Paris, she preferred to entertain rather than be entertained. The problem, compounded by her involvement in "trade," could not be disguised, if it could be ignored, and she probably suffered some embarrassment.

Lady Abdy throws some light on a curious facet of Coco's relationship with the duke.

"Coco was like a little girl before the duke and was very careful not to contradict him," she told us. Clearly Coco was very nearly, if not quite, out of her depth, but she faced up to the situation with great cleverness.

First, she said that she didn't speak English, while, in fact, she both understood it and took lessons.

Nobody, she emphasized, was to know. As she told Lady Abdy:

"I took them from a young secretary of the duke, an insignificant young man with a vague title. I had asked him to give me lessons without the duke's knowing about it. He was terrified that the latter would discover my little subterfuge and hold him responsible for it."

She apologized for her ignorance of the language with a smile.

"One of my English friends has absolutely forbidden me to learn English for fear that I would then understand the nonsense he tells his friends," she'd say.

But by obliging her interlocutors to speak French, she maintained her superiority over them in social as well as business discussions.

The acute sensitivity to every nuance, every occasion, that marked Coco in all her dealings was never more manifest than when, as all London waited to see what Coco would do, the daughter of the Duke of Westminster, Mary, made her debut in London society. The occasion was to be a large ball given by the duke's former wife, who, although divorced, was still called the Duchess of Westminster. The royal family was to be present. The duchess had invited Coco. Would she accept? On one side lay retreat in the face of the enemy; on the other, a dangerous situation verging on scandal. Coco decided not to attend, but this decision was by no means a retreat.

On the evening of the ball Coco gave a dinner, inviting the duchess and her daughters, Winston Churchill, and a few other intimate friends. When it came time to leave for the ball, pretending that she had to change, Coco urged her guests to go on without her. Then she went to bed and told the duke who, worried at her absence, had come in haste that she was ill. She had been expected at the ball; everyone was certain that she would make an appearance after having given a dinner in her *own* house, which was next door to the duke's. Her absence, noticed by all, made Coco the queen of an evening that, according to some dowagers, should have been her swan song.

That is the story, according to what Coco later let slip. Did she embroider on the facts? If she did, it remains one of the most beautiful gems in the Chanelian epic. And it is typical of the narrower path she had to tread in England than in France, where she mixed much more freely and often with a far less stuffy group.

If she held her own in England, the play was tiring, especially since her business in France remained active. Indeed, as the mistress of Westminster, it behooved Chanel more than ever to remain Chanel, the great fashion designer, for in her work she could hold onto her independence. At all times, she traveled back and forth to Paris for business reasons, seldom staying longer than two or three weeks in England at one time.

Finally, Chanel moved quietly back to Paris. Westminster was anything but quiet, however, as he pursued her. He organized a whole system of special couriers: three messengers—all titled, she later confided proudly—plied back and forth between Paris and London bearing the inflamed letters he wrote her several times a day. He added modest bouquets of wildflowers, which he picked at dawn and which she found at her bedside upon awakening the following day. "All I want from you are wildflowers picked by your own hands," she wrote to him. The duke complied, but jewels glittered under the petals.

Whenever they were together, the two lovers went either to Mimizan,* in the Landes, where the duke owned a house, or to Cannes, where they boarded the yacht for cruises, one of which was interrupted tragically in 1929 by the death of Diaghilev in Venice.

The occasion was one of high drama. As the *Flying Cloud* cruised among the islands off the Dalmatian coast in the Adriatic Sea with the duke, Coco, and Misia aboard, Serge Diaghilev, and old man at fifty-seven, was struggling against fever and delirium at the Lido in Venice in the care of Serge Lifar and Boris Kochno.

Serge Lifar told us: "He was being treated by a Venetian doctor for rheumatism and boils. I saw perfectly well that he was very ill, and so I sent a telegram to Misia and Coco, who were aboard the *Flying Cloud*. Westminster immediately gave orders to head for Venice. Coco and Misia raced to Diaghilev's bedside with the duke's personal physician, who diagnosed typhus."

When Diaghilev seemed to improve, Coco left Misia with him and went off again on the yacht. But she had hardly left Venice when she had misgivings and returned to Venice. Diaghilev had died at dawn in the arms of Lifar and Kochno, and Misia, completely bewildered and out of ready cash, had decided to sell her last diamond necklace to cover expenses. But Coco, arriving at this crucial moment, once more paid everyone's bills.

On August 19, 1923, Diaghilev's body, lying in state on its floating bed, was transported to the islet of San Michele, the cemetery of the Doges. There were only four persons in the black gondola that followed the catafalque: Serge Lifar, Boris Kochno, another of Diaghilev's loyal disciples, Misia, and Coco —altogether a humble and ghostly procession.

Coco recounted:

"We arrived on the island where there was a Russian cemetery. Boris Kochno and Serge Lifar, who had been embracing

---

*The duke had built a luxurious hunting lodge designed by Sir Herbert Baker at Mimizan, in the Landes, between Bordeaux and Biarritz, before World War I. It was situated on the shores of a lake and could be reached only by boat. His favorite guest was Winston Churchill, who loved to paint the Landes with its pine forests, its peasants walking around on stilts, and the play of light on sand, grass, and water.

and crying for hours, decided to follow the casket on their knees. And there I was following those two snails step by step. Toward the end I had had enough and cried, 'Get up immediately and stop all this nonsense.' That's all they were waiting for. They got to their feet but continued to embrace and weep even louder."

In 1924 the duke gave Coco the property of La Pausa, near Roquebrune on the Riviera above Monte Carlo, where she built a forty-room house. But, in spite of his passion for Coco, the duke remained the duke. Coco was not the only woman in his life, and she knew it, suffered from it, sometimes raged against it, her fury made even more violent by the attraction she felt for the mystic poet, Pierre Reverdy. His strange shadow began to haunt her, though she thought at first that he appealed to her only because he was the lover of Misia, still her best friend.

Under the circumstances, marriage to the duke became increasingly unthinkable, though it was probably never really in the cards. Coco's famous retort to the duke's formal proposal— "There are already three Duchesses of Westminster, but there is only one Coco Chanel."—is almost certainly apocryphal.

"Far too vulgar," Coco said later. And nothing horrified Mademoiselle more than vulgarity.

Valery Ollivier, friend of Etienne Balsan and of Coco, and one of the young lions of pre-1914 Biarritz, had this to say:

"I went to lunch at the Chapon Fin in Bordeaux. This extremely elegant restaurant was run by a certain Sicard who looked like a Chinese and who offered an outstanding cuisine. He had an excellent cellar. I entered the Chapon to find Coco Chanel at a table with Westminster. I went up to say hello to them and she said: 'If you're alone, join us.' The conversation was very lively, and I believe that at a certain point the duke reproached Coco for her reluctance to marry him. In any case, I never heard Coco pronounce that famous phrase. Not then anyway."

It is quite possible that the duke never really encouraged Coco to become his wife. Neither of them ever gave away any secrets, and no doubt the truth of the matter is far more complex than it appeared to be. Coco wanted an undivided interest in the duke, and, consequently, she preferred being his one and only mistress rather than his abandoned wife. Certainly she could not countenance the idea of being a mere plaything.

Yet the duke was far from reassuring in his regard for Coco's wishes. However ardently he wished to marry her, he insisted that she would have to drop fashion designing. She would be his wife, full time, living a life of leisure. One can well imagine what anathema such a life, together with the wealth of this all-powerful man, represented to Coco; the loss of the freedom and independence she had achieved, which, indeed, made her something more than a passing fancy in Westminster's eyes, was always to be resisted.

The implacable couturière preferred her eternal little hat, which she rarely took off during the day as she worked in the rue Cambon, to the duchess's coronet. She could not have both, and this woman who, since childhood, had been disappointed in love, as always, ended by sacrificing it. Later, she explained to Lady Abdy:

"God knows, I cared about love. I used to fall in love without reservation. But when I had to choose between the man I loved and dresses, I always chose the dresses. I have always been stronger than my desires. Work has always been a sort of drug for me, even though I wonder if I should have become Chanel without the help of men. Had I stayed in Auvergne, I would probably have ended up marrying a farmer and milking cows. Men can never understand that. They prefer to say to a woman: 'I'll marry you and you won't have to worry anymore; you won't need to work.' "

Coco held such thoughts in horror, for she understood the implications: "You'll have nothing else to do but to be here for me; you'll be free from your obligations and thus will always have time for me."

Few of her friends could understand her obsession for work, choosing rather to ignore the quality of Coco's life. But, of course, she paid for her independence: no husband, no children, no lasting love. In fact, she never understood children, though she rather liked them.

As Claude L. and Robert Chaillet told us: "She had the soul of an Amazon. 'Chaillet,' she used to say, 'he's a good guy because he adores his grandsons and loves his dog.' She had some great-nephews and she liked them. When they came to visit her, she wanted to see them without their mother: 'Children,' she used to say, 'are not natural when their parents are with them. Parents always feel obliged to suppress them with lectures.'

"In fact, she was timid with children because she didn't understand them. She didn't know how to talk to them. She envied people who could deal with them on an equal footing."

But where would Coco, the love-starved orphan, have learned how to smile at a child?

Robert Chaillet told us: "She tried having dogs. But the same thing happened as with children. Three years before her death, she bought two Afghan hounds. When they were shown to her she said: 'They're beautiful; send them back to the kennel.' "*

"She liked the *idea* of loving children," Claude L. added. "She took in her nephew. André Palasse, but packed him off to boarding school."

"Basically, I'm a virgin, she once told Robert Chaillet. "I've never borne a child."

Ironically, Coco had once wanted a child by the Duke of Westminster, who wanted any future wife of his to be able to bear a son, his first son having died at the age of fourteen. During their liaison, she forced herself to do painful exercises that were supposed to facilitate pregnancy, she confided to friends. She did not become pregnant, of course, but even at the age of forty-five this wild hope obsessed her. To accommodate her desire she might even have consented to marry the duke, giving up everything else she wanted in order to achieve fulfill-ment. Perhaps as a mother she would have expiated her original sin and joined the ranks of "normal" women, those upon whom motherhood confers a specific role sufficient unto itself.

But the child Coco so wanted to give the duke she could have neither by him nor by anyone else. In any case, the marriage never was to take place. The two drifted apart after a classic confrontation that no novelist would dare describe for fear of writing trite melodrama.

Nothing was missing: the moon, the prow of the *Flying Cloud* or the *Cutty Sark* (the duke had two yachts at the time) plowing through the foam, the night breeze blowing, tousling everyone's hair and giving every face a romantic cast. The setting was per-fect for Coco to play her royal scene with the duke.

The yacht had been at sea for three days. Coco, silent, hadn't

---

*However, her grand-niece, Mme Labrunie, says that what Chaillet recounts was only true at the end of Coco's life. In her youth she used to like beautiful dogs. She had at La Pausa a Danish dog called Gigot and a teckel called Dachsund. Later on, she had another teckel: Kelly.

uttered a single word and appeared scornful whenever the duke approached her. The reason was obvious: the duke had brought along a pretty young lady, a fashionable decorator. But he apparently tired of her charms rapidly. On the fourth day the yacht came into port and landed its fair passenger. That night the duke, all smiles, returned on board, a fabulous pearl necklace in his hands.

Serge Lifar tells it this way:

"Chanel was very proud, and she could not stand the idea of not being the only woman in Westminster's life. When the duke presented her with the necklace, which was worth a fortune, Coco, in a superb gesture of spite, allowed the pearls to slip into the sea.

"She wanted to be the sole, unique woman, and since she wasn't, she wouldn't stand for it any longer. That's all."

The estrangement of the couple was as inevitable as their first meeting, given their different needs, but Coco's and the duke's relationship remained perfectly amicable, even after the duke decided to marry Loelia Ponsonby.

Before his marriage, he wished to present his future wife to the woman with whom he had just broken off. Loelia has described the scene, which took place in Coco's house, not without humor:

"At the time, Mademoiselle Chanel had reached the pinnacle of fame. Her sober clothes, simple and uncomplicated, were considered the height of chic. Small, dark, and feline, her clothes suited her to perfection. When I met her, she was wearing a navy blue suit and an immaculate white blouse, with very light stockings (light-colored stockings were one of her credos).

"Describing her thus one might be tempted to think that she looked like a schoolgirl, but, in fact, she gave the impression of great sophistication.

"She was wearing a great many necklaces and bracelets that clinked and jangled at her slightest movement. Her drawing room was luxurious and richly decorated. She sat down in an armchair. In the background were two Coromandel screens. She offered me a small footstool at her feet! I felt as though I were before a judge who was about to decide whether I was worthy enough to become the wife of her old admirer. I doubt very much if I passed the test.

"The atmosphere was far from warm. Desperately searching

for something to say, I told her that Mrs. George Keppel had
given me a Chanel necklace as a Christmas present. Immediately, she asked me to describe the necklace.

" 'No,' she said coldly, 'that necklace certainly doesn't come
from my establishment.'

"And the conversation came to an abrupt stop."

Coco and Westminster remained in touch for as long as he
lived, but Loelia was only to be the third Duchess of Westminster. Married in 1930, they were divorced in January 1947. On
February 7 of the same year, Bend-or married for the fourth
time, the bride being Ann Sullivan. Shortly after, on July 19, the
Duke died of coronary thrombosis. At his funeral, Churchill pronounced the oration:

"Bend-or was my friend since the Boer War more than fifty
years ago. We had a somewhat adventurous journey down from
Pretoria to Cape Town in June 1900, and our relationship,
which started then, was never ruffled.

"As a companion in danger or sport he was fearless, gay, and
delightful. He was deeply versed in all forms of animal sport and
saw into the heart of them. In this and other fields, he was hap-
piest of all when he was giving pleasure to others. The arranging
of a shoot for his friends interested him more than his actual part
in it. I remember going deer stalking at Lock More several times
with him when he would not shoot himself or take a stalker, but
showed all his art of venery in bringing me to the right place to
fire.

"All the people on his estates were devoted to him, and he did
all he could to promote their welfare.

"Although not good at explaining things or making speeches,
he thought deeply on many subjects and had unusual qualities of
wisdom and judgment. I always valued his opinion. His
numerous friends, young and old, will mourn and miss him, and
I look back affectionately and thankfully over half a century of
unbroken friendship."

Mademoiselle Chanel received the news of the duke's death
with indifference. Later on, she talked of him with her intimate
friends. Of all the men who had loved her, he was one of the few
to have merited words of esteem, words that, in her last days, the
great Mademoiselle distributed with parsimony, as though she
were bestowing a rare honor.

8.

La Pausa

Coco did more than build a house, she invented a style of living for rich people on vacation."

Thus one of her friends described La Pausa, the house that Mademoiselle Chanel had built at Roquebrune-Cap-Martin, situated between Monte Carlo and Menton.

1928. Her idyl with the duke was at its zenith, but life in London and at Eton Hall had begun to pall. Of course there was the *Flying Cloud* with its sumptuous luxury, its uniformed crew, and its routine to distract her. But being the duke's "favorite cabin boy," as Westminster called her to his friends, or wearing a sailor's jersey marked with Westminster's coat of arms, as she often did in Deauville, was not very stimulating.

In any case, though Coco liked to escape from the rue Cambon between collections, she didn't like to stay away for too long. Her future was in Paris, and she *had* to immerse herself in Paris's atmosphere from time to time or risk seeing the source of her legend run dry. She had to be able to get back in one night on the train. Away from her kingdom she was nothing more than the duke's companion, one among many—a "kept woman," sniffed a few old English ladies, gossiping on the terrace of the Hôtel de Paris when Westminster's yacht hoved into view at the entrance of the port of Monaco.

Moreover, though Coco loved the sun, the sea depressed her. She didn't know how to swim and scanning the horizon for hours on end bored her to death.

Her solution was to set up a home in France. Of course Westminster had Mimizan, from whose windows one beheld a sea of pines stretching toward infinity. But the duke had entertained a great deal there, experienced a number of adventures about which Coco, who habitually threw gallons of No. 5 into the fire she kept burning day and night the year round for fear she would catch a whiff of gardenia or chypre—two perfumes she had always hated—had no wish to be reminded.

Coco was and wanted to be on her *own* home ground, to receive the duke in a place where she could enjoy her own rhythm of life. Mimizan was his; she wanted a place where she would feel less imposed upon. Though she didn't mind being waited on, she wanted to be able to take a few steps down a corridor without feeling as though she were reviewing an army, supercilious footmen lined up at attention as though on a parade ground.

Thus, at her urging, on a height overlooking the sea, the duke bought a five-acre piece of property, for 1.8 million francs. The name of the property, La Pausa, was a story in itself. According to a legend, which the good priest of Roquebrune always recounted to the children in catechism class, when Mary Magdalene fled Jerusalem after the crucifixion, she noticed a lovely garden, filled with olive trees, as she was traveling across the territory of Roquebrune. Since she was very tired, she paused there to rest. On the very spot rose a chapel, La Pausa, built many centuries ago and dedicated to Our Lady of La Pausa. The chapel was adjacent to Mademoiselle Chanel's property.

Whether the legend is true or not, it was in La Pausa that, later, amid lavender, hyacinths, and mimosas, a large and beautiful house had been built later to be sold to a Roquebrune family, the Mayens, from whom the duke purchased it. Two other little villas completed the property.

And thus it was that one day in 1929, at the opening of a Picabia exposition in Cannes, a twenty-eight-year-old architect, Robert Streitz, met Edouard Corniglion-Molinier, who was to become a hero of the Free French forces during World War II, and learned that Count Jean de Segonzac, whose house in Roquebrune he had restored, had recommended him to one of his friends who wished to build a house in the same region. The friend was Mademoiselle Chanel.

Today, Robert Streitz, nearing seventy, lives in retirement at Valbonne in the Alpes-Maritimes. He recalls:

"My first meeting with Mademoiselle Chanel took place aboard the *Flying Cloud*, which was lying at anchor in the port of Monaco. I asked her to describe what she wanted. She had no fixed ideas. Three days later I drafted a preliminary project, which Jean de Segonzac submitted to her. She accepted it almost immediately."

Shortly before his death General Corniglion-Molinier told his friend Emery Reeves, the present owner of La Pausa, how Robert Streitz had become the architect for Coco's house. Reeves told us:

"Streitz dreamed of building the 'ideal Mediterranean villa' without ever thinking seriously that he would some day realize his dream. Corniglion at the time was a young notary in Menton and often saw Streitz, his childhood friend. One morning as they were going down the Grande Corniche together, the young architect noticed a large garden planted with olive trees. 'There,' he said. 'That would be the perfect spot for my ideal villa.' Corniglion retorted with a smile: 'Well, old chap, this afternoon you'll come with me, and together we'll sell your plan for your dream villa!' The fact was Corniglion had been invited to a cocktail party that the Duke of Westminster was giving on his yacht. Before nightfall Streitz had indeed sold his plan to Coco and the duke, who were both most enthusiastic. The sale of the land took place in Corniglion's office. The only comment made by the duke was: 'I want everything built with the best material and under the best working conditions.' "

Coco made it clear she would be involved in the plans from the beginning. Her first request was significant. She told the architect, as he recalls:

"I want very much to have a large stone staircase in the entrance hall. I remember from my childhood the immense staircase, with its steps worn from use, in the orphanage at Aubazine. We used to call it the monks' staircase. That's what I want."

Robert Streitz went to Aubazine to have a close look at the staircase and to bring back photographs. He talked about his client to the mother superior of the orphanage, who still remembered her little boarder.

In her house Coco wanted a souvenir of her childhood: the staircase on whose tiles she had heard light footfalls.

Robert Streitz continued:

". . . And we signed the plans at Mimizan in the duke's house. This was the only signature between us. We never had a contract or any kind of correspondence. For me Mademoiselle's word was as good as gold. Nine months after the completion of La Pausa every last bill had been paid on the nail."

In his dealings with Coco, Streitz felt that the two most essential characteristics of her personality were intelligence and generosity.

"She was certainly intelligent. In discussions one always had a feeling of one's own inferiority. And when she was waiting for you, it was best not to linger behind the door, for you risked hearing her say:

" 'That is a complete idiot.'

"As for her generosity, one day, I was invited to lunch with her. I had just bought a secondhand car, which as luck would have it broke down that day. I was obliged to go to La Pausa by bus. We talked at length about my car, which she knew well for she had the same model in her six-car garage. When it came time for me to leave, she suddenly said to her Italian butler:

" 'Ugo, please get the papers of the Mors and give them to Mr. Streitz.'

"I thanked her profusely and promised to have the car back within three days.

" 'Not at all,' she answered. 'I'm giving it to you.' "

Fantastically generous as she could be, she knew how to defend her rights, and she spent a small fortune proving her ownership of a tiny piece of the La Pausa land that a peasant claimed as his. Avarice or pettiness? Probably neither. As a countrywoman she simply followed the custom of French peasants, whose boundary quarrels with neighbors help fill long winter evenings.

"Mademoiselle knew what she wanted." Edgar Maggiore, the contractor, sighed, making an eloquent grimace.

"We proved to her that the site she had chosen was not the ideal one. It was solid rock with spots of clay. It was dangerously out of plumb. She refused to listen to our objections, and we were obliged to build extraordinary foundations. Think of it, underneath the house there are supporting beams whose cross-section measures one yard! Moreover, for the roof she wanted only *handmade* curved tiles. Even then they were difficult to find. Since we needed twenty thousand of them, we had to look for them in villages as far away as Sospel. We bought the old tiles for a king's ransom, replacing them with new ones. . . ."

In short, thanks to Coco, there was a great deal of speculation in old tiles in Roquebrune around 1930. And, happy with the manna that fell on them from heaven, the peasants blessed Mademoiselle. There is an ordinance, dating from that time, and enforced to this day in Roquebrune, forbidding the use of all roofing material except curved tiles.

"She firmly insisted," continued Maggiore, "on having us work on the shutters so that they would have a weathered look. This upset the carpenter, who couldn't bear to see his brand-new shutters damaged and dirtied on purpose."

Her house had to be new, built to her specifications. But she wanted to give it a patina of age. Perhaps the reason stemmed from modeling herself like the duke, his frayed jackets, his shoes with holes in their soles: the slovenliness of the aristocratic rich. More likely, by giving her house an "old" look she was creating for herself the touching and childish illusion of a "family house."

Coco wanted the house that her father, had he returned from America thirty years before, would most "certainly" have built for the little girl who had waited for him in the dreadful loneliness of the orphanage. Perhaps it was there that she first dreamed up its plan.

Coco personally discussed everything with the architect and the contractor. The duke, to whom everything was submitted, rarely entered the discussions. Only once did he take Streitz aside, to point out to him that the plumber had made a false connection and that when he flushed his personal toilet the water came out hot!

"Mademoiselle," Edgar Maggiore told us, "used to come on the average of once a month to inspect the work. She came on the Train Bleu, got off at Monte Carlo, where a taxi waited for her and remained at her disposition throughout her stay. When her work kept her in Paris, we made the trip to see her if we had a delicate problem on which we wished to consult her. I remember sending the stucco worker to see her so she could choose the color of the plaster to be used on the façade.

"She was always very cheerful when she visited Roquebrune. One day she came out to the building site and sank up to her knees in mud. Instead of worrying about her ruined clothes, she burst out laughing. She was still laughing long after we had rescued her from her predicament."

The house, when completed, consisted of three main wings opening out on a patio, vaulted in the Roman style, paved with a hundred thousand sand bricks, and closed off by a high, wrought-iron grill.

The house cost her six million francs, excluding interior fittings, furnishings, and decoration, which was done by Jansen— that is, four times as much as the duke had spent when he gave her the property. But it was worth it. At the end, she was in her own home and the duke was now her guest.

Coco adored climbing trees. Since she didn't think that she had enough trees, she instructed Maggiore to find her some. Thus it happened that about twenty one-hundred-year-old olive trees were transplanted from Antibes to La Pausa! She had her gardener, Marius Angeli, plant rosebushes of every color around the house.

Every year on August 5 there is a procession in Roquebrune. Pilgrims follow the villagers, chosen to represent the major personages of the Passion, from the village to the chapel of La Pausa. In order to reach the chapel, which is next to the Chanel property but above its boundary line, one must come down an old Roman staircase that has always been a public throughfare.

Every August 5, Mademoiselle gave orders to Marius Angeli that the most beautiful roses of the garden be used to bedeck the portal through which the procession passed. "Better still," Marie Papucci, a Roquebrune woman who for many years helped in the kitchen, said to us, "she had a large table erected with a white tablecloth from which refreshing drinks were served to the men enacting the Passion."

According to one visitor, the interior of the house "was beige, . . . even the piano. . . ." Coco's bedroom took up five hundred square feet and was completely done in beige taffeta, including the curtains and bedspread; the walls were paneled to the ceiling with English eighteenth-century rectangular oak panels of varying dimensions, the bed and the chandelier were in wrought-iron, and on the floor was a large, blue rug.

The large adjoining bathroom was in white opaline. In the bedroom was a large fireplace in which wood burned all winter long. Mademoiselle did not like central heating. She agreed to its installation only in the reception rooms. The duke's bedroom was paneled and contained a sixteenth-century English bed in the Elizabethan style. Mademoiselle's bathroom separated the two rooms.

Although very different from English country life, a day at La Pausa preserved one of its main customs. Marie Papucci told us:

"Mademoiselle took her breakfast, consisting of coffee and toast, in her bedroom, which she didn't leave until one o'clock in the afternoon. Often she sunbathed on the terrace. . . . When there were a number of guests she liked to lunch in what she called English style."

This "organization," so different from traditional social life on vacation, was efficiently directed by a Russian refugee, Admiral Castelain, whom Mademoiselle treated as a friend and who took all his meals with the mistress of the house.

At La Pausa, Coco lived in a setting she had created for herself. The Coromandels that Misia had made her buy stayed on the rue du Faubourg St.-Honoré, and though Misia often came to La Pausa, she was invited into a decor that she had neither suggested nor imposed. At last, Coco, on vacation, was able to discover herself, assume her place in Society, the place she earned herself.

In those days, the Côte d'Azur was just beginning to come into its own. Apart from Monte Carlo, the favorite vacation spot of the rich, which at the time seemed to be flagging slightly, the rest of the coast consisted of immense deserted beaches where local residents watched, smiling ironically, a few crazy Americans swimming beneath a leaden sun.

The great discoverers of the Côte d'Azur were Philippe Oppenheim and, especially, F. Scott Fitzgerald. Oppenheim, who lived in Cagnes-sur-Mer, spent most of his time in Monte Carlo. His great friend was an American, Nevada Hayes, the widow of the Duc de Bragance, the heir to the Portuguese throne who renounced his right to the succession after the overthrow of King Manoel. The duchess, who was impoverished, was received by everyone on the Côte d'Azur, and Oppenheim was often her escort. Behind dark glasses, Fitzgerald observed social life on the Riviera, later describing it in his novels, which were serialized in the some of the most important U.S. magazines.

In 1924 Fitzgerald settled on the Côte d'Azur with his wife, Zelda, whose eyes reflected the Mediterranean, a mixture of "picture-book blue, essence of blue, and blue eyes." There under the sun and among the blue waves, they burned their youth away in a ferocious rage to live. Their days were already numbered, for Zelda, the marvelously beautiful Zelda, was soon to sink into madness. Fitzgerald, who realized what was happening, only felt inspired to greater extravagances, as though he were trying to get closer to his wife, to prove to himself that she was normal. He scribbled obscene graffiti all over Grace Moore's villa and bombarded duchesses in evening dresses with tomatoes. From the rocks of Cap d'Antibes, Zelda jumped into the sea with all her clothes on. One day, they both were found sleeping in their car, which was parked across the railroad tracks. Were they hoping for death?

Those crazy years on the Côte d'Azur inspired one of Fitzgerald's most poignant and heart-rending novels, *Tender Is the Night*. His heroines we can easily imagine dressed in the Chanel style.

Mademoiselle naturally became one of the queens of the Côte d'Azur, and it was there that she completed the revolution in conduct she had started fifteen years earlier: she sunbathed.

From that date elegant ladies would often abandon themselves to the rays of the sun. On August 2, 1931, the directors of the deluxe hotels along the Riviera, from Menton to Cannes, met and decided to stay open during the summer. A historic date! The kings of Sweden, Denmark, and Norway, the Crown Prince of Japan, the Maharajah of Kapurthala, Charlie Chaplin, Ernst Lubitsch, El Glaoui (Pasha of Marrakech), Maurice Chevalier, Rex Ingram (who discovered and launched Valentino), and his wife Alice Terry were all habitués. Sooner or later, many among them would be invited by Coco to La Pausa.

Some were not invited, of course. Sir Basil Zaharoff, for example, the famous arms magnate, nicknamed the "King of slow death," never received an invitation. One of the most mysterious and richest men in the world, he liked no one and refused to see anyone but the Duchess of Marcheda. He fled at the sight of a

Coco.

(*Above*) Coco and Etienne Balsan in a whimsical moment of donkey riding. *Photo: Collection of François Balsan.*

(*Right*) Coco on horseback. Posed side-saddle, she normally rode astride like a jockey. *Photo: Collection of François Balsan.*

(Left) The residence of Etienne Balsan, château of Royallieu near Compiègne. *Photo: Collection François Balsan.*

(Below) Etienne Balsan after winning a race on his Sauveur (1910). *Photo: Collection of François Balsan.*

(*Above*) Coco (*right*) poses in front of her boutique in Deauville. *Photo: Paris-Match.*

Coco (*left*) and Aunt Adrienne in Deauville, where they opened their first shop. *Photo: Paris-Match archives.*

A cartoon by SEM—Coco and her polo-player lover (probably Boy Capel). *Photo: Collection of Mme de Kermaingant.*

One of the first—early twenties—perfume promotional posters, drawn by SEM. *Photo: Collection of Mme de Kermaingant.*

One of the more beautiful portraits of Coco, in her early thirties. *Photo: Collection of Chanel, Inc.*

"For my dear Germaine with all my affection—Gabrielle Chanel." Seldom did Mademoiselle sign her name as anything but "Coco." *Photo: Paris-Match archives.*

Coco and Grand Duke Dimitri at a dinner party in Monte Carlo in the thirties. *Photo: Paris-Match archives.*

A charming portrait. *Photo: Collection of Chanel, Inc.*

avec toute ma tendresse et mon affection. Coco

"With all my tenderness and my affection, Coco"—a rare display of warmth. *Photo: Collection of Serge Lifar.*

Coco with Salvador Dali, a close friend for many years.
Photo: Collection of Chanel, Inc.

Coco dressed for a masquerade ball. She loved to wear fancy costumes.
Photo: Collection of Chanel, Inc.

Coco between the two black statuettes given to her by her decorator and friend Gérard Mille. *Photo: Willy Rizzo.*

Chanel in an astrakhan fur suit, a material she seldom used. *Photo: Collection of Chanel, Inc.*

(*Above left*) Pierre Reverdy, the poet. A white scarf and a cigarette in the corner of his mouth were his trademarks. *Photo: Paris-Match archives.*

(*Above*) The elegance of the thirties in St. Moritz, Switzerland. Coco is second from left. Henri Bernstein is fourth from the left, wearing a beret. Etienne de Beaumont is the white, wavy-haired gentleman. *Photo: Collection of Frank Duschnitz.*

(*Left*) Coco with her faithful friend Serge Lifar in Deauville in the thirties. *Photo: Collection of Serge Lifar.*

(Below) Black bonnet,
"claudine" collar. Coco loved
simple, youthful clothing.
Taken in her workroom. *Photo:
Collection of Chanel, Inc.*

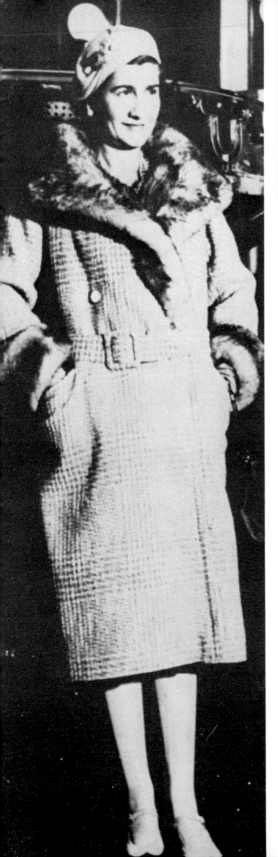

(*Above*) The quintessential Mademoiselle.
Photo: Collection of Chanel, Inc.

(*Left*) Coco wearing a smart traveling coat of Scottish tweed. *Photo: Collection of Chanel, Inc.*

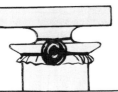

A Chanel No. 5 bottle is the frame—
Coco relaxes on the couch watching
a fitting. Drawn by SEM. *Photo:
Collection of Mme de Kermaingant.*

Coco and Baron "Spatz" von
Dincklage, after World War II,
during a winter vacation in
Villars-sur-Ollon, Canton de
Vaud, Switzerland. *Photo:
Private collection.*

After her comeback, Coco sits on the couch with her mannequins. *Photo: Willy Rizzo.*

Marie Hélène Arnaud, Coco's personal protégée and favorite model of the fifties, in front of the Chanel boutique on rue Cambon in Paris. *Photo: Willy Rizzo.*

МЕЖДУНАРОДНЫЙ ФЕСТИВАЛЬ МОДЫ

МОСКВА 1967

ШАНЭЛЬ

Ее духи среди которых знаменитый № 5
Ее последние создания : дамские костюмы,
ансамбли, платья, драгоценности
представленные ее манекенщицами

10 и 11 сентября

An example of the posters put up in Moscow to announce the presentation of the Chanel collection in 1967. *Photo: Collection of Chanel, Inc.*

Mademoiselle in one of her famous public poses. *Photo: Collection of Chanel, Inc.*

In her later years, on the staircase in her famous salon. *Photo: Willy Rizzo.*

Coco standing regally in a corner of her private apartments. An ornate
mirror and a Coromandel screen form the backdrop. *Photo: Willy Rizzo.*

A portion of Mademoiselle's elegant surroundings at the rue Cambon, including a suede couch and the beautiful Coromandel screens. *Photo: Willy Rizzo.*

Another fascinating study of Coco by Willy Rizzo.

Coco in one of her private apartments on the rue Cambon. *Photo: Willy Rizzo.*

Coco, her mouth full of pins, fits a dress. *Photo: Collection of Chanel, Inc.*

The grand parade in the salon of the rue Cambon. In the rear is the famous staircase where Coco used to sit to watch the *défilé. Photo: Willy Rizzo.*

A sophisticated pose in her private
apartments. *Photo: Willy Rizzo.*

(Left) The last portrait of Coco, taken at her residence in Switzerland, December, 1970. *Photo: Gianni Bozzacchi.*

(Below) In her residence of Sauvabelin near Lausanne, December, 1970, a month before she died. *Photo: Gianni Bozzacchi.*

photographer. Coco caught a glimpse of Zaharoff while he was on one of his solitary walks. She remembered that he was dressed in gray and that he wore a sort of little Tyrolian hat on the side of his head.

In those days, Zaharoff held sway over the Société des Bains de Mer de Monaco (SBM).* This mysterious man, whose pale eyes reflected the bright hardness of precious stones and whose long-nosed face ended with a very well-groomed, gray, pointed beard, had just acquired, for the sum of one hundred million francs, twenty-three thousand shares of SBM. His holdings were large enough to put Camille Blanc, the promoter and main owner of SBM and hitherto the preeminent figure on the Riviera, in a minority position on the board of directors. The story circulated that he had undertaken the operation in order to force the Grimaldis** to abdicate so that the could install the Duchess of Marcheda, whom he married, as a sovereign princess.

Zaharoff told a journalist who asked once what his favorite pastime was: "Win while gambling." And next to that? "Lose while gambling." Eight months after her marriage, Mme Zaharoff died. Her husband wasted no time in selling his shares in the SBM to the Dreyfus Bank—for three times what he had paid for them.

Then there was the American railroad king, Frank Jay Gould, who launched the resort of Juan-les-Pins. He got the idea while watching a documentary film showing men and women bathers frolicking on the sand beaches of Miami. Juan-les-Pins, it happened, also had a sand beach, a very beautiful one. The ex-brother-in-law of the magnificent Boni de Castellane, with whom he shared the wine bottles he sneaked into the austere family mansion in New York, hiding them in the fireplace in his bedroom, Gould had decided to flee the suffocating atmosphere of his puritanical family. He decreed that France was the only country where one could breathe and he added: "One can earn as much money there as in the United States."

Of course change was not so rapid everywhere. Protocol

---

*The corporation that owns and operates the gambling casinos and some of the best hotels in Monte Carlo, including the Hôtel de Paris.

**The Grimaldis were the first family to reign over the Principality of Monaco. The present ruler, Prince Rainier, descends from them by his maternal grandfather.

remained virtually unchanged. One day Frank Jay Gould had to seek the good offices of his friend, Edouard Baudoin, the promoter and director of the casino of Juan-les-Pins, so that Coco might be allowed to enter the gaming rooms in a short dress on a gala night.

Monte Carlo itself underwent a difficult time in the period between 1918 and 1939. The Russian clientele disappeared, and the exchange of the pound and mark made it impossible for either the English or the Germans to live in the style they had enjoyed before 1914. In 1925, Prince Pierre, father of Prince Rainier, confided to Elsa Maxwell, already famous, his anxieties over the economic future of the principality. As always she had an idea. She talked up Monte Carlo in the U.S. press, and in London and New York drawing rooms she inquired:

"You'll be in Monte Carlo this summer . . . naturally. . . . ?" Woe to those who didn't answer yes immediately. She looked them up and down with scorn, a warning signal of their imminent social failure.

But the work of the principality's "Minister of Pleasure" didn't stop there. She foresaw that the principality was going to have to open its gates to a much wider, though less rich, clientele than had been the case, a group for whom the casino was much too stiff and formal. Moreover, sea and sunbathing were becoming extraordinarily popular. Elsa, who had felt this revolution coming, pointed out that in her opinion it was useless to try to revive a way of life that was definitely out of date. She imagined a golf course, numerous tennis courts, an open-air summer casino, and a beach where one could swim and sunbathe. But there was no sand in Monaco! Elsa proposed that a small stretch of the rocky coast be transformed. "Where will we get the money?" Prince Pierre asked her. She brushed aside his objections and answered: "To make money, you've got to spend money."

The casino bought a piece of land, chosen by Elsa, on which was erected a pink stucco California-style hotel, designed by Addison Mizner. Elsa had the rocky beach covered with a coat of tar followed by a rubber mat. Then tons of sand were dumped on top.

Alas, rubber and salt water are not suited to each other, but such trivial failures did not deter Elsa. She promptly had another idea: build a swimming pool. When the contractor hired to do the job saw the sea only a few feet away from the projected pool site, he refused to start the work without the addition of a clause to the contract that guaranteed payment even if later "Madame Maxwell were declared not in full possession of all her mental faculties."

This time Maxwell scored. The swimming pool idea was brilliant, and it caught on immediately. In July 1927 the summer Sporting Club of Monte Carlo was inaugurated. Grace Moore, who lived in a villa at Mougins, was the star of the gala opening, presided over by the King of Sweden. One of the old croupiers told us the story of how one evening Yvonne Printemps, then married to Sacha Guitry, who was dining on the second floor above the roulette tables, accidentally dropped a hundred-franc coin, which landed on the number eight on one of the tables. The number eight came up and the house had to pay the famous actress 3,600 francs. Right after this incident the management of the casino had the gaming rooms roofed over.

Coco first met Elsa Maxwell in Paris at Lady Mendl's and the Count de Beaumont's, but she never invited her to La Pausa. Coco never forgave Elsa for the legend she had invented at the time of Boy Capel's death, according to which she, Coco, had sworn on the broken body of her lover to "dress all the women of Paris in black."

Indeed, Coco did not go out much, preferring to have people come to her. But she reveled in gossip, and gossip spiced all conversations at La Pausa. The twenties provided a climate perfectly suited to the flowering of situations from which love and humor were rarely absent. One of the most famous stories concerns one of the Dolly sisters, Jenny, who was a gambler. One evening she played baccarat at the same table with the Aga Khan, the former King of Portugal, and the Hungarian Prince Esterházy, who was the banker. The game ended with Esterházy and Jenny alone at the table. He lost fifteen million francs. With a honeyed smile she whispered to him: "I'm so glad. My grandfather was one of your serfs and you ordered him beaten by your overseer."

At the Hôtel de Paris, a Viennese steel merchant one day ordered a champagne bath for a young lady whom he had met in the street; an English actor called the reception desk at three o'clock in the morning to ask that twelve French cancan girls, then performing in a nearby cabaret, be brought to him; and a prince of the Italian royal family locked himself inside his room, using the pretext of urgent business in order not to be disturbed:

the next morning, the furniture in his room was found hacked up in a thousand pieces. "It wasn't period furniture," he announced calmly to the hotel manager, who apologized profusely.

It was in this atmosphere and under the gaze of Coco Chanel, who rarely risked more than a few tokens, that the Duke of Westminster once took on Nicolas Zographos, undoubtedly the greatest gambler ever seen around the tables in Deauville, Cannes, and Monte Carlo, where he played for a syndicate of Greek bankers. Still remembered is the game of baccarat during which Nicky, who held the bank against the Aga Khan, André Citroen, and James Hennessy, lost, in one evening, a cool 1.2 million dollars without batting an eye. This former Illyrian shepherd, discovered by the shipowner Athanasios Vagliano, was incredibly gifted in mathematics. Sacha Guitry called him the "human adding machine." "The whole thing is a matter of calculation," Zographos said. "There are three kinds of cards: strong, weak, and mediocre. You have to decide in a few seconds the worth of the two cards you hold in your hand and whether you should draw a third card."

And so it went. Coco, as much as Fitzgerald or Zaharoff, brought life to the south of France, shattering convention and introducing a new way of life such as had never before been seen. The reaction was immediate, even among her friends, who were enthusiastic about the style of life she had invented for herself. Bend-or even arranged a studio for himself in one of the two houses, where he painted watercolors, like his old friend Winston Churchill.

Without a ministerial portfolio for several years and rather on the outs with his party, Winston Churchill sometimes played Chinese bezique in the evening. Coco later recounted:

"When Churchill found himself with a bad hand, he never hesitated to cheat, rather clumsily in fact. One day I commented on it. He blushed with shame, just like a child caught in the act."

Churchill never stayed at La Pausa while Coco was living there, but he visited Mimizan, the duke's home, and it was probably there that she played cards with him.

"Churchill, cheat!" Emery Reeves, his literary agent, who bought La Pausa in 1953, exclaimed when I recounted the story to him: "It's impossible. He was much too much of a gentleman. He had much too much a sense of honor. He was much more likely to let Coco win out of gallantry. That Coco said this, doesn't surprise me at all! After all, she had to take a dig at Churchill, too!"

Jean Cocteau, to whom Mademoiselle lent the second little villa, La Colline, often came to stay. It was there that he came to recover from the serious case of typhoid that he caught in Toulon in 1931. Still very much addicted to drugs, despite two "cures" (paid for by Coco) in 1925 and 1928, he experienced a very strange adventure in Toulon. Forced to frequent extremely doubtful company in order to procure his opium, he was kidnapped by hooligans and locked up in the back room of a café. He succeeded in sending word to Coco. When she got his message, she immediately rushed to his help. She had a brilliant idea. Since she couldn't call the police without telling them that Cocteau was an addict, she called Marcel Thil, then a world boxing champion, and asked him as a great favor to lead an expedition to liberate Cocteau. Thil accepted the challenge with great enthusiasm and, accompanied by a few fighting friends, burst into the café. When the hooligans recognized him, they immediately lowered their fists, and Cocteau got out without a fight.

Cocteau introduced into Mademoiselle's little world his friend Christian Bérard, a talented painter, whom he had met in 1925 and who had done the decors for *La Voix Humaine,* produced at the Comédie française. Small and fat, he had a beard which he lovingly caressed, and a pink face like an overfed baby. His brilliant repartee made him an indispensible addition to Parisian salons, a success he enjoyed tremendously. He was mad about fashions and dreamed of designing dresses for Coco.

"You'd better stick to your painting instead of wasting your time on this foolishness," she retorted.

Resigned, Christian Bérard gave up. Later he realized his wish when he designed some models for *Harper's Bazaar* and in 1947 for Dior, thus bringing about his permanent falling-out with Coco.

Long ago she had been a little orphan. Now, under her own roof, one of the greatest French poets recited the first version of *Sang d'un poete.* Between tours, one of the epoch's greatest choreographers performed fantastic leaps in the moonlight for her alone. In La Pausa great artists found a calm, an atmosphere that they were never to enjoy again.

That, too, was part of Coco—a marvelous style of life that money alone could not explain.

High up in an olive tree, shading a garden where plants flowered in liberty, Coco came to rest on a branch like a bird.

9.

Mademoiselle, Glory, and the Poet

S HE had not broken with Westminster when she met the poet Pierre Reverdy. She had simply given up the idea of marrying the duke; she could not give him a child and his unfaithfulness offended her pride. Also, according to Lady Abdy, she wanted to make the duke jealous by taking Reverdy as a lover. And perhaps she was making a final attempt to arrive at unqualified happiness.

Reverdy was poor, taciturn, almost misanthropic. Largely unknown to the public, he was, to Cocteau, Picasso, and André Salmon, the greatest poet of his day. He earned his living as a proofreader at the newspaper *L'Intransigeant*. In the evening, escorted by his admirers, he sometimes rubbed up against the giddy round of Parisian social life.

There, standing on the threshold of the salons, he was like a moth, entering only with regret, for fear of burning its wings. At dawn, he worked on his heart-rendingly beautiful poems.

In those salons, Pierre Reverdy listened to and contemplated a famous, rich, greatly adulated, often silent woman who would speak from time to time in a firm and slightly hoarse voice. Though she was not yet the incorrigible chatterbox that she became in her latter years, Chanel had overcome much of her natural timidity. Her success was too complete for her not to extend it elsewhere, and especially in the salons in which conversational brilliance was the supreme virtue.

Coco's final ascent was paralleled by Paul Poiret's final descent. In the same period Sidonie Baba, the singer, had a rendezvous with Poiret, who had offered to share with her an invitation to the Comédie française. She found him on a bench in the Palais-Royal, sharing a hunk of bread with the birds in the gardens and digging into a small paper bag for some cherries, as his little seamstresses had done in earlier days. "It's too hot," he said in a gay tone of voice, "to be shut up in a restaurant."

He hadn't a dime. But he accepted his bad luck without any loss of dignity or pride or magnificence. He still lived in the same large apartment with terraces overlooking the rue du Faubourg St.-Honoré, where he had not paid rent for untold ages.

His country houses and boats had been sold long ago, then his furniture and his paintings— Vlaminck, Van Dongen, Derain, Dufy—then the curios, rare books, and famous autographs. After the deluxe souvenirs, the souvenirs of friendship disappeared.

When he had very little left, he ate salads. When he no longer had anything, he fell back on little restaurants in the market district where, as an old son of the quarter, he was still well received.

Always impeccably dressed, he adjusted his monocle to read the day's menu chalked up on a slate. "For me, Granny, it will be salt pork and lentils with a bottle of rosé wine."

Equally at ease at the Ritz or at Maxim's, he joked with the market porters and the fruit and vegetable hawkers.

In a moment of bitterness, he confided to a friend:

"They say that when a man is once launched it is for a lifetime. If they only knew!"

Once, some money donated by friends gave him a new spurt of energy. He immediately designed a hundred or so models and rented a Pullman car. Since Paris no longer understood his dresses, he decided to present them himself on the Côte d'Azur, in Morocco, Algeria, and Tunisia. The expedition was a fiasco. Afterward, he registered for unemployment compensation and from time to time borrowed ten francs from a friend.

When Poiret found himself all alone in his apartment from which the bailiffs had taken away the furniture, he had the satisfaction of being able to say to himself that he had never compromised. Apart from beach pajamas and evening pajamas, which were seen everywhere, and for which he claimed a distant paternity because of his culottes, everything seemed hideous to him. "Fashion is dying, fashion is dead!" he pronounced to all who would listen.

Fashion dead? In 1930? Not if one went round to the rue Cambon, where, if fashion were dead, one could cry out: "Fashion is dead! Long live fashion!"

"Perhaps I might hire him as a cutter," said Coco sarcastically. The remark, cruel as it is, was in line with a certain side of Mademoiselle's character.

The fallen prince once ruminated to journalist Anne Manson: "We should have been on our guard against that miss with the head of a young boy who was going to cause all hell to break loose and pull out dresses, hair styles, jewelry, and sweaters from her magician's hat."

How can Chanel's victory, her indisputable triumph, and Poiret's downfall be explained? By his extravagance, his total lack of financial prudence? Partly, but there was more, for the ascendancy of Chanel was more than the natural succession of couturiers: her arrival marked a revolution.

The amazing Paul Poiret's audacities help us to comprehend those characteristics that helped to make Mademoiselle's fortune. A great promoter and originator, he reigned over fashion for twenty years. He was the first to open a decorator's shop, which he called Chez Martine, after one of his daughters. He was the first to illuminate brilliantly the façade of his fashion house on the Rond-Point des Champs Elysées. He used furniture-cover material for his clothes and struck a blow at collars and stays. He was the first to dare to attack the corset. His waistlines were almost supple and, thanks to him, in the Bois de Boulogne, at the race tracks and theater first nights, the women wore dresses that did not resemble each other's. He implanted in the minds of society women, who still adhered to a few solid principles of bourgeois economy, the new idea that two or three dresses a year no longer sufficed. He loaded them with a thousand brilliant baroque inventions, sometimes too many. And therein, perhaps, lay his error. He was daring, but he was daring on a single level. The master of elegance in the Belle Epoque did not know how to adapt himself to the new world born after World War I. The Belle Epoque ended with the war and took with it the extravagantly sumptuous toilettes. Poiret had wanted to perpetuate the past at any price; he was a genius of the baroque era who could not bring himself to accept the rise of the uncluttered purity of classical forms. He was never able to give up his turbans, lamés, plumes, Persian motifs, and bouffant trousers.

One difference between Poiret and Chanel, for example, was in the reaction of each to the problem of copies. Poiret, sick at the idea that his models might be imitated, went so far as to forbid his customers even to *lend* the dresses he sold them, lest the admiring but economical friend have the dress copied by her own little dressmaker. Coco, in contrast, fearlessly proclaimed: "The more I am copied, the better it will be. It makes for free publicity that I don't have to pay for myself!"

Chanel was convinced that the success of a style meant its popular success. Yet, obviously, imitation and vulgarization do not for one moment replace the quality of a signed creation, and the clothes made in the rue Cambon workrooms were not available to just *any* clientele. Still, Chanel did believe that her ideas should *permeate* everywhere. Her objective was to give new "forms" to *women* and to furnish her rich *customers* with first-rate work, with clothes so perfectly made that they would not see them all over the place. That the "Chanel style" could be encountered in the street seemed to her proof that she had been absolutely right. *Vox populi, Vox dei* could have been her motto.

"Fashion should not come from the street, but it must reach down into it," she said.

Where Poiret needed ten yards of material for the folds of his Persian-style trousers, Coco used only one yard for her trousers, for which she charged Poiret's prices, and gladly accepted the possibility that the garment would be copied by the ready-to-wear manufacturers.

Poiret had based his ideas on a society still characterized by different "forms" of clothes for different social classes. He did not take account of the fact that a new conception of woman was emerging and that the society he knew was disappearing. Poiret's disillusioned remark regarding Mademoiselle's success— "Women were once beautiful and architectural like a ship's prow. Now, they resemble little undernourished telegraph operators"—sums up his attitude and his limitations. Ship's prows never sat in sports cars or danced the Charleston.

From the start, the Chanel style was called a *"miserablisme de luxe."* She didn't care. She triumphed because of her extraordinary sense of the future. A case in point is described to us by Mme Hélène de Leusse, head of the Chanel boutique in the early thirties:

"I remember going up to see her one day, because I had to attend a cocktail party or something of the sort. I asked her to lend me a 'dressy' dress. She answered: 'You astonish me. You seem to be rather avant-garde. How can you think of wearing a dressy dress in the afternoon? You haven't just arrived from the provinces!' "

For Chanel, there was no happy medium. You dressed up *only* for the evening, but then you really dressed up—or, one might say, undressed: low-cut evening dress, bare arms, paillettes, jewels. For cocktails, before dinner you had to wear a suit. She couldn't bear overdressed women. The dressy afternoon dress was good for provincials only.

Her revolution a success, she became· a queen and really began to assert herself. Her authority quickly developed into intolerance. (Her first differences with the perfume firm date from this period.)

Hélène de Leusse has told us of her conduct vis-à-vis other dress designers:

"When I began to work for Chanel in 1932, a dressmaker named Augusta Bernard dressed me. She made lovely clothes. I attached no importance to this since I was selling only fabrics and working in the boutique on the other side of the street facing the fashion house.

"One day, I finally saw Mademoiselle Chanel, whom I barely knew, again. She asked me to come up to her rooms. Once there, she immediately said: 'I hear that you are dressed by Augusta Bernard.'

"I replied: 'Yes. Augusta Bernard offered to dress me and, as I go out a great deal in the evening, she lends me dresses.'

"Mademoiselle Chanel replied: 'But that's unacceptable!'

"I retorted: 'But *you* have never offered me an evening dress.'

"She offered one to me and that is how I came to wear Chanel models.

"At that time, she and Patou were rivals. They competed for each other's models, literally stole them. It made me laugh because, when Patou offered 10,000 francs, for example—at the time that was a fabulous price for a mannequin—Chanel said 12,000. The auctioning was incredible!"

Fifteen years earlier, Coco had paid them one hundred francs and advised them to take rich lovers to support themselves till their next paycheck and better their circumstances!

Mme de Leusse continued: "The mannequins were American for the most part. The French girls of that day were much smaller and—how shall I say?— a bit low-slung in the behind. Patou brought over mannequins from the United States and Chanel stole them away by offering them double the money. The bidding war raged between the rue Cambon and the rue St.-Florentin."

Essentially, the difference between Chanel and her competitors was her scope. Her kingdom stretched beyond the rue Cambon and the fashion world. It extended over all Paris.

Did she become dizzy when she looked back on her past, the road she had followed to achieve prodigious financial success, her rich and unhappy love life?

Who, from now on, was worthy of Mademoiselle Chanel at the pinnacle of her success? Who could dare claim the right to be the successor of the men who had loved her—a gentleman rider, member of the cream of the "haute bourgeoisie," a handsome and wealthy English industrialist, an Argentine millionaire, a penniless Russian grand duke, a duke of a lineage more noble than that of the King of England?

But a poet, obviously, and one whose sole wealth was the stars in the heavens.

Coco cast the light of her name and her millions toward an unknown poet. The innumerable idiots in the gossip-ridden salons of Parisian high society smiled at the idyl.

All her life Coco fought against the exaggerated praise heaped on dress designers. She never accepted the use of the word "art" in connection with fashion. "We are artisans. I'm only a craftsman who works with her hands," she repeated over and over again.

She was marked, professionally, by pride—"because she was the *first*"—and humility in a world where, in the hothouse atmosphere, flattery and compliments flowed easily. "Genius," "artist," "prodigy" were words often used in the ladies' magazines. "Art"?

Coco knew what art really was. Her friends, the greatest writers, artists, and musicians of her time, had taught her about art.

And when some of them, like Bérard, smitten with the social vanities of this world, went so far as to design some dresses, she loaded them with sarcasm, for she had a sense of order and placed fashion design well below painting, music, and poetry. "It is a trade; it is not an art."

She saw him for the first time at Misia's apartment on the fifth floor of the Hôtel Meurice. There amid the fans, blue irridescent butterflies, baroque statues of blacks, and Venetian glass, Misia received the best minds and talents of the day. And there, for Coco, it was love at first sight, even though she tried to resist the impulse for some time. Reverdy fascinated her.

She often spoke eloquently of him. He was obviously the man whom she respected the most, and, of all her loves, the one of whom she was the most proud. But he also caused her the most unhappiness.

She could see him for what he was, vibrating with hate for a society that had failed to recognize his genius but also uneasily wanting to remain unknown, always sincere, tormented by an unshakable but at times faltering faith, adoring the absolute.

Reverdy was a Mediterranean from head to toe, his hair black and thick, his skin swarthy. He couldn't stand still for five minutes, first talking animatedly in a warm, harsh voice, then suddenly closing up into savage silence. Abruptly, he would flee, to the abbey at Solesmes, impatient to regain the solitude within which he had almost buried himself alive with one companion: the words that he tore out of nothingness. Later, he would return, longing to see his countless friends—Apollinaire, Cendrars, Max Jacob, Picasso, Braque. There were many others.

All his friends became rich. At times, poor and suffering, he was jealous, but he refused any and all concessions, for he drew his talent from sources inherent in silence and obscurity.

He was a reticent man, full of strange modesty, and in his blood ran all the heat of the wind and sun of Narbonne, his native city. Because of a word, he would explode, denounce, plunge into a brawl.

"I was born to be a boxer, a bullfighter," he said to his best friend, that other bullfighter manqué Pablo Picasso. "But thank God poetry, like painting, is a man's work and tough, a violent combat that is decided in one single round," he added.

According to Misia, "Reverdy arrived in Paris one day in

1910, coming from Narbonne, in the southern wine region where the inhabitants are of a rough and hot temperament. He came to try his luck in the capital with the idea of meeting Max Jacob, whose poems had bowled him over. He met him soon after, and an indestructible friendship flowered immediately. Max Jacob, a bit of a tramp, a bit of an alcoholic, but with a tenderness that could wring tears from you, had been converted to Catholicism (from Judaism), and his poetry is a mixture of humor, naïve faith, and delightful whimsicality. Under Jacob's influence, the young poet from a family of free-thinkers converted, with absolute ardor, as befitted his uncompromising and impassioned soul."

During World War I, Reverdy founded a literary review called *North-South*. It brought him immense admiration and a great number of friends, but with the disappearance of the review—it is the fate of such literary reviews to be eternally ephemeral—his friends also vanished.

The simplicity with which he lived was due to an ascetic quest rather than to poverty. Though he did want to remain unknown, it was not a gesture of defiance but almost a method for the salvation of his poetic integrity.

"To work on an empty stomach and in a cold state," was the dictum that he offered against "the systematic disorder of all the senses" advocated by Rimbaud and picked up unanimously by the surrealists, beginning in 1920. Reverdy believed in remaining lucid so as to "seize the object on the wing." And he did this by a "quasi-total subordination of the body to the mind, so as to get at the lyricism of reality."

He had married a woman whom hardly anyone had ever seen. His friends knew only that she was unbelievably beautiful and a dressmaker. He shared a small attic with her in Montmartre. She spent long evenings waiting for him, quietly seated beside a lamp, a book on her knees, sometimes falling asleep in this position so that he would find her thus on coming home in the early morning hours. Painter friends dreamed of painting her portrait, but none of them got to know her well enough for that, except Braque perhaps. One evening in 1925, Reverdy calmly announced the decision that was to stupify the artists of his circle. He and his wife were leaving Paris; the world was finished for them; they were going to install themselves at Solesmes, an old

Trappist abbey that Reverdy had decided to enter as a lay brother.

His true friends understood that this passionate and tormented soul needed to seek refuge away from the sophisticated Paris world that tempted him and in which he felt that he was going astray. He spent two years in the abbey, in perfect spiritual joy, without once seeing anyone outside. He wrote: "A free thinker, I freely chose God." His poems spoke of air smelling of "water and leaves" and of solitude "full of bells and prayers."

Everyone expected that he would enter formally into the order and that his wife, Henrietta, would join the Ladies of St. Cecilia in a nearby convent. But again he surprised his circle. After two years of seclusion, he no longer set foot in church. His wife attended alone, never missing a mass.

And then he suddenly landed in Paris, saw his friends again, began to frequent the salons, and met Coco. It was 1927.

Misia stood aside, abandoning Reverdy to Coco and urging her to read his poems of secret dreams, lugubrious melancholy, deceived hopes, and frustrated passions.

Reverdy's poetry has been described as "melting ice." It is amusing to imagine Coco, leaning on her elbow and poring over his verses.

Theirs was undoubtedly a tumultuous love affair, fated to be brief. Though they had similar attributes, both had chosen their separate ways early in life. It was inevitable that they eventually should draw apart.

A mystic, married, Reverdy could not renounce his faith, which was inseparable from his art; nor Coco, fashion. At least each knew what could not be demanded of the other. Still, Reverdy was afraid—afraid of Coco, of her world, of her possessive instinct, which threatened to swallow him up.

Each loved in the other what the other had refused to be in his life. Even though they knew that their affair could only be a momentary digression from their normal existence, they could not refuse to belong to each other. It was the prototype of impossible passions.

George Auric testifies to this:

"Of course she led a luxurious life, the kind it is difficult to imagine today. *Nothing but the best.* She received a great deal

and lavishly, and she went out a great deal. She liked to surround herself with brilliant people. She adored Jean Cocteau as
well as SEM, the famous caricaturist. She had become exces-
sively social, and this was one of the main reasons for the fiasco
of her idyl with the poet Pierre Reverdy. She loved him very
much and she tried to cast him in her mold, but she realized that
this was impossible. She could not, for example, ask Pierre
Reverdy to spend his evenings with SEM!"

Faithful to a different set of values and personal demands,
Reverdy quickly made his decision. Despite the power of seduction that Coco exercised over him, he suddenly remembered
Henrietta, so beautiful and so touching in her simplicity, so different from Coco. Henrietta—whom he could not leave abandoned on the mystical path he had opened up for her. He
wrenched himself away from the brilliant woman who moved
him so and disappeared, again shutting himself up in the Trappist abbey. There he led a veritable recluse's life until his death.

After a long period of complete silence, a new volume of
poems appeared in 1937. In *Ferraille,* and especially in the verse
significantly entitled "Coeur Tournant," the most beautiful
poems he ever wrote, Coco must have recognized certain echoes
of their love.

They saw each other again from time to time during Reverdy's
clandestine visits to Paris.

"She conserved an immeasurable esteem for Reverdy until the
end of her life. She always spoke of him with warmth and admiration. I believe him to be the only person she had always admired, perhaps because he escaped her. She never spoke ill of
him."

And with a malicious smile, Georges Auric, who must have
been thinking of several scenes he had witnessed, added: "And
she was capable of saying horrible things about her friends!"

Was Coco's metamorphosis, which dates from this period, due
to the bleeding of this secret wound, her love for Reverdy? Her
moments of pensive silence disappeared. She became aggressive
in her speech, talking, chattering and scoffing. Her behavior
toward her friends changed.

Perhaps she could not forgive Cocteau his fame—the fame
that had turned its back on Reverdy—for she began to attack
him, reproaching him for taking drugs (though she continued to

pay for his cures), for a certain dilettantism (a false accusation), and for wasting his time playing the social game (which was true). Cocteau's genius touched on everything in the arts, opening up new horizons, notably in the cinema. Perhaps he dispersed his efforts too widely, so that one searches his graceful poetry in vain for the depth of thought that was a part of Reverdy's work. In any case, Reverdy had become the model poet and writer in Coco's eyes. His talent, his independence, his asceticism made him unique. She could not accept that others could write without experiencing the ordeals that Reverdy had imposed upon himself.

"You're not a real poet," she flung at Cocteau.

And he, sensitive to her criticism, his cuffs flapping, replied: "Stop it, Coco. You're going to make me cry."

Even Apollinaire, whom she probably had caught only a fleeting glimpse of before his illness cut him down on November 11, 1918, was not safe from her sarcastic remarks. A serious war wound, which necessitated trepanning, had added the glory of the soldier to the fame of the poet. One day, André-Louis Dubois found Coco very irritated. "You know what they tell me? Apollinaire has been trepanned. What is this idiocy?"

"I tried to persuade her that it was true but she refused to believe it," Dubois told us.

"Her passion, the passion of her life, prevented her from recognizing the talent of a poet perhaps even greater than Reverdy. She would have gone on foot to Solesmes to see Reverdy if he had asked her to."

In the circumstances, anything was preferable to silence, so Coco talked.

About 1933, an incredible rumor spread among Coco's acquaintances and caused the gossip writers to make all sorts of suppositions. "Mademoiselle is going to get married." And Coco did everything to confirm the rumor. She was seen everywhere with the gentleman, and they lived together in a small hotel on the rue Cambon, the Family Hôtel. She had sold her residence of the rue du Faubourg St.-Honoré, perhaps because it held too many memories. The Coromandels were divided between the rue Cambon and the Ritz, where Coco still maintained an apartment and where in 1955 she took up permanent residence.

Sophisticated and cynical, looking out at the world from

behind glasses that never left his nose, Paul Iribe had dared her
to live with him, and she had taken the challenge.

Iribe was born in 1883, at Angoulême; he was of Basque origin. Black-haired and thick-set, he seemed to mock everything
with his biting wit. One of the most celebrated caricaturists of
the time, he had, since 1910, exercised considerable influence
over the decorative arts. Moreover, he had once been a designer
for Poiret, though he often had disappeared in the middle of the
working day to rejoin his friends (Poiret's also) Derain and
Vlaminck to go fishing in the Seine at Chatou.

Iribe had a great success with his drawings, whose style, typical of the graphic arts of the day, were reminiscent of Aubrey
Beardsley and were published widely, notably in the celebrated
and mercilessly satirical review *Assiette au Beurre*.

All Coco's friends agree that she loved him, to an
unimaginable degree. She involved him in her business affairs. In
the thick of her perfume battles with the "Société des Parfums,"
she sent Iribe, furnished with a power of attorney, to attend the
meeting of the board of directors of the perfume firm. With
Coco's money, he created a publishing house—the Chanel editions! She edited an ephemeral review, *Le Témoin,* in which she
appeared on the first page disguised as Marianne. She did more
for him than she had done for any other man, envisaged a life at
his side, with Iribe sharing her fashion throne like a prince con-
sort.

It was a passion full of crises. "He dominated her and she
couldn't stand that," recalls Serge Lifar. "Soon she began to hate
him as much as she loved him."

At La Pausa, in the summer of 1935, Iribe was on the tennis
court, chatting with friends. When Coco appeared, he turned
toward her, looked at her and suddenly fell to the ground,
having suffered a heart attack. He died several days later at
Menton without regaining consciousness.

Coco's grief was inconsolable; her bout with destiny had again
left her the loser. Misia, her constant friend, saw that she had
medical attention, but when Coco recovered, her eyes were hard.
Capel killed in a car accident, Reverdy a recluse, Iribe dead—it
was too much. Solitude once more took over the life of the
orphan from Auvergne. Fame? Yes. Happiness? Never: this was
her destiny.

Then she steeled herself. She refused to accept the last blow by pretending that she had never loved Iribe. Not long after Iribe's death, Serge Lifar was shocked upon hearing Coco say: "Oh, Iribe! He's finally dead, that one! He won't be seen anymore."

And Coco's confidant, for whom her affection never faltered, added rather sadly: "And then, all her life, at bottom she had been looking for happiness, and she never really found it. So she took her revenge with fame and success. She was never very happy in love, though she looked for it everywhere, with me, with women. But starting with a certain dose of egocentricity is a handicap for loving and being loved. That was Chanel's drama."

Later, in 1966, when the time had come for old age and resignation, Coco permitted a German journalist to ask her a few questions about her private life. Her replies were bitter.

Q: Based on your own life, what would you tell women in a few words?

A: Is it possible to say much in a few words? Well, I'm going to surprise you by saying that I think it is best for women to follow conventional moral standards if they want to be happy in life. Otherwise, they will need to be armed with heroic courage—and in the end they will pay the terrible price of solitude. I know something about that. There is nothing worse for a woman. Solitude can help a man to realize himself, but it destroys a woman. It is preferable that she stay with her husband, even if he has become fat and boring, rather than be alone.

Q: Why didn't you ever marry?

A: Because of my work, I suppose. The two men I loved never understood that. They were rich and didn't understand that a woman, even a rich woman, might want to work. I could never have given up the House of Chanel. It was my child. I created it starting with nothing. "Why should we marry?" I said once to the Duke of Westminster. "We're together, people accept it." And I pointed out a couple at the other end of the room who were exchanging banal remarks like most married couples. "If that happened to me," I said, "I would flee." I never wanted to weigh more heavily on a man than a bird.

Q: Or that a man weigh more heavily on you?

A: As you can see. Running away from boredom makes one gain weight! Few people are aware of it, but I never knew what happiness was. Except at seventeen or eighteen, when I had a few good moments. Do you know anyone who is truly happy?

Q: But still, wasn't it self-realization that you were seeking?

A: I was too young to know what I was looking for. When I was a child, I sought love; I didn't get it. Later, undoubtedly, I found more love than I wanted.

Q: You are in the habit of addressing reproaches to women.

A: Exactly! They can be reproached with honesty. But I will never cheat. I will tell them what I always wanted to say to them: If I had children, and particularly boys, I would do everything to seem beautiful to them, more than for a lover. Lovers! Jump out of the window if you are the object of a passion, I would say to women, flee if you feel it. Don't dream of a grand passion. That's not love. Love is warmth, affection, tenderness, decency. There are so many ways of loving and being loved. Remember this—passion disappears, boredom remains.

Indeed, she was bored.

10.

The Gentleman from Neuilly

A MAN of medium height, slim (he remained slim; he valued his good figure), with beautiful blue eyes, Pierre Wertheimer possessed almost irresistible charm. The number of women who were in love with him was legend. Known for his suave and sweet character, he became tough and pitiless when talking business. Then not a mean word was spared, especially in his discussions with Mademoiselle.

"But the next day I would receive flowers!" said Coco.

A man of highly refined taste, he had discovered Soutine and owned a beautiful collection of the artist's best paintings. A fine horseman, he also kept a great stable that still is celebrated and now belongs to his widow. He fulfilled an ambition when his famous Lavendin won the Epsom Derby.

Pierre Wertheimer played the most influential male role in Mademoiselle's life. She met him in 1922. Thereafter he was her partner at all times. Nothing was missing in this partnership: frequent scenes leading to serious threats of breakups, quarrels about business interests, moments of sincere feeling, and certain reciprocal admiration.

Their love of money bound them together. They wanted to escape from one another but realized that they needed each other. It was a tragicomedy with a hundred different acts in which both partners alternated between feelings of hatred and friendship and battled to win their points of view and to retain their self-respect. Sometimes in the same day it would be "that crook who cheated me" and "that dear Pierre." Such were Coco's temperament and feelings toward this man.

Pierre Wertheimer was discreet enough to remain in the background, and few people suspected the extent of his role in Mademoiselle's professional life. Was she grateful to him? Surely. Especially since without him she perhaps would not have become the Great Mademoiselle. On the other hand, without her he would have remained simply Pierre Wertheimer—a perfume industrialist. Perhaps he would have been a bit less wealthy. But that would have bothered him very little since before meeting Coco, he was well versed in the art of making money and had numerous possessions, including a racing stable, a yacht, and a high social position. He also had a reputable business enterprise, Bourjois perfumes, which was bought at the beginning of the century by Ernest Wertheimer, an extremely dignified forebear who resembled a character from Balzac. A photograph of him wearing a black hat still hangs in the hall and watches over the destiny of the firm.

Persons who worked with and observed Chanel and Wertheimer confirmed the fact that the two experienced complex feelings of envy, trust, distrust, hatred, and fear toward each other.

"If it had been love which had united them, it would have been the horrors of love," a lawyer, one of the indispensable intermediaries in their imbroglios, commented recently. It was not love but business into which Coco, at first completely ignorant and alone, threw herself, her claws unsheathed, alternately seductive and vicious. Shrewd, peasantlike, at times reminiscent of a shady horse dealer, she argued her case against financial advisers and lawyers, and she won, which was a great stroke of luck for the two principal associates of the Chanel Perfume Company.

Since their relationship had all the characteristics of a loveless love story, a go-between was needed to start it off.

This go-between was Théophile Bader.

At that time Bader was nearly sixty years old. He had succeeded in just about everything. Starting in 1895 with a small store, selling flashy finery and trinkets and graced with the audacious and optimistic appellation of Galeries Lafayette, transforming it in 1899 into a firm listed on the stock exchange under the same name, Bader made the Galeries Lafayette into a great Parisian commercial temple extending over 130,000 square yards, of which 35,000 were reserved for sales merchandise, offering nearly 300,000 articles in 120 departments. It became the largest of the capital's department stores and perhaps the most perfect symbol of Parisian chic. In its ready-to-wear departments, all the women—or at least those neither too wealthy nor too poor—could be certain of finding youthful and sometimes even daring elegance.

"In Paris, the wives of high functionaries, notary publics, military officers [Madame de Gaulle when her husband was only a captain], do their shopping at the Bon Marché. Those of engineers and doctors—and the women who work—dress at the Galeries," wrote a fashion reporter in 1928.

How did this success come about? Théophile Bader had three excellent ideas: mail-order sales, of which he was one of the precursors in France; the opening of branches in the larger provincial cities; and the creation of a buying exchange so as to benefit from wholesale prices. Twice a year, close to seven hundred thousand catalogs, an enormous figure for that time, carried temptation into French households. And Théophile Bader—Papa Bader to his associates—read over the proofs himself, correcting the prices and inconsistencies with a red pencil.

He was almost a happy man. He was rich, honored in the highest degree by being awarded the Grand Cross of the Legion of Honor, and he could afford to leave his austere office on the Boulevard Haussmann to go to the race tracks and mingle with the fashionable people. But even the sober, astute, brilliant Théophile Bader discovered that fame and fortune were not sufficient to open all doors. A man's fortune must be "old."

How did Bader meet Mademoiselle? It is common knowledge that as a young milliner Coco bought her hat blocks at the Galeries Lafayette, and that she got them at favorable prices.

Claude L. recalls: "Around 1920, Coco, who was a young and beautiful woman, understood perfectly well how to make use of Papa Bader, how to work on his ambition and worldly inclinations. He was extremely flattered by the attention she paid to him. She knew how to put him at ease, which she did not do just to be nice but because she must have said to herself: 'The

Galeries Lafayette can help me to sell my perfumes or anything else I like.' "

Did they agree to do something together? Was it only worldly vanity that impelled Théophile Bader toward Coco, or did the shrewd businessman understand what the name "Chanel" might have to offer—especially when the vogue for No. 5 began and the only obstacle to an increase in sales lay in the makeshift character of its production and marketing?

Théophile Bader had two young friends, the brothers Pierre and Paul Wertheimer. Pierre, who had money to invest, owned, along with his brother, one of the biggest perfume factories in France. Since Bader knew that Coco possessed a perfume of rare quality, he decided to introduce Coco and Pierre.

The decisive encounter took place at Longchamp race track in the spring of 1923. If one can believe the legend, as Wertheimer recounted it later, everything happened very quickly and for the best.

"I am going to introduce you to Mademoiselle Chanel. She is a dress designer and has an idea: she wants to launch a perfume," Bader supposedly said to Wertheimer.

And to Coco: "Mademoiselle, you have just made a perfume that is very good, and I think it will have a much greater future than that of being sold in only one shop, even one so wonderful as yours. I present Monsieur Wertheimer, who has the most important perfume factory in France and who, in consequence, possesses an extensive distribution network."

The dialog was very much to the point:

"Would you like to manufacture and distribute my perfumes?" asked Mademoiselle.

"Why not? But if you want this to be done under the name of Chanel, we will have to form a company," replied Wertheimer.

"Form a company if you like, but I'm not interested in getting involved in your business. I'll give you my calling card and will be content with 10 percent of the stock. For the rest, I expect to be absolute boss of everything."

If that is the way it went, Coco was, out of character, satisfied with fame and power alone. In any case, she soon would want a fortune, too.

The company, Parfums Chanel, was set up in 1924, establishing a partnership between Pierre Wertheimer and Coco Chanel. In spite of all sorts of disagreements, quarrels, and misfortunes, the partnership was incredibly long lasting.

"Think of it! At the beginning we got along so well together that we hired only one lawyer between us, P.M.* confided to us.

Several years later, the differences arising between Coco and the gentlemen from Neuilly—as she called the people of the perfume firm—were to mobilize a veritable army of top-notch corporation lawyers.

The contract that was drawn up gives an invaluable explanation of Coco's astonishing juridical adventures during World War II and of how she managed to become one of the most highly paid women in the world. One key clause read:

> Mademoiselle Chanel, dress designer, . . . founder of the company, brings to the company the ownership of all the perfume brands sold at the present time under the name of Chanel, as well as the formulas and processes of the perfumery products sold under this name, the manufacturing processes and designs registered by her, as well as the exclusive right of said company to manufacture and put on sale, under the name of Chanel, all perfumery products, makeup, soaps, etc., excepting what is listed under the title "Conditions." This right is strictly limited to those objects usually entering into the perfumery trade and gives the Chanel Perfume Company the right to use the name Chanel only for the aforesaid products.

"You noticed the word 'makeup,' " commented P. M. later. "The first brawls began because of this word. The company brought out a cleansing cream. Chanel immediately served a writ prohibiting us from bringing out a beauty preparation. The way she understood it, her name was to be used only for perfumery and not for beauty products. The suit lasted five years. This occurred before World War II, around 1934."

When Chanel lost her first suit against the perfume company, she then submitted the defense of her interests to a young international lawyer, René Aldebert Pineton, Comte de Chambrun, the son of General Aldebert de Chambrun, president of the First

---

*One of the administrators of Chanel, Inc., working for Pierre Wertheimer and still active now at Chanel, Inc., Neuilly.

National City Bank of New York, and an American, Clara Longworth. In 1936 the young Chambrun opened his law office on the bank's premises in the Champs Elysées.

His father said to him: "Here's office space and a telephone. Install yourself."

"Ever since then," René de Chambrun told us, "I haven't budged.

"One day, my first client, a young and elegant woman, arrived.

" 'I am Mademoiselle Chanel,' she said. 'Do you know Pierre Wertheimer?'

" 'Only by name. I am better acquainted with his famous horse Epinard!'

" 'Well, that Wertheimer is a gangster. Are you ready to listen to my long story? Are you ready to fight?'

" 'I am just starting out, Mademoiselle Chanel. I have all my life before me.'

"And that is how I became Chanel's lawyer."

Other important clauses of the contract:

> The Company is forbidden to put on sale any other article, whatever its nature may be, under the name Chanel, without the express written consent of Mademoiselle Chanel. Mademoiselle will retain the right to have manufactured herself and to sell on her own account in her shops in Paris, Deauville, Cannes, and Biarritz, all beauty preparations bearing her name at the present time or those which may be sold in the future by the Chanel Perfume Company.

At the time that these agreements were signed, Chanel must have said to herself:

"If they want to tie my hands (despite the good faith that still seems to reign) and don't want to give up anything to me, I must be able to have the perfumes manufactured elsewhere if I so desire."

She began to do her own manufacturing: "After all, I'm not obliged to sell what the Parfums Chanel sells!"

Another clause:

> The Chanel Perfume Company may put on sale only first-class products, since Mademoiselle Chanel, as owner of a fashion house in which only first-class luxury articles are made, would find it det-

rimental to herself if perfumery products of an inferior quality were put on sale under her name.

This reasonable clause was later used and abused by Coco. She forbade the company to launch new perfumes, and she forced them to take off the market those already launched, with the pretext that she did not like them.

The above-mentioned Company will be obliged to take back from Mademoiselle Chanel, at their cost price, the stock of perfumes, scent bottles, boxes, or raw materials existing at Mademoiselle Chanel's present supplier, if she so desires.

"And," added P. M., "we did not have the right to resell the perfumes to other companies. All that was lost. For example, there was a perfume of Chanel's called Une Idée. It was presented in rather special packaging, different from that of No. 5. Well, Chanel had it withdrawn once it was out! Strictly speaking, she had not given her accord beforehand. As soon as it was put on sale, before you could say Jack Robinson . . . !"

Coco's leitmotif rapidly became: "I signed something in 1924. I let myself be swindled."

There were three or four more suits before the war. Claude L. told us:

"She didn't institute proceedings with the idea of winning: she wanted to make a row, to be talked about, to have people say that things weren't working out between Mademoiselle and the people manufacturing her perfumes and that they weren't any good. The suits were a form of pressure politics."

Any idle pretext for argument sufficed.

"I entered the Chanel Perfume Company about 1938," P.M. told us. "Before that I was with Bourjois, but Wertheimer had 'had enough of buttonholing that damned woman.' When I married, I warned my wife: 'My main activity is to take care of Mademoiselle Chanel's lawsuits.' When I returned from captivity in 1945, I hadn't yet reached Paris when I received a message: 'The lawyer is calling for you because there is a new lawsuit with Mademoiselle Chanel.' "

Coco was especially exasperated by the fact that the company of which she was president did not at first distribute dividends. The reason was that there were heavy expenses and investments.

The company had to be housed, first on the rue du Faubourg St.-Honoré, then in Neuilly. Pierre Wertheimer invested hundreds of thousands of dollars in publicity in the United States.

Coco was not appreciative. Every month she called in her accountants and said to them: "Go around to the Neuilly factory to see what those gentlemen are up to!"

The accountants went there, audited everything, brought back verified figures. Still, Coco was convinced that she was being robbed by pirates. She became obsessed with the idea that she was being swindled.

No dividends! While other companies launching perfumes at that time were earning a lot of money! It was ridiculous to have such a famous company, with a president, a board of directors, specialists with the best "noses" in France, and not be able to get one franc out of it. And the height of "dishonesty" occurred when the Bourjois Company began to *manufacture* the Chanel perfumes. In short, the Bourjois Company was living off her!

P. M. remembers with amusement some almost grotesque scenes. One occurred in 1934:

"A report was drawn up as a result of the general stockholders meeting. In principle, Mademoiselle Chanel should have been present as president. Actually, she never came. Then one day she declared: 'No, I wasn't there. I won't sign.'

"There was a new 'adviser' behind her. Result: she didn't sign and the next day demanded that the proceedings be declared null and void, because in the minutes it was stated that she was present, that she had presided, etc.

"To calm her down, we called a special general meeting, which confirmed the decisions of the preceding one. She didn't attend this one either, but we had stipulated in the minutes that she was not present. We put that on record by adding that this meeting had been held to confirm the preceding one. This time she agreed to sign!"

The same year, at another general meeting over which Coco did not preside, the shareholders had to decide what attitude to adopt in the face of legal proceedings instituted against it by its own president!

The quarrel reached its highest point in the 1930s. Even Paul Iribe joined in, anxious to protect the interests of his future wife.

According to P. M.: "It was worse than ever. That's when the cleansing cream incident occurred.

" 'You don't have the right to make a cream, and furthermore I demand that you give me all the balance sheets, all the books, all the minutes and reports, all the profits and losses of the past ten years during which I have been president. Else, I will go to court,' Mademoiselle said.

"Then, incredible things happened. One day, Paul Iribe, armed with a power of attorney dated September 12, 1933, came and ostensibly attended the meeting when he didn't have the right to do so! He held no stock, knew nothing about the business. We could have thrown him out. We didn't do so because he was Mademoiselle Chanel's representative. Theoretically, we permitted him to preside over the meeting! But, naturally, when the minutes were presented to him he refused to sign."

At the end of 1933, the "Société des Parfums de Neuilly," anxious for better management and taking into consideration the bitter criticism of Mademoiselle, decided to reorganize completely. In particular, they replaced the managing team that had not been giving full satisfaction. Probably to ridicule Parfums Chanel, Mademoiselle immediately hired for her fashion house the commercial director that had been fired.

The misunderstanding between Coco and the gentlemen from Neuilly soon became overwhelming. By the end of 1934, she was no longer president of the perfume company. She instituted lawsuit after lawsuit, trying to get her money out once and for all. The case was set to be heard in 1940.

"Ah! Coco, what a woman!" cried Chambrun. "I would always defend her tooth and nail. I have nearly five hundred pounds of Chanel files in my cupboards.

"One day, she came into my office white with anger. 'Well!' she said, 'I am being taxed as a spinster, can you imagine that. After all, I'm not a spinster.'

" 'But Coco. . .'

" 'If Wertheimer wants me to be in his box at the Grand Prix at Deauville, let him pay my taxes. I'll only go on that condition. No. Ask him to pay my Swiss taxes, too. I never go to the owner's enclosure at the races. You meet too many snobs. I go to the public enclosures. So let him make a gesture!' "

It was, in a sense, true. Coco never went to the paddock. When she owned a racing stable, she could be seen near the post on the public enclosure side, a fact that has been confirmed by her trainer, François Mathet, who by a curious coincidence is married to Etienne Balsan's niece.

"A Chanel stable is an exaggeration," François Mathet told us. "I met Mademoiselle Chanel through René de Chambrun, who was a classmate of mine.

"René is a racing fanatic and in 1961 he suggested to Chanel that she buy some horses. The idea was not displeasing to Coco. Didn't her associate and personal enemy have a celebrated stable? In short, she asked me to buy her a foal and a filly, which I did in 1962 at the sale of yearlings in Deauville. Coco became the owner of Soldo, since resold in England, and of Romantica.

"That was the Chanel stable, red casaque, white arm badge, red jockey cap. She wanted a white casaque, but that color was already taken. Coco adored horses in her youth. She had even ridden at the training of the racehorses belonging to Etienne Balsan. Apropos of this, I remember an anecdote. Coco said to me one day that when she arrived at Balsan's at Royallieu, she had no riding clothes and Uncle Etienne said to her: 'Go get some at a tailor in Compiègne.' The latter made her a jacket, which she told me became the inspiration for the line of her famous suits.

"Romantica was an excellent mare. She won her first race at Tremblay, ridden by my jockey, Yves-St.-Martin. She also won at Deauville and was even a favorite for the Prix de Diane. Alas, the day before there were severe rainstorms and Romantica did not like soggy ground.

"Coco's greatest joy came on the day that her horse came out in front of one of the many horses belonging to Pierre Wertheimer's stable. That time she triumphed totally!"

Chambrun was at Chanel's when she learned by way of *Le Figaro* that, thanks to Lavendin, Wertheimer had just realized his dream of winning the Epsom Derby.

"Now he'll be completely impossible," concluded Coco.

"On the contrary, he'll be so happy that you can get anything out of him," replied Chambrun.

Chambrun had hardly finished his phrase when Pierre Wertheimer was announced at the bottom of the rue Cambon stairs.

"Monsieur Pierre is coming up to see you, Mademoiselle."

Wertheimer climbed the steps a bit faster than usual and rushed into the apartment, where Coco was waiting.

"How out of breath you are, my friend. Do sit down," she said.

"Is that all you can find to say to me?" answered Pierre, nonplussed. "Aren't you going to kiss me?"

"Kiss you? Why?"

"What? But look here, I've just won the Derby. Everyone knows that. Didn't you know it?"

"Ah! No, this is the first I've heard of it," replied Coco very calmly. "That's how good a friend you are! You win the Derby and you don't even telephone me!"

Coco and Pierre, a perpetual comedy in a hundred different acts that ended on July 12, 1964, with a letter:

My dear Pierre,

I was very touched by your personal letter. As you thought, all my desires are now fully gratified by the latest modification in our agreements, to which you allude.

I am persuaded that the future reserves for us both as much satisfaction as our collaboration has brought me till now. But as I told you, from now on I am depending above all on your moral support.

I embrace you tenderly,

Pierre Wertheimer died several months later, on April 24, 1965, at peace with Mademoiselle. That same year, Chanel broke with her lawyer, René de Chambrun, after thirty years of "good and loyal services."* Perhaps she was giving up her juridical battles! But no, soon after, the fight began again.

In 1967 Mademoiselle asked Robert Badinter, a brilliant young international lawyer, to take her interests in hand.

"I'm Jewish," he said. "Perhaps you didn't know that, Mademoiselle."

"Yes," replied Chanel, "and that doesn't bother me at all. I have nothing against the Jews."

"That's how I became Mademoiselle Chanel's last lawyer," Badinter told us.

---

*They were reconciled two years later.

11.
Triumph and Challenge

As World War II approached, with Boy Capel and Paul Iribe dead, Etienne Balsan, the Grand Duke Dimitri, the Duke of Westminster, and Pierre Reverdy married, Coco found herself alone more than ever. A solitary and haughty queen, she sometimes broke her silence with futile, nonstop conversations. It was as if, by stopping, she feared being overwhelmed by stirred-up memories of her dead and unhappy lovers and her childhood . . .

". . . She yapped out a continual stream of personal anecdotes devoid of any interest . . ." Alice Halincka said of Coco in her *Memoirs,* though she was referring to dinner and society, meetings where conversation rarely reaches a high level.

"She had the physique of a swarthy Gypsy." Alice Halincka added, but then women rarely found Coco beautiful or interesting. She only impressed men that way.

While Coco may have been an unhappy woman, she nevertheless managed to become the foremost dress designer of her times and an incomparable hostess. She was closely identified with the revolution in style and manners that was the sign of the period, and as Sachs so eloquently put it: "She created a feminine personage such as Paris had never seen before." And whose majesty knew no bounds. . . .

The following lines written in 1928 by the Princess Bibesco

show us what Coco—baptized "Tote" in the book, autocrat of the third fashion international—had become in universal fashion. ". . . She drains the wealth of about ten capitals and of at least three continents. . . . All the women who wear Tote sweaters, her flower, her dress, or her striped scarf have twins and would recognize their lookalikes in New York, London, Rome, or Buenos Aires. . . . Tote's bicolor scarf has made them correligionists. . . .

"One could say that civilization starts with Tote's customers and ends with them. Isn't the product that she exchanges for the most solid currencies in the world quite simply her intelligence? The precious matter, imponderable, inexhaustible, and forever renewed with which she floods the world market every six months."

Literary exaggeration? That would be forgetting who Chanel was. By 1935 she employed nearly four thousand women and had sold twenty-eight thousand dresses in Europe, the Near East, and the Americas. In 1932 she had taken the United States by storm.

"The world of fashion and the movies are all agog. Gabrielle Chanel, famous Paris designer, is in this country launching her new job of telling a galaxy of stars what to wear. Those who know their movies are wagging their heads. Those who know Chanel are saying she'll do it. The betting runs high.

"It all started at Monte Carlo," wrote Laura Mount in *Collier's* of April 1932. "The Grand Duke Dimitri, of the Romanoffs, quite casually introduced Samuel Goldwyn, of the movies, to Mlle Gabrielle Chanel of Chanel. Pleasant talk, pleasant compliments, big inspiration, big contract—and the great Chanel had agreed to come to Hollywood to design clothes for the movies. Admittedly, it's an experiment, a gamble, but on a million-dollar scale."

In the United States, still very much shaken by the upheavals of "Black Thursday" (October 24, 1929) and with bankruptcies, suicides, and unemployment as part of everyday life, the event that shook the movie world was the imminent departure of Chanel for Hollywood!

She hesitated for a long time. What could she gain from the trip? Publicity? Wealthy American women were already her customers and Paris haute couture was being deified in the daily press. The wealthy women wore original models; the "less rich among the wealthy" wore exact or more simplified copies. Several thousand copies of greater or lesser taste and in different fabrics could be made from the same model.

Poiret, of course, had refused these "compromises." For Coco the problem was entirely different. Though she made inimitable dresses for the women who could afford them, she also created a certain style. Why not sell her models to U.S. ready-to-wear manufacturers since all that was needed were women from California to the East Coast willing to wear "$10 Chanels"? They certainly wanted them. Might as well give them the clothes they wanted—without the label, of course! And what better way to advertise the models than by dressing film stars?

Thus Chanel made her decision to go to the United States—to Hollywood!

"I tell you it will start a new era in the movies," Samuel Goldwyn said to Laura Mount. His rosy face was flushed and determined. "Women will go to our movies for two reasons: one to see the pictures and stars; two to see the latest in clothes."

The article continues:

"The world of fashion is watching it, and the world of celluloid. Everybody in both worlds has passionate theories about what the idols are for success, but one thing they all seem to agree on: Chanel has picked herself the hardest job she has ever tackled. The world-famous fashion dictator now tells the duchesses and countesses and queens of the talkies what is chic. And it is just possible that in the talkies they'll talk back!

"In fact, at least ninety-five percent of the people who know all about movie stars and their ways with their clothes think they will. Their general attitude is an eyebrow raised way up to here, and something gloomy about 'It isn't what Chanel is going to do to Hollywood—it's what Hollywood is going to do to Chanel.'

"It must be explained that this skeptical 'Oh, yeah?' attitude is no slur on Chanel's genius.

"The idea sounds good; even the pessimists agree to that much. Mr. Goldwyn and Mlle Chanel are positive that it will make good.

"Chanel herself has no fears about the outcome of her experiment. She is full of excitement and eagerness to try it. 'But it will be so interesting, so amusing! To design clothes that will be seen in every small village of the world, in every city, in every

country! That is fascinating, stimulating. I shall work day and
night to make it succeed.'

"The gloomy prophecies she poohpoohs, and in her voluble
French that's a very convincing sound. . . . For a tidy sum, neat
but not gaudy, the great dictator of Paris is to migrate to
Hollywood for several weeks each spring and fall to design
clothes for all pictures released by Samuel Goldwyn and by United Artists.

"This takes in a list of stars that reads like a Burke's Peerage
of the talkies: Gloria Swanson, Mary Pickford, Ina Claire,
Norma Talmadge, in other words just a great big crowd of
celebrities.

"It's an open secret, for instance, that if Chanel or anyone else
designed for Bebe Daniels a dress that depended on utter simplicity for its effect, Bebe would take one look and pin a big rose
on it before she'd wear it. Clara Bow would pin two roses, a
rhinestone buckle, and a velvet bow with fine streamers! Maybe
not precisely, but you get the idea. . . .

"This is why the doubters remain stubbornly doubting. In the
movies and out, people who know fashions and movie stars, almost all are taking bets that Chanel is going to have hard if not
impossible sledding in Hollywood.

"And the chief reason for this poisonous pessimism is their
knowledge of movie stars themselves. The little matter of pinning
bows and roses, already cited, is merely a hint of general conditions in likes and dislikes among the leading ladies. Not among
one special group of them, but all stars, in all studios. . . . Laying
down the law to them about what they should wear, apparently
is just one of the things that will not work. Getting them to give
up their favorite styles, their favorite shops, their favorite notions
—it is, as Chanel may soon sadly say, 'to laugh.' For it seems
that most of them have exquisite ideas of their own about how
they should dress. Well, anyway, ideas. . . .

"And there are two other reasons for the pessimistic sighs.
One is the fear of monotony and the other is the sad lesson of experience.

"How can any genius, Chanel, or anyone else, be able to
supply—year in and year out—all the main fashions for all the
stars and all the pictures involved in this new scheme of things?
They ask you that and tell you the answer: no one can. In the

past the studios have found it hard enough to keep individuality in movie clothes even with all the large collections of all the largest houses in Paris, Hollywood, and New York to choose from. Surely no single brain is fertile enough, no imagination varied enough, to replace all of them year after year. Not even if it were a Chanel, a Lanvin, a Molyneux, a Vionnet, and a few other couturiers all rolled into one.

"Then there is the little lesson learned by experience. This idea has been tried before in a smaller way, and has always promptly come to grief. There was the time that Erte, the French illustrator and designer, went in for uplift in Hollywood and went out in a terrible huff after Lilian Gish positively refused to wear such-and-such that he decreed was right. And the time that Gilbert Clarke, trained by Lady Duff Gordon, resigned from M. G. M. because of a similar set-to, with Greta Garbo doing the refusing. . . .

"The very fact that none of Mr. Goldwyn's rivals have made any move to sign up other Paris fashion creators is proof that they really mean it when they predict that Chanel will soon come up against the same thing. The day after the news broke about Chanel's contract, Elsa Maxwell called up Walter Wanger of Paramount.

" 'Should I get Patou?' she asked. The answer was an impressive combination of sounds with negative overtones. . . .''

The die was cast. The uncontested queen of Paris fashions prepared to leave for Hollywood. She would go for several weeks in the spring and fall to design exclusive models for Sam Goldwyn's stars.

"The only important dissenting opinion on this whole matter, aside from Mr. Goldwyn and his associates, comes from the Countess de Forceville of Bergdorf Goodman, in charge of dressing the more high-hat Broadway productions. So emphatic was it, that it must be included.

" 'Since it is Chanel, I say it will work,' " the Countess de Forceville told Laura Mount. " 'No one else in Paris, or in the world, could do it, but Chanel can. If they never listened to anyone before, the stars will listen to her. If she designs a dress, they will love it. She will never go stale—monotony is impossible for her. All the more important styles we have been wearing for the past ten or fifteen years were born, in their first form, in Chanel's mind. It will be a triumphant success and the movies will be better for it.'

"But even this staunch supporter agreed that it will be no easy job. On these semiannual jaunts to Hollywood, it appears, the great Chanel will have to take her backbone with her—and her entire French vocabulary. For though clothes may not make the man, in the talkies they certainly make a man-size job."

Meanwhile the economic crisis in the United States was worsening. In March 1932 forty thousand unemployed marched on New York City's City Hall. By the end of the year there were fourteen million unemployed in the United States. Incidents multiplied. In July war veterans marched on the Capitol.

In November Franklin D. Roosevelt was elected. The New Deal began.

Coco left like a queen, accompanied by Misia. In New York Maurice Sachs joined Coco. He was just recovering from one of those crises of mysticism that came over him periodically. In the midst of the last one he had married the daughter of an American minister. But once again, weary of virtue, he had taken up his old habits, and so, accompanied by ephemeral youths, he escorted Coco to Hollywood.

Speeding toward California in a special train, painted entirely white, the journalists were overwhelmed by Chanel's life style. They discovered real champagne, caviar, Paris mannequins, and French wit. Their cables were raves that added fuel to the fire as the world capital of the movies awaited the arrival of Parisian chic. When the hour drew near, the exclusive world of Hollywood stood expectantly on the train platform of the Los Angeles station. Greta Garbo welcomed Coco.

"Two queens meet" headlined a daily Hollywood newspaper. But Garbo, who for some was the femme fatale incarnate and for others nothing more than a complicated and pretentious little schoolteacher, modestly stood aside for the couturière. Later Coco dressed her, thus perfecting the famous silhouette. Remodeled by Chanel, Greta would leave the screen at the peak of her glory.

Coco discovered a very strange Hollywood. The talkies, only a few years old, had completely upset the rules of the game, resulting in the dramatic disappearance of most of the great silent screen stars. Those who left could not adapt themselves to the less conventional, more supple, and delicately expressive style of acting required by talking movies.

Yet the departure of the silent stars saw the birth of new stars, among them the dazzling Marlene Dietrich, whose role in *Blue Angel* revealed her immense talent and remarkable figure. Schoolboys the world over dreamed of her as she first appeared, disheveled, charming, ravishing in her tacky negligee, with her admirable legs, her cigarette, and her hoarse voice. She continued to make films under the direction of Josef von Sternberg, who had discovered her. Madly in love with his creation, filling the world with the sounds of his promises and quarrels, constantly swearing he would leave her, Sternberg created more and more elaborate films in which Marlene, a splendid creature coiffed in plumes and covered with jewelry, offered herself to the admiration of the masses. Marlene and Coco grew to have great sympathy for one another, and Dietrich became one of Coco's most loyal friends and customers.

With Marlene, Coco discovered the fabulous city, focal point of the dreams of hundreds of thousands of people for whom Hollywood had opened up the gates of the imagination. With Marlene, too, Coco discovered the reality: Hollywood had become settled in its ways.

First, there was the Depression. It was considered to be in very bad taste for stars to display flashy luxury at a time when unemployment plagued millions of Americans.

Second, a rigid code of behavior had been imposed on Hollywood. As a result of a few scandals, a formidable and uncompromising White Terror, inspired by the clergy and the formidable women's clubs, had begun to do battle with the idols of the screen. An army of detectives was delegated to enforce a standard code of good behavior: divorce was forbidden and certain stars were forced to abandon the screen. The most famous stars had very simple homes, and it was considered good form to receive the minister of the local church around the domino table. In short, in Hollywood during those years you had to be pious, docile, and smiling.

The stars who resisted were struck down without pity. Blacklists were drawn up. Actors were subjected to minute examination of their conduct and morals, and becoming an actor was a goal equivalent to seeking knighthood. The Hollywood employment bureau had the great satisfaction of providing the movies with several thousand unemployed who were as strong as policemen, pure as Boy Scouts, and temperate as Quakers.

Finally, of course, there was a backlash. The censors were forced to temper their ferocious verdicts with a little indulgence. Still, hypocrisy flourished. Hollywood pursued a style of life that was both puritanical and debauched. An outgrowth of this climate was the Code of Decency, the bible of movieland. Maurice Sachs was highly amused by the text of the Code and had it framed.

During one of the many receptions given in her honor, Coco met a young actress who was then largely unknown. She, too, was never addressed by her name; like Coco, she was known as "Miss." Dressed in baggy pants, her bony face covered with freckles the color of a Connecticut forest in the fall and framed by wild hair, she wandered around like an underfed lunberman with a pixy face through studios filled with platinum blonde hair, bovine eyes, and abundant bosoms. She was in the midst of making *Little Women,* which, when it came out in 1934, was an immediate success and made her a star. Her name was Katharine Hepburn. Forty years later, she was to star on Broadway in a musical, which, for the first time in the history of musical comedy, presented the story of a real and still living person: *Coco.*

One of the sacred cows of Hollywood at that time was Eric von Stroheim, at the peak of glory for a film that almost no one had seen: *Greed.* Feared and dreaded, his genius overwhelmed the movie colony, though no one wanted to let him make a film, for he had nearly ruined Goldwyn. Monocled, disdainful, and faithful to his best creation—his impersonation of a Prussian *junker*—he returned in great pomp from the filming of *Greed* with twenty-eight reels of film representing seven hours of projection time. The producers threw themselves at his feet, but he remained intransigent: "No cuts."

Coco met von Stroheim during a reception. He kissed her hand with his usual ceremoniousness. Ten minutes later, joining the circle surrounding the heroine of the party, he pronounced in sepulchral tones: "You are a dressmaker . . . I believe. . . ."

"What a ham," Coco said later, "but he really had style!" She forgave him.

In spite of the social whirl, Coco didn't forget her work. It was difficult, and she was forced to compromise on certain of her criteria for elegance. In the United States, where she felt lay the future and survival of couture, Coco the shrewd Auvergnat was ready to make certain concessions.

On February 21, 1932, the following item appeared in the *London Sunday Express,* written by their Hollywood correspondent:

> You probably remember how, early last year, Sam Goldwyn announced, in a voice bursting with pride, that he had secured the services of no less a dress designer than Mlle Gabrielle Chanel of Paris. For a time there was silence. Then Sam Goldwyn made public Chanel's manifesto to the world: This and this were fashionable, she proclaimed, and these and those were not. The general trend of it was that any costume was OK so long as it was made by Mlle Chanel. On one thing she was particularly insistent: lounge pyjamas were the quintessence of bad taste and no lady would be seen dead in them. *Tonight or Never* is the first Hollywood film gowned by Chanel, and in one of the first scenes of it Gloria Swanson appears in lounge pyjamas!

Chanel undoubtedly made a triumphant entrance into the U.S. movie world, but not without accepting compromise. When she abandoned her movie preoccupations to take a close look at the worlds of fashion and society, she departed Hollywood as she arrived: in triumph.

Before leaving for Europe, Coco stayed in New York for a while. A clever diplomat, she ingratiated herself to the two queens of American fashions: Carmel Snow of *Harper's Bazaar* and Margaret Case of *Vogue.* Forgetting that they were competitors, the two magazines praised Coco to the skies—all the more enthusiastically since their respective editors, both Russians, knew what Coco had done for émigrés. Hadn't she been the "boss" of the czar's cousin, the Grand Duchess Marie, who prior to coming to New York, where she successively became a photographer, director of a fashion house, woman of letters, and lecturer, had supervised Mademoiselle's embroidery workshop?

Furthermore, New York was then having its Russian hour: the survivors of the Diaghilev ballets, Colonel Basil's, Leonid Massine's, and Balanchine's troupes, were creating the beautiful nights of the Metropolitan Opera.

The boxes were filled with millionaires, Russian princesses—real or fake—exiled grand dukes, and penniless European aristocrats in search of heiresses or simply in search of dinner invitations.

Tradition had it that the Opera never filled until after the first act. One night, Coco and Misia had been invited by one of her customers to attend a performance. During dinner, the hostess told Misia, who was anxiously and nervously waiting to see once again the ballet company for which she had done so much: "Don't worry. The second act only begins at ten o'clock."

Misia answered: "In Paris the spectators are attendant upon the dancers. For they have their talent as an excuse . . ."

The party immediately left for the Opera. But when the curtain rose, Misia was overwhelmed by too many stirring memories. After an hour, a lump in her throat, she leaned toward Coco and whispered: "Please, let's go. I can't stand it anymore . . ."

Coco apologized to her hostess, and the two women left before the last act, leaving their hostess in the belief that if Parisian chic insisted on one's presence for the first act, it also decreed that one should leave before the last act. And so are social customs sometimes born.

Informed of her presence in New York, a great many of Coco's clients rushed to invite her. She discovered New York drawing rooms with all their snobbery and social barriers. The Americans were thrown into raptures by titles of nobility, and everyone was looking for ways to ascribe one to himself.

Used to the discreet luxury of the old European world, Coco and Misia were amused to discover such residences as that of a very wealthy woman whose Park Avenue apartment had been transformed into a Spanish patio. In her house on Fifth Avenue, Mrs. O. K. Vanderbilt had covered her walls with authentic Renaissance paneling, bought at great expense in a château on the Loire. However, since the panels were much too high, they had been cut down to the proportions of her rooms, On Long Island, certain millionaires had spent huge sums of money building exact copies of European châteaux.

It was all very amusing, of course, but the round quickly palled. Soon tired of social life, Coco turned her attention to business. She spent the rest of her stay in the United States studying the structure of the U.S. fashion industry.

In New York there were practically no haute couture houses,

but large stores such as Saks, Macy's, and Bloomingdale's had departments devoted to the reproduction of Paris models. A month later the same model would be on sale for a few dollars at Klein's, in Union Square. Alice Halincka has described this unique store in a way that would have made Paris designers and ready-to-wear manufacturers shudder, just as Coco did when she visited the store.

"Klein's consists of one or rather two large dirty buildings erected in downtown New York. Dresses are sold there by the thousands. The customer helps herself; she picks out the desired number of dresses and tries them on in large communal dressing rooms with mirrored walls always crowded with women waiting to get a look at themselves in the mirrors. There are no saleswomen to help them choose and try on clothes. The former usually sit on ladders chewing gum and watching the customers. Signs in every known language—Polish, Armenian, Yiddish, etc., etc., admonish:

" 'Don't try to steal; our detectives are everywhere.'

"These notices alternate with others: 'Sticking chewing gum under sinks is forbidden.' "

"Enormous colored women undress next to the Polish peasant woman or the ravishing chorus girl. Dresses are cut by the thousands in exact duplication of the Paris model, only the fabric is different."

Chanel's trip ended with this commercial vision of the United States. She returned home fascinated and irritated. The New World had intrigued her, but saturated with what she had seen, Coco announced upon arriving in Europe that she needed "a bath of nobility."

An occasion presented itself. The War Service Legion, founded in 1918 by Lady Londonderry and Lady Titchfield, was in need of money. Coco suggested showing her models in one of the houses that the Duke of Westminster had put at her disposal. On May 14, 1932, the following item appeared in the *London Daily Mail*:

The exhibition of models by Mademoiselle Chanel the French dressmaker at 39 Grosvenor Square has now been opened more than a week. Since May 6th, the collection has attracted between 500 and 600 people daily and manufacturers have come from all over the country to see it. Many women have brought their dressmakers with them for Mlle Chanel has allowed the collection to be copied although the dresses are not for sale. Among those who have visited the exhibition are the Duchess of Sutherland, the Duchess of Beaufort, the Marchioness of Cambridge, Lady Titchfield, Lady Derby, the Countess of Portarlington, Viscountess Gage, Lady Desborough, Miss Gertrude Lawrence, and Miss Iris Tree.

It was a new triumph for Coco, who went home, elated, to continue creating.

"And so there it is, the real imitates the fake. . . ." SEM's joke provoked a smile in the salons of the rue Cambon, for the International Association of Diamond dealers had asked Coco to design precious jewelry, an impressive accolade for someone who had never created anything but costume jewelry.

Around 1934 Coco went into costume jewelry on a large scale. She surrounded herself with "artisans" found in Paris society, and it was considered the height of chic to design jewelry for Coco. Etienne de Beaumont excelled at it. A past master of futilities, he dabbled in almost everything: fashion (he designed models), decoration, and his many marvelous costume balls, which were sometimes attended by Coco. Ten years earlier, after falling out out with Diaghilev, he had even tried to organize his own ballet spectacle in his sumptuous town house on rue Duroc. But it was a flop.

"He's just an amateur. . . ." Coco explained with disdain.

Misia, whose divorce from Sert had just been finalized, was having financial difficulties. She had left her luxurious apartment in the Hôtel Meurice and had moved into a flat on the ground floor of the building on the esplanade of the Invalides. The same enchanting atmosphere existed still, but to earn a living Misia designed jewelry for Coco and did interior decoration for people in society such as Lady Colfax and Elsie Mendl.

In addition to being preoccupied with the design of costume jewelry, Coco owned some of the most beautiful precious jewelry in the world. But she rarely wore these sumptuous jewels. She preferred to slip them anonymously among the Chanel jewelry, most of which were actually copies of the real ones, which she kept locked in a safe.

Sometimes she showed them to friends, such as Serge Lifar: "One day, I think it was around 1965, she opened her safe in front of me, took out her jewelry and covered herself with it. She looked like an idol, an icon. There were masses of it, enormous diamonds, gigantic emeralds, pearls, it was like the treasure of Ali Baba."

But it wasn't enough for Coco just to create jewelry. As with everything else she touched, she had to bring out the deep philosophical implications, to define a style and, better still, an art of life. The art of wearing jewelry. Later, in 1969, she explained it further in a television interview with Jacques Chazot:

Q: Jewelry, for example, you have beautiful jewelry?

A: I only like costume jewelry. I only like fake jewelry because I think it is a provocation, that it is disgusting to wander around loaded down with millions around the neck just because one happens to be rich. Jewelry isn't meant to make you look rich, it is meant to adorn you, and that's not the same thing at all.

When costume jewelry is well made—and that which I make is well made—you might as well get rid of the real thing. For I've also got a demolition industry . . . for certain people. I think that going out in the evening covered with diamonds is idiotic. Fake diamonds are made for that. It's a whole industry, too. . . .

Q: It's not much different from the theater. . . ?

A: Yes, it's very different . . . but inevitably it looks theatrical and when making fake jewels, one must avoid making them look more real than the real ones.

Q: By that you mean that one shouldn't be able to tell them apart if one mixes real and fake jewelry together, as you often do I believe. . . ?

A: One should mix them, that's skill. To insist that a woman wear real jewels, is exactly as if you asked her to cover herself with flowers not made in silk, real flowers . . . they'd be faded in a few hours. It's the same thing . . . if you wear fake flowers why not fake jewelry? It's very important for a woman who has a great deal of jewelry that she wear it as though it were fake. Women dress aggressively, like imbeciles. They're stupid.

In 1935, of course, they were still intelligent since they dressed, perfumed, and adorned themselves at Coco's.

Yet things were going to change.

1936. On May 3 the face of France changed. The voters had just given the Popular Front a majority in parliament, with 146 Socialists and 72 Communists. Léon Blum succeeded Albert Sarraut (Radical Socialist) as prime minister. For the first time three women held ministerial portfolios.

Amid unfurled red flags and stirring choruses of "l'Internationale," the people discovered joy and proclaimed their right to leisure and idleness. The masses surged forth to make history, in a world not made for them. They demanded the forty-hour week and paid vacations and developed a tremendous aspiration to enjoy life. Gigantic strikes suddenly paralyzed factories, workshops, and stores. Workmen, salesmen, and seamstresses occupied their places of work, stopping the machinery, to the great indignation of those who had never worked a day in their lives. They danced and sang in the factories, finding joy in a fleeting laziness. The "haves" were terrified. During the night of June 8 French employers signed the Matignon agreements: the forty-hour week was granted, and paid vacations became part of the law. Later, when summer came, millions of people saw the mountains and the sea for the first time in their lives. Horrified, the smart ladies of Deauville, Biarritz, and Juan-les-Pins indignantly watched crowds cluttering the beaches. It was the end of a certain way of life.

Meanwhile, work did not start up again. In the fashion world, where salaries were among the lowest and work conditions the worst, the workers discovered hate. It is difficult to work during one's entire life in close proximity to the most ostentatious and futile luxury, earning a meager salary, without nourishing resentments.

In the rue Cambon the strike was total. In the showrooms where the marquises used to sit there was singing and dancing. Factory workers waltzed while Mistinguett sang.

Coco, whose reputation as a demanding boss was well known, was completely dumbfounded. Her employees demanded a weekly salary. She refused. The strike continued. A tough woman, she recovered her cool.

They taunted her. She refused to give in. They insulted her. She fired three hundred workers. They refused to leave.

Coco tried sweetness next. She offered to give them her fashion firm so long as she continued to run it. They refused. Slowly, as fall came, the strikes dwindled. Like so many employers, Coco was forced to make concessions, to yield.

Work started up again. But a spring had snapped inside Coco. People had dared to stand up to her. A certain conception of the world—the poor work docilely while the rich play—had been torn asunder. Coco was scared. She never forgave her employees, and her sudden closing in 1939 was perhaps a secret revenge.

After 1936 she stayed away more and more often from the rue Cambon and gradually seemed to lose interest in her work. In any case, it wasn't very important to her anymore. Skilfully greased, the machinery continued to work. Coco was needed only to prepare the models for the collections. She frequently sought refuge at La Pausa, where, in the shade of the olive trees, she abandoned herself to solitary meditations.

Or so goes the most charitable explanation. A more harsh explanation for her behavior also is to be found: Coco's supremacy was threatened.

A star had risen out of Italy: Elsa Schiaparelli, "Schiap" to her friends. She was born in Rome in the Corsini Palace; her mother was a timid woman who lived in the shadow of her husband, a good man, a coin collector, and a misanthrope. In the backdrop of her youth existed St. Peter's Square and the moiré robes of the princes of the Church. They may have inspired her vocation.

By the time she was fifteen she had developed a passion for purple, and later she insisted that her admirers wear purple ties so that everyone would know that they were courting her.

While in England she fell madly in love with a gentleman lecturer, M de Kerlor, a theosophist and a practitioner of yoga. She was eighteen when she married him.

She spent World War I in New York, where her daughter Yvonne—Gogo—was born and her husband disappeared.

Returning to Paris after the war, she went with a friend to Poiret's, where she tried on a blue coat that she liked very much.

Poiret watched her as she pirouetted around. "That coat is made for you," he said to her.

"Yes," answered Schiap in Italian. "But I can't afford it."

"I'll give it to you," said Poiret.

Another day while visiting an Armenian friend who made sweaters, she made a few suggestions. The Armenian followed her ideas and the models sold very well.

And so Schiap entered the world of fashions. At first she moved into a small Left Bank apartment, where she made sweaters and skirts. From there she moved into an attic on the rue de la Paix, where she had one salesgirl. From the attic she went down to the second floor, and in 1929 she established herself on the Place Vendôme. The famous playwright Anita Loos, author of *Gentlemen Prefer Blondes,* was one of her first customers. After World War II she was incapable of adapting herself to the new conditions then existing in high fashion. She preferred to retire and to devote herself to painting in her private house on the rue de Berri.

The battle between Schiap and Coco lasted almost ten years, but in 1938 a number of Parisian ladies abandoned Coco for Elsa, her flamboyant colors and her parachute-shaped dresses.

"Chanel launched sailor sweaters, the short skirt," said Schiap. "I took her sweater, changed its lines, and there, Chanel is finished!"

Elsa acted on the assumption that one could make rich and beautiful society ladies believe always that the world is futile, amusing, and absurd. At a time when people, realizing that they were reaching the end of an epoch and hoping to enjoy it down to the last, frenetically pursued pleasure, such a definition of life was bound to have a certain success.

But Coco continued to feel that her work had not yet seen its day. She was convinced that she brought a valid contribution to the art of dressing women as well as to a certain style of life and that this infatuation for the extravagant Italian would be short-lived. "Fashion," with its superficial seasonal changes, Chanel opposed with an unshakable conviction in what she called "style." For her, the Chanel style was far from dead.

Of course, history proved her correct. And yet Chanel's position was paradoxical. For her peremptory objections to Schiap's extravagances, she was accused of directly contradicting her own avant-garde battle against the old style. Coco answered this accusation with a resounding "No." A novelty is not necessarily modern just because it is new, she maintained. Chanel's modern spirit derived from the fact that she placed herself within a classic tradition. Schiap's "futurism" was an optical illusion, and Coco denounced it: Schiap, she said, had nothing to say of the future.

The substance separating these two couturières, whose rivalry was the continuing subject of society gossip for years, was made clear much later.

In Cristóbal Balenciaga's sober salon on the Avenue George

V (sober because it had been decorated in his image) we talked about Coco, who had recently died. We recalled her successes:

"You see," said Balenciaga, who, like Coco, has inspired dreams in millions of women, "Coco had very little taste, but it was good. Schiap, on the other hand, had lots of it, but it was bad."

Yet Chanel's victory over Schiap was far from over in the late 1930s, and Coco became more and more bitter, tired, and discouraged. She rarely set foot in the rue Cambon, for she found it difficult to forgive her customers who had allowed themselves to be tempted by Schiap's extravagances. She was in her mid-fifties. Was she to retire at the peak of her glory? Did she fear that if she were to continue she would fail, like Poiret?

She must have asked herself these questions and many others. But we will never know what finally made her decide to close up. Perhaps it was the outbreak of war.

War was declared in September 1939. Shortly afterward, Coco closed her workshops. She did it without anyone's ever suspecting her decision.

"I had the feeling that we had reached the end of an era. And that no one would ever make dresses again," she said later.

She was wrong, but if one rereads today what happened to French couture during the phony war, one can well understand that Coco wanted no part of it. In a dying world, nonsense pervades everything—especially fashion.

Thus, as war broke out, fashions were supposed to form part of the war effort, as indicated by the following press releases:

The uniform is worn by men who are in the most privileged position of all, that in which one gets killed. No one, of course, has ever dreamed of objecting to this situation. So let's let them have it all, including the uniform.

A few models in the new collection deserve special mention; take, for instance, the ensemble "False Alarm," a three-quarter-length ermine coat over a dinner dress in Moroccan crepe encrusted with blue stones. "Offensive" brings together a printed silk blouse and a fairly long skirt made in a woolen fabric in the same tone, a short jacket with printed silk lapels, and a small bag of the same material for the gas mask.

This was a war in laces, a war without battles, a war of boredom, a war of entertainment for the troops.

During the phony war, Coco's world—the world of the mid-1920s—came back to life. But she wasn't to be seen. She traveled.

Having gotten over their fears, the people made spectacles of themselves. Twenty thousand nurses, from the best families, waited to devote themselves to the wounded. Every Thursday, at tea time, women from the American colony rolled bandages in the American Church on the Quai d'Orsay. Surrounded by a rustling and distinguished swarm of blue capes and white veils, the Minister of Colonies inaugurated a welcoming center for black soldiers on leave.

For nonmobilized actors, entertaining the troops presented a challenge. From the headquarters at Vincennes to the bunkers of the Maginot Line, the idle soldiers made a perfect audience whose enthusiasm was easily aroused.

Dressed in an outfit that grazed the ground, a top hat with gauze streamers on her head, Cécile Sorel, the great actress of long ago, haunted the waiting rooms of ministers, where she was greeted with great deference:

"What can I do for you, Madame?"

"I want to serve."

Alas, she was too old. In the same way, the distinguished Henri Bernstein offered his services to Jean Giraudoux, the playwright and commissioner of information, but without success:

"You are like one of those battleships that for the moment must remain in port," Giraudoux answered him.

To give Coco her due, she managed to escape the traps that caught her contemporaries and often had them foundering into the grotesque.

As the year ended, Jean Giraudoux considered the fact that "no one had ever seen a bird alight on the Führer's shoulder during his walks" to be an omen pointing to the evil fate that awaited the armies of the Third Reich.

Never before had there been so many benefit galas. Most of the theaters and movie houses, which had closed, reopened.

In the fashion houses the biggest hit of the winter collections was the hostess gown, which succeeded the "Air-raid Warning" outfits that were never very popular with customers despite their ingenuity: elegant, one-piece ensembles, the type of thing a lady hotel thief might wear, perfect for the air-raid shelter, easy to put on, roomy, equipped with many pockets suited for carrying papers, playing cards, crème de menthe, etc.

One day Coco called on one of her old friends, the Countess Greffulhe, ex-queen of the pre-World War I years. The peerless model for Proust's Duchess of Guermantes received callers seated under a heated tent. Clearly, even if coal was unavailable during the winter of 1940, social life had returned to its old habits. Paris society amused itself by talking of nothing but strategy and politics. Despite the slogan "enemy ears are listening," no one kept his mouth shut at Lipp's or Maxim's, where every evening one saw as many officers as at Vincennes during the day.

"When I saw all this foolishness," Coco said later, "I was glad that I had closed my fashion house."

Slowly Coco sank into oblivion, and was more often than not absent from Paris.

Though no one doubted that history would remember her name, as it had Worth's and Poiret's, who would have guessed that fifteen years later she would make such a prodigious comeback?

Let's assume she was finished. Indeed, many thought she was. What had contributed to the genius and success of this woman in the period between the two wars? Certainly there was the revolution in fashion for which Chanel was largely responsible. But there was a great deal more.

Coco lived at the very heart of Paris life after World War I. She reigned over society and was part of everything that went on; indeed, she often was the instigator of social events. She was at the heart of all artistic life, the friend of painters and poets.

But we should go even further: Coco intuitively understood her century better than almost anyone else. The later war years saw the birth of surrealism, an incredible revolution in the worlds of poetry and art. When the world of art lost its elitist character, a new costume was needed, and Coco provided it. She dressed the world and imposed a style of life that everyone immediately adopted.

We know that a certain sense of modesty made Coco deny that she was an artist or that fashion was an art:

"It's simply a craft," she said, "a manual trade like any other. In my case it's the business of dressing women and doing everything possible to make them elegant."

This comment says a great deal about her character. Undoubtedly the creation of a dress or a suit is not in the same category with the works of Picasso, Stravinsky, or Cocteau. The loveliest of suits only lasts a few seasons. But Chanel went beyond fashion. She dedicated her entire life to a precisely defined goal, and nothing could make her deviate from it.

The saying, "Chanel isn't a fashion; it's a style" meant only this: underneath her apparently modest work lay an aesthetic inspiration, a profound sensibility, and a sureness of taste—the very essence of the innovating artist, one who contributes decisive landmarks in the search for beauty in life.

Part II

12.

Exile

1 939-1954. Coco spent fifteen years of her life away from fashion, away from the workrooms of the rue Cambon. Only the boutique, which had remained open during these years, retained the flavor of the luxurious atmosphere of yesteryear.

People no longer hurried up the staircase leading to the first floor. The shutters were kept closed. The mirrors reflected only a single, ever-elegant silhouette, returning to the apartments on the second floor where friends sometimes came to visit.

For fifteen years, from the Hôtel Ritz to 31 rue Cambon, from La Pausa to Switzerland, Coco Chanel spent her retirement on the edge of oblivion and of history, cut off from the kind of life that had nourished her celebrity.

May 10, 1940. From Strasbourg to Rotterdam, 3,000 German tanks and 120 German divisions flung themselves against the French army.

Thirty-four days later, on June 14, Paris was proclaimed an open city. Beneath a radiant summer sun, millions of men, women, and children, mingling with routed French army divisions, fled along the French roads, machine-gunned by Stukas. Some lucky people rode by in automobiles, but only for as long as their gasoline held out.

This desperate journey brought Coco near to Pau, in the

Pyrenees. There she took refuge in Lembeye, where before the war she had bought a piece of property for her nephew André Palasse. There, too, Coco found Etienne Balsan, a long-time resident, grown older, married, but still mad about horses. He was the man through whom Coco had bought the property.

On June 16, Marshal Pétain became premier of France; on June 18 he requested an armistice, which was signed on June 22.

Paris slowly recovered its inhabitants. A section of the Ritz was requisitioned by the German army. However, the hotel management was able to keep Coco's apartment free for her. She returned to it soon after.

Parisian life gradually returned to a more normal state. Some of the fashion houses opened, and in October 1940 they began to present their collections. The showings were attended by Germans belonging to the embassy or the wives of the General Staff, some of whom (among them Goering, who escorted his wife Edda) accompanied their spouses.

Some of the designers were able to remain open during the bleak hours of the Occupation because of the efforts of Lucien Lelong, the president of their association. Lelong, according to fashion journalist Simone Baron, "obtained special dispensations permitting them to buy deluxe fabrics without using ration tickets."

But these fashion houses soon found a changed situation. As Lelong said, "A new class of rich people, black marketeers, and collaborators, thanks to their wives, provoked a sudden change in the dress world. The old wealthy and aristocratic clientele almost totally disappeared, replaced by the butter-egg-and-cheese people, the spoiled darlings of the war. These nouveaux riches caused deluxe ready-to-wear, unknown to the public before 1939, to make remarkable strides. Dozens and dozens of elegant boutiques opened on the rue du Faubourg St.-Honoré and then on the rue de Sèvres, and the new clientele brought an enormous success to this fashion, which was not high fashion but imitated it very well and was cheaper in the bargain."

Only the House of Chanel obstinately kept its doors shut. "That period was singularly lacking in dignity; it was a filthy mess!" said Coco years later.

Millions of Frenchmen were taken prisoner. In September, the Occupation authorities proclaimed the first anti-Jewish measures, and on October 4 the first transit camps for Jewish foreigners were opened.

"Let Paris be the Reich's Luna Park," said Hitler. The Germans insisted that Paris must once again become "gay Paree" for the sake of worldwide public opinion as well as for the morale of the German troops. The cinemas reopened, except for the Berlitz, which showed an exhibition entitled "The Jew and France." The theaters also opened; Jacques Copeau became the director of the national theater, the Comédie française, and Serge Lifar the director of the Opéra ballet.

There were 550 thoroughbreds in Paris ready to compete, and on November 10 the race tracks opened. German officers were admitted free of charge to the paddock, where they strode about amid Parisian society. That same day, the Gestapo arrested a French engineer, Jacques Bonsergent, the first Parisian shot by the occupying forces.

The Third Reich offered yet another visage to the Paris of arts and letters, to its artists, intellectuals, and musicians. Under the pretext of Franco-German cultural exchanges, many drawing rooms began to open their doors to the elite of Nazi Germany. "They are so well mannered," said some prominent people belonging to the "smart set."

Among the German soldiers was a diplomat belonging to the elegant entourage of Joachim von Ribbentrop, minister of foreign affairs of the Third Reich. Tall, with blond hair and blue eyes, a handsome, distinguished-looking Aryan, Hans Gunther von Dincklage was born on December 15, 1896, in Hanover. In 1935 he divorced his wife. His close friends had nicknamed him "Spatz," which means "sparrow."

Coco fell in love with Spatz. Had she, as rumors had it, known him before the war? Possibly, because Spatz was a playboy who belonged to the international "smart set" between the two wars.

Dincklage entered France on November 9, 1928; he lived successively at 14 Avenue Charles Floquet, 150 rue de l' Université, and 64 rue Pergolèse. He also worked as a spearhead of the Fifth Column, his role being to spread defeatist propaganda in French circles.

Numerous investigations made by the French counter-espionage services showed that Spatz Dincklage was an important Abwehr agent under the orders of Colonel Waag. On July

9, 1947, by ministerial decree, he was deported from France, and this measure has never been revoked.

The handsome Spatz Dincklage now lives on an island in the Mediterranean. He devotes himself to erotic sculpture and paintings, believes in the occult, and claims to be in frequent communication with Admiral Canaris.

In 1941 Coco was nearing the age of sixty, the age for a last love, or at least a loving friendship. Coco went out very little during the Occupation. She sometimes attended the Opéra to applaud her old friend Serge Lifar. She disdained the chic restaurants, where, as Lifar wrote, "the young counselors from the embassy and the young German officers, enjoying their first moments of glory and pleasure of belonging to an elite, thronged about in their green infantry uniforms, black uniforms of the tank corps, and the navy gray uniforms of the air force. The young girls and women of Parisian society or the artistic world came there to have some fun, hard to find in a Paris empty of warmth. Fashion had not yet had time to change, but the shows . . . were already beginning to transform the trends, and the new silhouette, which would last until the end of the war, was starting to appear.

"I spent long evenings with Chanel who, because of her inactivity, had returned to her first loves, music and singing. Accompanying herself on the piano, she sightread the greatest bel canto scores. I was struck by her musical talent. . . ."

When he greeted Serge Lifar at a reception, Pierre Laval, leader of the Vichy government, recommended: "Insofar as you have any influence in Paris, protect the Auvergnats, and above all Chanel. . . ."

Thus, during the war her social life almost nonexistent, Coco had to be content with long conversations with intimate friends and a romance with Spatz Dincklage, a passionate admirer of music. In the soft, padded, protected atmosphere of her apartment on the rue Cambon, she was insulated from the turmoil going on outside.

Was she at all interested in what was happening in France and elsewhere in the world? Coco passed the black years of the war with her back turned to any involvement—and this in a divided country where it soon became necessary to take sides, where a minority chose active resistance. Events barely touched her unless they concerned her directly.

But can Coco's behavior be explained so simply? As with everything about Coco, there is ambiguity, mystery. She was seen everywhere with a German, Spatz Dincklage, a servitor of the Third Reich and Hitler. In 1942, however, the BBC honored her by citing her for having helped one of her English friends, Vera Bates Lombardi, to leave Italy clandestinely, and at the end of the same year, when she was living at La Pausa with Spatz Dincklage, at the request of her architect Robert Streitz, then a member of the Resistance, she spontaneously agreed to intercede for a friend of his, Professor Serge Voronov, who had been arrested by the Gestapo.

Under Pétain and Laval, the country devoted itself to "intellectual and moral redressment." The return to the land, the youth camps, and the hunting down of bad shepherds (Jews, Communists, and Freemasons) were the antidotes to all evils. The leitmotif of Vichy's propaganda was "We must atone." In matters such as the forty-hour week and paid vacations set up by the Popular Front Government in 1936, France had sinned, and the Vichy slogan was strongly taken up by Parisian circles. Profiteering and black market operations made it possible for those who had the means and few scruples to rise above the vicissitudes of daily life. Never had there been so many dinners, lunches, receptions, concerts, and play openings. Atonement was made by third parties—such intermediaries as Jews, for example.

An ordinance was promulgated requiring that any business whose owner or owners had left the country would be subject to the jurisdiction of *"administrateurs provisoires,"* persons solely responsible for the proper administration of the commercial sector of the economy.

Pierre and Paul Wertheimer had left France for the United States, selling their holdings for a low sum of money to someone in whom they had confidence—a plane designer and manufacturer, who then became the legal owner of Bourjois perfumes and of the shares in the Chanel perfume company.

Coco again took up arms against the Wertheimers as a direct result of the war. Exercising their rights as majority owners of Parfums Chanel, the Wertheimers had set up a wholly independent U.S. subsidiary: Chanel, Incorporated. In this company Chanel had no control and virtually no participation, and it was in the United States that No. 5 sold most briskly.

If the loss of income were not enough to goad Mademoiselle into fighting action, the "change in ownership" in France was too good an opportunity for her to pass up. Typically, she used all the means at her disposal without realizing that there are times when certain actions, even in competitive commerce, are not acceptable. To her mind, Wertheimer's absence was simply one more weapon to be turned to her advantage. After all, she reasoned, she was not, during the war, receiving any dividends from the sale of perfumes in the United States.

The war on the company escalated dramatically. Coco now attempted to take over the company. She had tried this before the war, without success, but this time she held powerful weapons: she was an Aryan who had been known to be anti-Semitic and, like her friend Pierre Laval, she was an Auvergnat. Also, thanks to Spatz Dincklage she was in good favor with the Germans.

The legal advisers for the perfume company told us: "Coco returned to attend a board of directors meeting of the company, the first held since that attended by Iribe, her representative. Then, in circumstances that have remained relatively unknown, with vehemence and savage ruthlessness, she had the company declared abandoned by its owners (the Wertheimers) and a gentleman named Georges Madoux* designated commissioner.

"She installed herself at Neuilly. There was a ghastly board meeting. In front of a cousin of the Wertheimers, Raymond Bollack, who had remained in France and who had served in both world wars, Coco railed against those who she thought had fleeced her fifteen years earlier.

"She said: 'Those Wertheimers in America are still the owners of the firm. Raymond Bollack should know it since he is their cousin and is still present here at this board of directors table!'

"We counterattacked immediately. Since Mademoiselle had German support, we searched for our own, and it was not too difficult to find such support in the Paris of those years if enough money were offered as a bribe. Thanks to the 'goodwill' of a German who was amply rewarded, we fabricated some antedated

---

*According to Madame Lâbrunie (Coco's grandniece), Mademoiselle had chosen Madoux to protect both the interests of the Wertheimers and of herself. Madoux knew the Chanel business very well because from 1924 until 1931 he had been the commercial manager of the "Société Anonyme de Parfums."

false stock transfers, which made indisputable the purchase of the business by the plane designer and manufacturer. Thus, the latter's lawyer was able to appear before the German authorities and declare that the business now belonged to a plane manufacturer assisted by Baron Robert de Nexon, who had just been liberated from a French prisoner-of-war camp.*

"It worked. Robert de Nexon then became a member of the board of directors along with several figureheads and, at another board meeting, we put Madoux out, despite Mademoiselle's insulting remarks to Robert de Nexon, who in the meantime had been elected president of the firm. During the rest of the war, Mademoiselle Chanel had no further say in the matter. . . . "

So Coco had lost again, and most ingloriously. But what did she care? On the rue Cambon, the sale of No. 5 continued— thanks, in all territories occupied by the Third Reich, to the French company and throughout the rest of the world, to the U.S. company.

The U.S. company, independent of the French firm, expanded at an incredible rate. Claude L. explained to us the reasons for these prodigious strides:

"Until 1941, the sales of perfumes to the United States stabilized at about half a million dollars per year (about two million dollars in today's currency). Today, this figure was increased tenfold and this great increase began in the period 1940–1945.

"This was due first to the fact that No. 5 is probably the only perfume whose quality remained the same throughout the war, although it was necessary to fabricate the concentrate in the United States. But the initial essences continued to come from Paris, especially the jasmine from Grasse. With a great deal of foresight, the Wertheimer brothers sent people to France to round up stocks while it was still possible to do so.

"Their exploits were worthy of James Bond: gold had to be sent into France clandestinely, the jasmine taken out and brought into the United States. Some 700 pounds of jasmine were received, more precious than its weight in gold. None of the competitors was able to do as well.

"Then, the Wertheimer brothers, with extraordinary commer-

---

*Robert de Nexon, first cousin of Adrienne Chanel's husband, had been a close friend, in the earliest years of the century, of Etienne Balsan.

cial acumen, decided to undertake a vast publicity campaign. The annual advertising budget quickly reached several million dollars, but the budget was more than matched by an increase in profits. Between 1940 and 1972, a promotional budget totaling sixty million dollars was spent on the American market, most of it before 1950. Coco, as sole owner of the business, could never have come near to investing that sum."

When the Wertheimer's launched a huge publicity campaign to promote Chanel perfumes, they also opened up an irreparable breach (to Coco), even though the scheme was most successful. Coco now felt all the bridges were burned between her and the Wertheimers.

1943–1944. In occupied Paris, behavior changed. The landing in North Africa and the victory at Stalingrad opened many eyes, and though fashionable Paris continued to lead a rather frenzied social life, it was no longer under the pretense of "Franco-German intellectual exchanges." Many salons closed their doors.

On the other hand, the theaters were constantly full, and in those black years French theater saw plays from Paul Claudel, Sacha Guitry, Jean Anouilh, Jean-Paul Sartre, and Jean Cocteau. One of the latter's plays, *The Typewriter,* presented for the first time in 1941, was canceled at the request of the occupying forces. The following year, Cocteau courageously defended the great writer Jean Genet, prosecuted for theft, despite the risks involved in that period of moral order. Genet was condemned to only three months in prison. In 1944 Cocteau put on *Antigone* again, and Coco went to work creating the costumes for it.

Serge Lifar told us: "She lived then at the Ritz in two little maid's rooms. She had two suits and several blouses. In 1944 she did nothing except create costumes for *Antigone*. Then, some time before the Liberation, she returned to live entirely on the rue Cambon. Since I was living at the Hôtel de Castille, two steps away from her, we continued to see each other almost daily."

June 6, 1944. Americans, English, and Free French landed in Normandy. "The battle which is taking place on our soil does not concern us," proclaimed Marshal Pétain. The Resistance attacked. In Paris, some smiled, others spent the hours before Liberation making bargains and deals in fear of denunciation. In fashionable Paris, people observed each other carefully, weighing respective chances, because the Resistance had announced, via the BBC as well as by tracts, its decision to call people to account for their conduct during the Occupation. For those compromised by ultracollaboration, it was the hour of desperate flight to Switzerland or Spain or of decision to stay and face up to punishment, of maintaining one's dignity. For others, menaced by disgrace rather than by prison, for all those who, in good faith, had thought that they could protect someone or something or, more simply and stupidly, had not been able to resist the charms of a social life subtly orchestrated around and by the German embassy, it was the hour of reciprocal lapses of memory and few mutual services: *nobody* had seen *anybody, anywhere.*

August 1944. Paris rose up at the announcement of the approach of the Leclerc Division. On August 24, General de Gaulle descended on the Champs Elysées.

As far as Coco's circle was concerned, the first to be affected was Serge Lifar. He was accused for having remained at the head of the Opéra and of having entertained Hitler (false) and many Germans (true). When the excitement died down, he explained how his conduct had allowed him to protect, often successfully, many artistic works or to intervene for people threatened by Vichy or by the occupying forces.

At first, only one house was open to him—that of Coco Chanel, disdainful of last-minute compromises. Spatz Dincklage had, of course, followed the German army. Later, Coco confided to one of her friends: "I couldn't walk around the apartment even half-undressed because Serge might be hiding in a closet." Fifteen days later Lifar came out of the rue Cambon and gave himself up to the Purge Committee of the Opéra.*

In the meantime, Coco herself was arrested by the F.F.I. (which she called the "Fifis") and held for three hours. She never spoke of it, but from that time on she nourished a ferocious hatred for the Resistance and for Gaullism.

What did they reproach her with? Her liaison with a German? No doubt. But it was also true that Coco had been the only de-

---

*He succeeded in exonerating himself, and the Purge Committee made him retire for one year. Several years later he returned to the Opéra. He explains his attitude with admirable frankness in his *My Life,* a remarkable document on social life in Paris during the Occupation.

signer to keep her fashion house closed. Neither the hazards of war, nor the Occupation, nor restrictions, nor the Liberation had kept the collections from being presented in all the other Parisian temples of elegance.

Serge Lifar told us: "At the Liberation, Coco behaved like a queen: Marie-Antoinette on her way to the scaffold. She left with the two Frenchmen who had come to arrest her without speaking a word, her head held high."

One of those who had fought off her attempt to take over the perfume firm declared to us: "She was not a coward. She could be ignoble but she was never cowardly. At the Liberation, she was in an awkward situation, but she faced up to it. She didn't run away. She didn't throw over her friends who were compromised. She confessed to me that she was frightened but said that she had succeeded in dominating her fear.

"That is real courage."

13.
Mademoiselle, Forgotten

ONE victory follows another, but how different they can be.

In Paris in 1945, victory had a bitter taste. Admitted to the victors' feast, but seated below the salt, nicknamed the "sick man" of Europe and giving up all pretense to being a great power, France licked its wounds and tried to overcome the internal divisions between "Resistance Fighters" and "Collaborators."

If 1918 saw the birth of a new world, 1945 saw its premature death. The prewar elite was discredited in the eyes of the young, in whom the recent past had instilled a skepticism about the establishment.

The literary and artistic worlds felt the birth of a new sensibility imbued with a sense of nothingness, more tragic and more committed. Paradoxically, in those "tomorrows that no longer sang," one was supposed to forget, enjoy life, and rebuild all at the same time.

In this new sensibility, everything that was written, painted, or expressed was done *outside* the slowed-down world of Society. The avant-garde deserted Parisian high society, in which it had been so tightly meshed between the two wars. After 1945 the two worlds were rarely to meet—or, to be more exact, Society was to adopt and cultivate its own writers and artists outside the mainstream. Neither Albert Camus nor Jean-Paul Sartre nor

André Malraux, far and away the dominant intellectual figures of the immediate postwar years, were drawing-room lions. Those whose names continued to shine brightly, the poet Aragon and the artist Picasso, for example, found a second youth in politics or solitude, far from the social anarchism that had so delighted them in the past. Jean Cocteau, disillusioned too, confided to a friend: "It is difficult to last. . . ."

The indefatigable Etienne de Beaumont tried to revive his famous balls, but those who had heart and talent stayed away. The sun of the prewar social leaders had set. Social life had become an anachronism, surviving through kickbacks and playbacks in the press. Henceforth Society would be manipulated mainly by public relations men.

Most of Coco Chanel's world had foundered. Far from couture, to which she no longer had any ties, from a world whose evolution left her pensive and perplexed, and from intellectual and artistic life, which continued without her, Coco sank into oblivion. Then, to add to her plight, death once again struck down those near her and those whose talent and company she cherished.

Between 1945 and 1956, the poets Max Jacob, Leon-Paul Fargue, Antonin Artaud, and Paul Eluard, the actor Louis Jouvet, the painters Christian Bérard and Marie Laurençin, the musician Arthur Honneger, and the writers André Gide, Paul Valéry, and Colette disappeared. And so did many others who once had dined at 29 rue du Faubourg St.-Honoré and at the rue Cambon: the writer Jean Giraudoux and the director Charles Dullin, among them. In England in 1950 Nijinski died without ever regaining his power of reason.

Nor must we forget all those who died tragically, victims of the times: the writer Drieu la Rochelle, who took his own life as disdainfully as he had led it; Robert Brasillach, the poet, shot for having seen in Naziism only the splendor of Nuremberg's cathedrals of light; Maurice Sachs, whose voyage to the depths of nothingness ended with a bullet in the neck in 1945 near Hamburg, where he had worked for the Gestapo—which finally assassinated him—as a radio announcer and as a spy in a political prison.

It was the end of an epoch of which Coco had been one of the queens. Over sixty years old, for the first time in her life Coco Chanel had no future.

So she traveled, dragging her boredom behind her, from the Côte d'Azur to Lausanne, getting as far away as possible from Paris, where, ever since the Liberation, it was as though fumes of sulphur clung to her.

In Switzerland she rejoined Spatz Dincklage, who had taken refuge there. They spent some time together in Villars-sur-Ollon, a ski resort in the canton of Vaud, making short trips to Italy. Their idyl seems to have lasted until around 1950. Mademoiselle's Swiss friends—her three lawyers, her dentist, Dr. Vallotton, her doctors, a rheumatism specialist, Dr. Theo de Preux, and an eye specialist, Professor Streig—often saw them together, and there were rumors of a possible marriage between Coco and the German.

Those who knew the baron remember him as an impoverished, aging playboy who nevertheless managed to keep up the pretense of wealth and fun-loving youth. Then one day he disappeared from Mademoiselle's side and settled on a Mediterranean island. She never spoke to her friends about Spatz Dincklage but continued to send him an allowance. Perhaps he still receives one.

Coco had known Switzerland before the war and liked its calm, its cleanliness, its mountains, its hotels, and the discretion of its banks.

Somewhat insensitive to the ups and downs of international politics, but good accountants, hard workers, and respectful of property rights, the Swiss were for Coco the most reasonable of people. And they were serious, in contrast to the French, who were forever wrapped up in their petty quarrels and perpetual demands.

She had taken her nephew, André Palasse, who suffered from tuberculosis, to live in French-speaking Switzerland. She bought for him successively a house in the vineyards of Lavaux, an apartment in Chexbres, also in the vineyards between Lausanne and Vevey, and finally a villa hidden among the woods above Lutry. Whenever in the region, Coco always came to visit her nephew, of whom she was very fond, staying with him from time to time. Otherwise, faithful to her old habits, she stayed in the big hotels: the Beau Rivage at Ouchy, which she eventually abandoned because of a badly toasted piece of bread, the Palace, the Royal and the Central, in Lausanne.

Coco's Swiss friends remember her as a charming, simple, and lively woman. She entertained them frequently, either in the hotels where she was staying or in restaurants in "old" Lausanne. She was especially fond of the Pomme de Pin, La Bossette, and the Chalet Suisse, situated on the Sauvabelin hill. Her menu varied very little. She almost always ordered vegetable soup, filet mignon, unbuttered rice, and fruit compote.

For Coco this was vacation-style retirement. She went dancing with her friends and shopping, especially in the less expensive stores such as the Bazar Vaudois, whose handbags she particularly liked.

She dined out, here and there, quite often in Dr. Vallotton's home, for she was fond of him and later invited him and his wife to stay at La Pausa. It was there that Mme Vallotton remembers hearing Coco sing Yvonne Printemps' songs in a duet with her great friend Maggy van Zuylen, mother-in-law of Baron Guy de Rothschild, who married her daughter Marie Hélène.

"Couture? She hardly spoke about it," Mme Vallotton told us. "It was as though it did not interest her anymore. Or almost not. . . ."

Still, one day Mme Vallotton wore a blouse that Coco did not like; Coco could not resist taking a pair of scissors and making a few changes on the spot.

One of her close friends described to us Mademoiselle's daily life.

"At the beginning of each stay she would sleep a great deal, resting up from the fatigue of life in Paris. In the morning, if she hadn't an appointment with one of her doctors or lawyers, she would stay in her room reading fashion magazines or the latest novel. She had herself driven to the Sauvabelin hill, near Chalet-à-Gobet, just below Lausanne. There she took long walks alone before climbing back into her car, which followed her slowly."

Coco loved the hill of Sauvabelin. There, near a lake in the middle of woods where deer roamed, she bought a villa whose cheerless gray walls rose in the middle of a property planted with grass, trees, and boxwood. Unfortunately, however, the trees were not sufficient to protect the house from the prying eyes of neighbors, and Coco soon forsook her Lausanne house, which became simply a legal residence for tax purposes, and went back to living in hotels, where she felt more at ease.

Meanwhile, at the rue Cambon, Mademoiselle's other

headquarters, the Americans had followed the Germans as customers for Mademoiselle's famous No. 5 and the new red-label perfumes, numbers 1, 2, and 31, the latter named "Mademoiselle Chanel." These perfumes were created in 1946, well after the liberation of France, when Coco was suing Chanel, Inc., New York; Chanel Ltd., London; and Perfums Chanel, Neuilly.

Pierre Wertheimer returned to Paris to try to settle matters, but Coco was often out of town and after all the nasty business of the war they tended, of course, to avoid each other. Matters were turned over to the lawyers.

The dispute did not involve only the red-label perfumes. There was the matter of the general evolution since 1940 of the U.S. company, of which Coco owned 10 percent. She had been brushed aside, while the Wertheimers, who had run the business skilfully, but to their own profit, felt that the enormous investment they had made gave them the right of control. Both camps were preparing to sue in France, in the United States and in England.

When Coco returned from Switzerland, completely cleared of charges of collaboration, she sued the Wertheimers for abuse of their majority position. In return, the Wertheimers sued for counterfeiting.

"In France," Robert Chaillet told us, "her suit resulted in a confrontation between her lawyer and Paul and Pierre Wertheimer. An examining magistrate discharged the case, advising Mademoiselle Chanel to give up her suit, which could very well turn against her. Mademoiselle was furious.

"In the United States, however, things were different, for there minority shareholders are much better protected than in France. An expert was about to be brought into the case. In order to avoid this, René de Chambrun, then Mademoiselle's lawyer, and the lawyer for the perfume company got together out of court. A gentleman's agreement was concluded. The Wertheimers bought up Coco's shares. A deal was made concerning the 'red perfumes,' in compensation for which Coco accepted a clause stipulating that these could only be sold by the perfume company, which, of course, in view of the fantastic success of No. 5, obviously had no desire to sell them.

Unfortunately for the lawyers and the perfume people, Chanel was not party to the gentleman's agreement. Again, she saw herself as being sold short. She rejected all overtures and agreements and, almost alone, decided to take on the company—in her own way.

Claude L. told us:

"At about that time she came into contact with a rich American industrialist who made and sold refrigerators. What story did she tell him? I have no idea. In any case, they began to manufacture the red perfumes, intending to sell them in the United States. We had them seized in customs, as we were legally entitled to do, and went to see the industrialist in question. He was completely unaware of the agreement Coco had with us. She had brainwashed him. He withdrew, advising her to make a deal with us."

Coco was beaten, but not for long.

Armed with new samples, she descended upon perfumers, letting them understand that these new items were the only perfumes worthy of the glamorous label "Chanel" and of whose composition she, Coco Chanel, approved. For the Wertheimers, the situation was getting out of hand. All Coco had to do was make a few statements to the U.S. press, and the perfumers would start demanding the red perfumes from the Chanel perfume company, perfumes the company had no right to make and Coco had no right to sell.

An agreement *had* to be made. It was an impossible situation. Coco had set a careful trap. She was especially furious that although the war was over, because of the relationship between Parfums Chanel, Chanel, Inc., and herself, she was receiving only 10 percent of the 10 percent royalty Chanel, Inc., was paying Parfums Chanel. According to René de Chambrun: "Coco thundered: 'I'm getting out of the company!'

" 'It's impossible,' I told her, 'but you can demand damages.' '

" 'I'll ask for all or nothing!' Coco answered.

"In order to calm her and to try to convince her, we consulted my colleague, Maître Chresteil.

" 'Chambrun is right, Mademoiselle. You cannot withdraw your capital. Ask for damages and then the return of your capital. Otherwise your suit is lost in advance,' he said.

"The next morning, Coco arrived in my office. She had slept on the problem. In her right hand she held a large bag, which she deposited on my desk and from which she took several perfume bottles.

" 'That's for you,' she said. 'Give these bottles to Josée [Mme

René de Chambrun, daughter of Pierre Laval] and ask her what she thinks of them.'

"As soon as Coco left, I telephoned a Russian friend who was a chemist for Coty and was said to have the best 'nose' in the world. I asked him to drop by my office in the late afternoon.

"When he came, I showed him the samples. He smelled and went into a trance; overcome with emotion, he shouted: 'Fabulous! Wonder of wonders! It's No. 5, but even better!'

"Coco came back to my office the next morning and told me that the sample was indeed an improved No. 5 but with a higher cost price.

" 'Do I have the right to have it made in Switzerland and to give it to a few friends?' she asked pointblank.

" 'Legally you have the right to, but I don't see what you're aiming at,' I said.

" 'Wait and you'll see!'

"A few weeks later she sent perfume bottles to her old friends Bernard Gimbel, and Stanley Marcus—people well-entrenched in the U.S. perfume trade. A few days passed. Then one afternoon, Pierre and Paul Wertheimer, accompanied by their entire management staff, burst into my office.

" 'Exactly what does she want?' they asked in chorus.

" 'She wants . . . she wants 2 percent on all gross sales of all perfumes sold throughout the world; she wants these perfumes made in Switzerland.'

"The conference lasted until two o'clock in the morning. Finally the Neuilly company gave in. Pierre Wertheimer did so willingly, delighted at the idea of a reconciliation with his false enemy."

After May 1947, Coco received 2 percent on the gross amount of perfume sales throughout the world, in the region of $1 million a year. She also received a sum calculated to cover past royalties.

At sixty-five, her squeeze play successful, she had become, from the income standpoint, one of the richest women in the world.

"Now I am rich," she confided to a friend.

Rich, but alone. Rich, but idle. What good had been gained from this last battle?

Death now struck down her last friends. The Duke of West-minster died in 1947. His friendship and esteem for Coco had survived their separation.

In Switzerland, at La Pausa, on the rue Cambon, the years slipped by, carrying past memories away. Coco gradually was forgotten.

On October 16, 1950, the incomparable Misia died in Paris. The beautiful, intelligent, passionate, devoted, mean Misia was no more. In her, despite their many quarrels, Coco lost the one who had guided, counseled, and formed her, opened to her the doors of intelligence and sensibility—Misia, without whom Gabrielle Chanel would have been just another dress designer.

Coco received the news by telegram and left La Pausa for Paris on the next plane. She rushed to Misia's bedside and locked herself in the room. She called for forty ice cubes. As she applied them to the dead woman's face, the skin hardened, the wrinkles faded. Two hours later Misia looked thirty years younger—just as she had in her glorious days when, like a queen beneath her diamond tiara, she presided over the premiéres of the Ballets Russes.

Coco had nothing left. Nothing but money, jewels, and houses in which she was bored. She had become a living ghost with only No. 5 to evoke her name.

1945. 1946. 1947. The years that succeeded each other were much alike. Bad years for high fashion's venerable survivors, all those ex-greats; Paris was no longer the couture capital. Fantastic years for American ready-to-wear manufacturers, who were out to conquer the feminine market throughout the world. And for them New York became the clothes capital.

No one gave away anything to anyone. No holds were barred. America waged and fought the first battles in this game with an artillery barrage of "sensation headlines" in western newspapers:

"The scandal of French luxury! An insult to our fighting boys!"

A Pentagon committee proposed to the administration "that newspapers, magazines, and agencies be prevented from publicizing French fashion."

In 1947 U.S. magazines waged psychological warfare with great skill:

"Two American models can be cut from the fabric needed for

one French model! The French tell us that they are poor! That they lack fabrics! They have the nerve to ask us to supply them with more!"

Meanwhile, an unknown Parisian named Dior was putting the finishing touches on his bomb, fashion's secret weapon, imagination.

The scene: Avenue Montaigne, whipped by glacial winds under snowy skies. The time: ten o'clock on Wednesday February 12, 1947. Waves of mink coats and English overcoats were beating against the well-guarded door of a private town house. Only those who held a white invitation card were admitted:

"Christian Dior requests the honor of Mr. or Mrs.————'s, presence at the presentation of his first collection, at 10:30 A.M. Avenue Montaigne."

Immediately upon entering, everyone rushed toward the large pearl-gray salon, taking a seat amid the frenzied hubbub so typical of openings. It was a music Paris had almost forgotten.

At the entrance, a liveried doorman screened the visitors, denying entry to several journalists. Guests passed under a satin canopy and found themselves in a vestibule hung with Toile de Jouy, where attractive hostesses sprayed them with Miss Dior perfume.

The "old stand-bys" of every Parisian event crowded into the show room. Before the war many of them had rushed to Coco's salon: Etienne de Beaumont, who naturally had designed jewelry for the new couturier; Christian Bérard, who had become a typical Parisian celebrity (theatrical decors, gossip, witticisms, fashion sketches) was seated on the carpeted floor, his red beard resting against the white coat of his dog Jacynthe.

The journalists were present. The omnipotent editor of *Harper's Bazaar,* Carmel Snow, forever young, who, for years, had always seemed to be napping during the collections yet remembered every detail of each dress. Twenty years before, Paul Valéry had cruelly described this blue-grey haired and rosy-complexioned American who had done so much for French fashion as "a Louis XV chilblain." Marie-Louise Bousquet accompanied her, ready for battle. A few seats away, the rival *Vogue* team, led by Michel de Brunhoff, waited.

"Number one," announced a voice.

Stupefaction: the dress parading by was well below the calf.

Then came the second dress, greeted by a silence so profound that one could have heard a pin drop. For thirty years, no one had seen a dress like it: accentuated waistline, corseted bodice from which the bosom protruded provocatively, molded shoulders. The skirt was long and pleated. The mannequin pirouetted, revealing a petticoat. Ever since Chanel had relegated petticoats and corsets to the attic, no one had dared to make such a dress.

Applause burst forth. Bérard's plump hands gave the signal. He greeted each model with loud and shrill "ohs" and "ahs" of admiration. Of course, he *had* made a few sketches for the collection.

The conquering hero, Christian Dior, appeared with the last model, a wedding dress. He had a distinguished bearing in spite of his Norman peasant face, his prematurely bald head, and his prominent paunch (he ate a box of chocolates a day).

Everyone rushed over to hug him. He received two very moving tributes: the accolade of Lucien Lelong, whom Dior had left just a short time before, and the simple compliment of a little old lady, Madeleine Vionnet, who had, long ago, been dubbed the "sorceress" because of her dazzling technique: "It has been a long time since I have seen anything as beautiful."

But Carmel Snow pronounced the word which was heard around the world: "It's quite a revolution. Your dresses are wonderful; they have such a *new look*."

The New Look!

The day after the presentation, the news was spread on the front pages of newspapers throughout the world: "In Paris, dresses have dropped around the ankles." (Paris itself did not hear the news for a month, for the press was on strike.)

The new style was a catastrophe for the ready-to-wear manufacturers in New York, who had thought, thanks to the silence from Paris, that they could call the shots.

The morning of February 13, the United States learned the news: hems had dropped, waistlines had returned, and shoulder padding had disappeared. Every newspaper and every radio station announced it with commentaries ridiculing what Paris wished to impose on women.

But the word was out, and dress manufacturers and retailers were scared. They knew that with the end of the war, women, tired of sleazy dresses, rationed fabrics, and austerity measures, would throw themselves on these luxurious models.

The garment industry had billions of dollars' worth of dresses and coats in stock. If this Frenchman succeeded in outmoding their stocks, many bankruptcies would follow. From Paris, the buyers cabled: "Catastrophe. Women will go for this like a bee for honey."

Conferences were held at Bergdorf Goodman's and Marshall Field's. They all had heard Carmel Snow's answer to an NBC reporter:

"God help those who bought before seeing Dior's collection. He is a genius. He has changed everything."

Carmel Snow was the oracle. If she wrote in *Harper's Bazaar* that the New Look was a must, all America would follow her.

An enthusiastic lady announcer exclaimed: "Dior has done for French couture what the Paris taxis did for France at the battle of the Marne."

It could not be helped. The U.S. buyers returned to Paris and rushed to Avenue Montaigne.

By the end of 1949, 75 percent of couture exports bore the Dior label and represented 5 percent of the total of French exports.

In the United States, especially, Dior was violently attacked.

The Women's League, that powerful association that once held in check even Hollywood producers, came out against the "abominable display of arrogant bosoms" in which Mr. Dior invited women to indulge. Evening dresses such as these would "lower the standards of public morality."

"My wife has become insupportable: she eats nothing but ten prunes a day in order to acquire your wasp-waist. Life at home is hell. Go to the devil!" a Mr. Appleby wrote to Christian Dior.

They ranted against the waist cincher. Corset manufacturers were delighted, as was the brassiere industry.

Christian Dior went to New York. He was greeted by crowds of journalists. Aroused by the League, matrons brandished placards:

"Down with the New Look!"

"Burn Mr. Dior!"

"Christian, go home!"

But in Dallas, Stanley Marcus told Dior: "Permit me to

express to you the gratitude of the entire American ready-to-wear industry as well as that of all those who sell dresses in our country. The fashion boom you have inspired has given new life to our industry and retail businesses in less than three months."

The New Look had triumphed.

Coco learned of Dior's success through the press. Curious, then furious, she left Switzerland and returned to Paris. She saw Christian Bérard and covered him with insults, reproaching him for working for Dior and thus participating in the ruin of French couture.

"Stop taking yourself for France and crowing 'cock-a-doodle-do,' " Christian Bérard grumbled furiously to Coco.

And, yet, was it simply jealousy on Coco's part? Perhaps it was mostly jealousy. But it was something else, too.

In announcing the New Look, *Time* entitled its article "Counter-Revolution."

And that is exactly what it was. Waist cinchers, girdles, corsets, and ribbons flowered, just as in the years before 1914. Dior women were much less free than their mothers had been when dressed by Chanel, for Dior's designs inhibited freedom of movement.

Yet Dior had saved French couture, and the textile industry was swamped with orders. Women who could afford to now were able to gratify their taste for luxury after a long period of austerity. But once again high fashion insisted on divorcing itself from the street. Much too elaborate, the New Look models were difficult to copy. While a number of very elegant women were divinely dressed, the average woman was rather badly turned out in clothes whose very nature required impeccable cut and adjustment.

Dior returned haute couture to Poiret. Coco, perplexed, understood this, and in retirement, fidgeted impatiently.

The New Look ran out of steam rather rapidly. Dior himself evolved, and while today his firm has survived him brilliantly, first under the direction of Yves St.-Laurent and then of Marc Bohan, nothing remains of the spirit of the New Look in the creations of Avenue Montaigne.

14.
Comeback

M ADEMOISELLE is making a comeback. . . ."

After 1950, this rumor was periodically bandied about in the world of women's magazines, fashion journalism, and haute couture. One thing helped support the rumor: Mademoiselle was bored and grumpy.

The New Look was at its peak. Women had again taken up all those appurtenances from which Chanel had liberated them after World War I: in the showrooms and workrooms of Parisian fashion establishments they were back to tucks, taking clothes in at the waist, wearing corsets.

With a wave of their wands, the famous designers rubbed out breasts one year, narrowed and almost obliterated shoulders the next, and then put shoulders back in their proper place for the following collection. Momentary inspiration sent waists oscillating wildly between the belly button and the chest. Even the head was affected—for example, "This year heads will be worn small."

Coco poured withering sarcasm on all this foolishness: "If I have a large head, must I jump into the Seine when those gentlemen decree that this year the head will be small?"

Few of "those gentlemen" found favor in the eyes of the merciless Mademoiselle.

"Dior? Lucubrations tacked together on cardboard! Grès?

Drapes hung up on corsets!" And then: "The upper part of the dress is easy to make, like the first act of a play. Real skill is needed to finish a dress and I am the only one who knows how to make a skirt."

The art of dressing fashionably soon became dependent upon the art of being informed ahead of time. Two months before the presentation of the collections, cleverly doled out indiscretions kept alive the suspense. The fashion houses of Paris became "laboratories," carefully guarded for fear of "leaks." The object was to present a collection all of whose characteristics were the contrary of those signaled in advance: the "sack" dress was expected and instead the "string-bean" line appeared.

The divorce between the street and "official" fashion was complete. Thus, when haute couture, six years after the New Look was introduced, still had been unsuccessful in establishing a "style," a manufacturer dealing in expensive ready-made clothes launched thousands of sweater models of all kinds and colors and prices on the market, with enormous success. Fifteen years after the rue Cambon had closed, Mademoiselle Chanel's ideas were continuing to gain ground.

Chanel, who was seen more and more frequently in Paris, declared to her few intimates:

"Fashion has become a joke; the designers have forgotten that there are women inside the dresses. Most women dress for men and want to be admired. But they must also be able to move, to get into a car without bursting their seams! Clothes must have a natural shape."

She installed herself at the Ritz and once again received her friends in her rue Cambon salon.

French author and novelist, Michel Déon, who met Coco during this period, wrote:

"The upper floors of the rue Cambon were deserted. She sometimes walked through the silent workrooms where pieces of fabric, dress dummies fallen over onto tables, rusting sewing machines were left trailing about. Life had stopped there in 1940, having barely survived the Popular Front strikes. Mademoiselle had no regrets and no bitterness, never imagining that one day she might bring back to life this graveyard from which so many fashion criteria had sprung."

When and how was the idea of rebirth conceived?

"There is an increasing tendency to consider dress designing

as an art when not as a veritable philosophy! It seems to be forgotten that dress designing is a craft. There are some people who
know this craft and others, more numerous, who *think* they
know it. The present crisis is due to this. I have thought it all
over and have come to believe that I still have perhaps two or
three things to say."

The rumor of Coco's comeback continued to circulate, until
finally there was an official announcement: "Chanel is going to
make her comeback in Parisian fashion in February," read the
headline in a Paris daily in December 1953. The most extravagant reports spread through Paris on this subject: "She is making
a ready-to-wear house," said some. "She is going to present a
collection of creations such has never been seen," said others.

Meanwhile, as the speculations about her comeback collection
multiplied, Mademoiselle kept herself invisible. Denied interviews with her, the press ran biographies, embellished by time,
especially since the war had prevented most of those who
thought they knew Coco from writing their memoirs. Through
Maurice Sachs and Jean Cocteau the younger generations discovered the astonishing story of Coco Chanel and were fascinated by it. In the absence of recent photographs, old ones
were published, and the newspaper or magazine reader, gazing at
a Coco stretched out on her sofa, was invited to dream about the
pleasant days that dated from "before" the "last war."

Several months before her return, Mademoiselle was already
monopolizing the pages of the fashion magazines, and her past
loves were as well known to the young journalists as were those
of the most contemporary dress designers and stage and screen
stars. Who among those in the limelight of the day could rival
Coco with her lovers and her sparkling salon?

Indifferent to the rosy compliments with which the press covered her, Coco had no illusions, either, about the true feelings of
her colleagues—sometimes even being unjust in her comments.
When Cristóbal Balenciaga, who admired Mademoiselle and for
whom jealousy did not exist, declared, "Chanel is an eternal
bomb. None of us can defuse her," and sent her a bouquet of
flowers in the form of a heart upon her official return, Coco
sneered, "Flowers for a coffin. They shouldn't be in such a hurry
to bury me."

It had not taken long for Mademoiselle to get in form and
begin sharpening her claws.

She looked up her old forewomen one by one.

"Come quickly," she said, "we have only ten green years before us."

One of them, Mme Lucie, who had set up on her own in the rue Royale, returned in August 1953, and became the head of the rue Cambon establishment.

"Bring along the little one, too," said Mademoiselle. The "little one" was another old employee, Mme Manon, who later was to have the difficult task of dressing Mademoiselle.

She recalls: "That is how we reopened the house, with two workrooms. We were all greatly excited. Mademoiselle had such guts! At that moment, we didn't think that we would become so important again."

On the ground floor, in the boutique that had remained open since 1939, the salesgirls smiled, happy at no longer being only the guardians of a defiled temple. "Nostalgia for the fashion house, though we had never known it ourselves, was very strong, especially after the end of the war," Mme Isabelle, manager of the boutique, told us. "Mademoiselle was bored. She still felt the need to create. We were delighted when we learned that she was going to open the fashion house."

With the utmost secrecy, Mademoiselle hired young debutantes as mannequins, among them Marie-Hélène Arnaud, aged eighteen, tall and slim, with large laughing eyes, daughter of an old friend and fellow student of Georges Pompidou, then a director of the Rothschild Bank, whose wife was to become a faithful customer.

Indifferent to rumors and sarcasm she was provoking, Coco reinstalled herself on the third floor.

The large showrooms on the first floor remained closed, and the dust continued to accumulate on the sheets covering the gilt chairs. It was only later, when success returned, that Coco worked there. For the moment, she went to work, scissors in hand, with a single fitter, a white-haired old lady, and one mannequin. She took refuge in a small room two steps away from her apartment.

She was nervous; beneath her beige suit the muscles were tense. Wearing her usual hat, she crawled about on her knees to make sure that a hem was right. When evening came, she rose to her feet fit and fresh, not a single wrinkle disturbing her clothes and her hat still set at the same angle. She almost never took off her hat in public because it served to hide bald spots; she was already seventy.

The years had hollowed and wrinkled her face, but it remained deeply tanned, burned by the sun. Her coal-black eyebrows, glowing eyes, high cheekbones, and gaunt neck made her resemble a bird of prey. Her hands were white, as though polished by their constant handling of fabrics. Fine and delicate when in repose, they became transformed when she went to work, twisting and knotting the fabric, forcing it to take the form she desired in accordance with her own mysterious rules of geometry. Cecil Beaton, an old friend, wrote: "They seemed strong enough to shoe a horse."

Coco worked passionately—desperately—hard and remained silent. Was she afraid? If so, it was for the first time in her life.

It was hazardous to attempt such a comeback at a time when designers' reputations went out of fashion as fast as their collections. It was sheer madness to want to dress the grandchildren of the women she had dressed fifty years earlier.

Perhaps it was the magnitude of the risk she was taking that fascinated Coco. The stakes were certainly high. Yet she was bored and, driven wild by the current trends in fashion, she wanted to return; she had to.

Of course, these reasons seemed too simple at the time, too naïve. Their simplicity hardly fit in with the sophisticated atmosphere of the fashion world. Writers, struggling with the puzzle of Coco's return, set forth their own inventive theories:

"The vogue for No. 5 was losing ground. Her sensational return would, particularly in the United States, be excellent publicity for it. The perfume company had insisted that Coco reopen her doors." Yet despite the preponderance of these theories, they were not based on the facts. No. 5 had never before sold so well.

"What do you wear at night to sleep?" On American television screens, the famous smile turned into a pout. The full, scarlet lips half-opened. A slight blush rose to the cheeks. First silence, then, in a lascivious stage whisper, the celebrated mouth lisped: "Chanel No. 5." As if suddenly becoming aware of what her answer meant, Marilyn Monroe burst into laughter.

No. 5 was by far the most popular perfume in the world; its fabrication used up about 80 percent of the French production of jasmine.

No. 5 losing ground?

Long before there was talk of her return, Coco Chanel and Pierre Wertheimer met on the terrace of the Hôtel Beau Rivage at Ouchy on the banks of Lake Leman.

Friends, enemies, partners? All three at once. They had not forgotten their juridical-commercial controversies during the Occupation and immediately after the war. But they were nevertheless happy to be together, like members of the same family after a long quarrel. The tone was courteous. They did not speak of their previous differences and the conversation bore on past days and common friends, many of whom were dead. Though white-haired, Wertheimer was still handsome, his voice as calm and steady as ever.

As they took a short walk together, Coco rested her gloved hand on his arm. They were simply two wealthy and distinguished persons, followed by their automobiles (a Rolls Royce for Wertheimer and a Cadillac for Coco), taking a walk along the lake shore.

"Pierre, let's launch a new perfume."

The words were uttered almost as though Coco had been suddenly inspired by the idea; her tone of voice was tender and soothing.

"A new perfume? Why?"

"We haven't brought out anything since 1924!"

Coco's "we" was sublime. The perfumes with a red label, which she had tried to launch alone, resulting in the ruin of her associate, were somehow forgotten. Perhaps Wertheimer had the good taste to smile at this curious evocation of the past, but he did not agree.

"You can't really be thinking of such a thing. It's far too risky. To launch a new perfume today would require enormous expenditures for publicity. And why do it? We are living on No. 5. The Americans don't want anything new. They want No. 5. Your new perfume would harm the old one."

To Pierre Wertheimer's astonishment, Coco yielded and did not insist. He closed the door of her car with affectionate deference, almost disappointed that she had not been more eager to argue with him. But, after all, he probably thought, Coco was no longer young. Perhaps she really did wish to live in golden retirement enjoying the income from No. 5.

Coco ordered her chauffeur to drive slowly along the side of the lake while she sat on the cushions in her car, strangely silent, meditating. What ideas were racing around in her head? Unquestionably her idleness had never before weighed so heavily upon her as at this end of an afternoon when her suggestion of introducing a new perfume had been turned down. What was she to do? Why not go back to designing?

Perhaps it was that she was not just an old lady. More likely she wanted to play a trick on those gentlemen of the perfume company who were burying her too quickly, in her estimation.

The difficulty was the means. It would require money, lots of it, more than she had available, on a continuing basis. The obvious source of funds was the perfume company, but so far initial contacts had not proved successful.

La Pausa had been sold,* as well as the buildings on the rue Cambon, except, of course, for number 31. She had money, but only enough to venture so far. Wouldn't her age, the times, new fashions, and her now painfully arthritic hands make it difficult for her?

What difference did all that make? She couldn't die there, on the shores of that lake, almost forgotten, leaving the women of the entire world prey to the heavy hands of the Parisian designers!

Several days later, she was again living in her apartment at the Ritz, which she now called her "white-collar habitat."

In the autumn of 1953, Robert Chaillet, financial adviser for the perfume company and soon to be Mademoiselle Chanel's personal financial adviser, received a telephone call from René de Chambrun, Mademoiselle's lawyer.

Chambrun said to Chaillet: "I'll tell you a good one. *She* is taking *that* up again. You should speak about it to Pierre Wertheimer."

On her side, Mademoiselle did not wait for the Wertheimer's decision. She hurried to protect herself from what might happen. She contacted Carmel Snow, the high priestess of New York fashion, through a great friend they had in common, Marie-Louise Bousquet, head of the Paris office of *Harper's Bazaar,* who maintained a brilliant salon in her apartment in the Place

---

*Gerard Mille, a friend of Chanel's and a talented decorator, arranged for Emery Reeves, a literary agent and friend of Winston Churchill, to buy La Pausa. Sir Winston often visited Reeves there and was named an honorary citizen by the neighboring village of Roquebrune.

du Palais Bourbon. In case the gentlemen from Neuilly declined to help her, she was looking for a way to sell her models to one of the mass-production manufacturers of New York's Seventh Avenue.

Several days later, Carmel answered with the following cable:

> KNOW TOP WHOLESALE MANUFACTURER WHO WOULD BE INTERESTED IN COPYING THE MODELS YOU WILL CREATE stop MARIE-LOUISE VAGUE AS TO DETAILS stop WHEN WOULD YOUR COLLECTION BE READY stop DO YOU ANTICIPATE COMING OVER WITH IT stop WILL YOU SUPPLY FABRIC TO COPY stop DELIGHTED TO BE OF ANY HELP. CARMEL SNOW.

Coco received this cable on September 24. On September 30, she answered with the following letter:

My Dear Carmel,

This will acknowledge your cable and confirm my reply. During the summer I thought it would be fun to work again because work is my entire life. I probably told you before that one day or another I might resume my activity of creating a new style adapted to a new mode of living and that I was waiting for the proper time to come. I feel that this time has come.

The paradoxical Parisian atmosphere of today, where more and more women go to collections of dresses they cannot afford to buy, has led me to do something entirely different.

One of my prime objects is naturally to wholesale through one manufacturer in the United States on a royalty basis. Nevertheless I feel that what I am doing will have a tremendous appeal throughout the world.

My first collection will be ready on November 1, and I think it would be wise not to make any move before receiving the offer of the top wholesale manufacturer whom you have in mind. Possibly the best would be for him to fly over to Paris. Of course nothing would please me more than having you over here, too. For the time being I do not anticipate presenting the collection myself in America, but that might come later.

As ever,
Gabrielle Chanel

René de Chambrun, when he gave us these documents, confided: "Coco wanted to be able to say to herself and to others: 'I can make a comeback on my own. I don't need the Wertheimers.' In fact, Pierre must be given credit for not hesitating to act."

At the headquarters of the perfume company on the Avenue de Neuilly there were mixed reactions to the news. There was a twofold danger: either she would make a successful comeback and again would be able to use as she pleased the open-sesame of the name Chanel, or she would fail in the attempt and this would have bad repercussions on the sales of the perfumes. Another danger: Mademoiselle might sell licenses for stockings and underwear like any vulgar Paris designer, and that would end the incomparable prestige of the perfumes.

Robert Chaillet told us: "I spoke to Pierre Wertheimer about this comeback.

" 'Does it interest you?' I said.

" 'It is too fantastic. Obviously, it interests me.' he answered."

Pierre Wertheimer did not share the apprehensions of the other gentlemen of Neuilly. He had known her for a long time. He knew that, though Coco was only too happy to create problems for the perfume company, she would be miserable if she lost contact with the different persons who were handling the business. For thirty years their innumerable suits against each other had created solid ties between them.

He regarded Coco's appeal, though indirect, as nearly an order. He considered it an insult that she would appeal to anyone else.

An agreement was signed, under the terms of which the perfume company would be responsible for half of the fashion expenses as a publicity investment on behalf of the perfumes. Regally seated on her suede sofa, Coco nonchalantly assured Robert de Nexon, a company director: "The collection won't cost more than fifteen million francs, at the outside."

One year later, Mademoiselle Chanel and the "perfumes" had each lost thirty-five million francs and the rue Cambon company had not a penny left.

To one of the few journalists who were lucky enough to talk to her in the winter of 1953, and who asked what she was planning to present in her collection, Coco, superb as ever, answered, "How can you expect me to know? Until the last day I alter, transform. *I* create my dresses on the mannequins themselves."

And anticipating the question to follow, she added, "Why did I return? I was bored. It took me fifteen years to realize it. Today, I prefer disaster to nothingness."

No assistants, no documentation, no dress patterns prepared in advance, no preconceived ideas, still less any outside inspiration. Henceforth, Mademoiselle proudly gave lessons in modesty to her young colleagues. "That young 'boy' will really show us all right," said Poiret the Magnificent of her in 1920. Twenty-four years later, he died penniless. Even as the seventies began, Paris designers were still afraid of the old lady.

"From Picasso to Kisling, from Proust to St.-John Perse, from Honegger to Satie, the masters of their day were never in danger of being challenged," wrote Paul Morand in *Venises*, "and Gabrielle Chanel, who was dressing women in her jerseys in the Deauville of 1915, is still dressing them in 1970."

In the first week of February 1954, few invitations were more sought after than a card signed with the name Chanel. Coco had naturally chosen February 5, and from two o'clock on the shop's salons were full. The press, well represented, was ready to give out dithyrambic praise in case of success or to tear to pieces in case of failure.

"The French press was shockingly vulgar, stupid, and nasty. They jeered at her age," wrote Michel Déon, perhaps with some exaggeration.

The cream of Paris society was present, mixed in with top-notch buyers and foreign journalists. The old customers were there, highly excited and moved by this comeback: Mme Lopez Wilshaw, Countess Pastré, Lady Abdy, Mapie de Toulouse-Lautrec, Princess Bibesco. In the gleaming mirrors (the tarnished ones had been replaced: "I am reopening my fashion house, not a museum," said Mademoiselle), they searched for the reflected image of their youth, before furtively raising their eyes to the top of the staircase, but no, Mademoiselle was not there.

On the newly painted gilt chairs, they sat crowded together any which way. Sacrilegious, or simply unaware of the etiquette to be observed, young journalists sat on the celebrated steps, not knowing or caring that twenty years earlier not even a countess would have dared to be so bold without a personal invitation from Chanel. Later, her fame reestablished, Coco was to make them pay dearly for this insolence.

On this day, the duchesses were relegated to the tenth row.

Carmel Snow, fashion dictator on the other side of the Atlantic, found a place on an edge of one step. Mme Castanié, editor-in-chief of *L'Official de la Couture* (the Paris fashion bible), arrived three minutes late. She remained on the sidewalk, the door closed even to her. All the staff members of the English, French, and American editions of *Vogue* stood on their chairs and twisted their necks. They all wanted to see. And then they saw the first model—a black, collarless, tailored suit—parade by in glacial silence.

It was a fiasco, at least in the opinion of the French journalists. Some old-faithfuls exchanged sorrowful glances; others did not hesitate to whisper that Chanel was finished.

The next day an *Aurore* reporter wrote: "A touching retrospective. The mannequins resemble those of 1930, without breasts, without waistline, without hips."

But therein lay Coco's revolution, perhaps. It escaped the notice of the French. The mannequins had breasts, waistlines, and hips, but in their proper places.

"The dresses gathered at the waist, with puffed sleeves and round neck lines, only suggest a faint evocation of an era that it is difficult to pinpoint, perhaps 1929–1930. Everyone had come hoping to find again the atmosphere of the collections that had bowled over Paris in years gone by. But there is nothing of that left, only mannequins who parade before an audience that cannot bring itself to applaud. A rather melancholic retrospective," concluded the *Aurore* reporter.

Dissimulating his melancholy with sarcasm, Lucien François wrote in *Combat*, under the headline "With Coco Chanel at Slocum-in-the-hole in 1930":

"With the first dress we realized that the Chanel style belongs to other days. Fashion has evolved in fifteen years. . . . Chanel, meanwhile, has become a legend idealized in retrospect, making us forget that already in 1938 her vogue had been mortally injured. . . . Not even dresses from 1938! The spirit of dresses dating from 1930. . . ."

In 1961 the same journalist was to write: "It is indisputable that Chanel's influence is the basis for the vogue, in 1961, of the style of the Roaring Twenties." Indeed, because of the United States, from the end of 1954 the Chanel style was "in the street."

On the night of this first presentation of her collection, Coco did not appear before her friends. She had watched the mannequins parade from the top of her staircase, where she could see without being seen. Then she had disappeared.

"I dreaded the next day," remembers Mme Manon. "She said: 'They'll see! We are going to start our collections again.' And thus we began to carry on."

"It is then that I saw her for the first time," wrote Simone Baron in *France Soir*. She was wearing a white tweed suit, a straw sailor hat, lots of gold jewelry, and very little makeup. She was vehement and passionately exicted. I heard her speak: 'Pooh! People don't know what elegance is anymore. It is the contrary of vulgarity. Me, I think only of women and not of fashion houses. It is not possible to bamboozle them to such a degree. Once I helped us to achieve liberation; I am beginning again. For fifty years I have done everything—the accounts, the dresses, the administration, everything. They will see what I am still capable of doing!' "

Claude L., her lawyer, told us:

"She accepted her defeat with a great deal of dignity, a dignity based on her self-confidence. 'The French are too intelligent, they will return to me,' she said. She behaved as if it were the others who were mistaken, intoxicated by the taste of those 'little pederasts'—Coco's designation for other designers. Not bitter, she blamed neither herself nor those who had helped her. The press—at least the French fashion journalists—were those really responsible. As to the customers, they would understand quickly."

And, in fact, they were going to understand, via the United States. Indifferent to historical nostalgia, the American woman immediately saw what was eternally modern in the Chanel look: the breasts and hips in their places, a certain elegance, freedom of movement, and the look of youth.

While the French press remained silent or sarcastic and the French customers kept aloof, daring buyers, almost all of them American, who had purchased models were flooded with orders in New York demanding originals or copies.

"American fashion has Chanel written all over it," marveled the French.

In March 1954, *Life* commented as follows about Chanel's comeback:

"She has influenced all today's collections. At seventy-one, she brings us more than a style—she has caused a veritable tempest. She has decided to return and to conquer her old position—the first."

Harper's Bazaar and *Vogue* praised her tirelessly. Chanel had a gift for dressing women in such a way that they felt good inside and out.

"When I get up in the morning," said a young American, "I ask myself what I am going to put on for the day. And immediately I know that I will choose my two-year-old, two-piece Chanel."

Coco's designs also enjoyed masculine approbation. The real secret of the Chanel look was its eternally young aspect, which made men say: "How lovely you are!" Not: "What a pretty dress you are wearing!"

Chanel's U.S. success forced the other designers to change. The U.S. reaction seriously affected them since the commercialization of their labels and the sale of their original dress patterns to the Seventh Avenue buyers represented one of the principal sources of their income. Some five thousand women in the world, it was estimated, had the means to buy haute-couture clothes. The majority of these women were American, but, far more important, in the United States the models were diffused rapidly and on a large scale. After 1954, the U.S. secretary or mother, whether she knew it or not, wore a two-piece outfit inspired by Chanel, which sold for $24.95 in her neighborhood dress shop. Line-for-line copies put on the market by the manufacturers who had reproduction rights of original models bought at the rue Cambon sold for $150 in deluxe shops in New York, Dallas, or Los Angeles. Finally, "made-to-order" outfits were sold in the United States for $500 with the number of models limited and each necessitating 150 work hours.

In Hollywood, the young stars became aware that Chanel was also a designer. The older ones remembered her 1932 visit; and those who had not yet sunk into Sunset Boulevard-type apparel were among Coco's first customers, followed soon after by the newer stars such as Grace Kelly, Suzy Parker, Lauren Bacall, Elizabeth Taylor, Rita Hayworth (married to Aly Khan then), and Romy Schneider.

Passing through Paris in January 1954, Marlene Dietrich came to see her old friend. The most beautiful grandmother in show business was singing every night in a Las Vegas cabaret.

Almost nude beneath a transparent mousseline dress, she remained at fifty-odd years the unequaled example of the glamour girl.

The dialog between those two *monstres sacres* was brief and equal to their legend:

"Why have you begun again?" asked Marlene.

"Because I was dying of boredom."

"You too!"

Marlene ordered several suits. Her fitter found order forms dating from 1933 in the archives of the rue Cambon and discovered that her measurements had not changed. But Marlene did not dare ask Coco to make her dresses for her show—it was not in line with the Chanel style!

All this success was still to come. The initial reaction in France and England was bleak. But, in any case, the following week, without hearing any comforting echoes from across the Atlantic, Mademoiselle went back to work. There had never been any question of giving up, and though orders did not flow into the workrooms, Coco pretended to be delighted: "At least that gives us time to prepare the next collection."

It was obvious there was to be another, for summer. She left the small room on the second floor and began to work in the large fitting rooms on the first floor. She hired new mannequins. To be a mannequin at Mademoiselle's did not involve simply modeling dresses; above all, it meant being the *object* on which Coco worked, cut, and pinned.

Apprenticeship was long. Those selected had much to learn: how to walk, fix their hair, dress, perfume, and remain standing for hours at a time under bare, harsh lights, before Mademoiselle—seated, standing, on her knees, or on all fours.

Many gave up.

"Now, walk," Coco would order.

The mannequin would walk a few steps. Coco, buried in her immense armchair, eyes half-closed, did not look at her. She seemed lost in meditation. Nerves on edge, the girl would walk three times around the salons, grazing the mirrors, while Coco remained silent.

Not knowing what else to do, the mannequin would sit down. She would be on the verge of hysteria.

"Are you tired already?" Coco would shout. "Continue."

Actually, it was in the mirrors that Coco studied the shimmering play of the fabrics. With the tenacity of an ant she would study new textiles to see how they fell and moved. "A Chanel suit is made for a woman who moves." When Coco fixed the sleeves of her models, she never intended them to be sewn on. She simply wanted to see what happened with different fabrics.

"It was dreadful," a mannequin at that heroic epoch (who refused to give her name) told us. "Mademoiselle did not create, she enveloped us in material. For example, she made a shoulder on which she mounted a sleeve. Then she made us walk and for half an hour we had to raise and lower our arms. Mademoiselle wanted to see what the new material would give. This exercise would occur five, ten times during the afternoon. By evening I was all in, swearing not to return the next day. Then she would smile charmingly and say, 'See you tomorrow.' And the next day we were all there.

"One day I cracked and left. I shall always regret it."

She was silent for a moment, stirring the cup of tea before her.

"You see, how can I explain it? After that I worked in many fashion houses. I was head mannequin at [here she gave the name of one of Coco's bitter enemies]. I have worked for other designers, almost all nicer and in any case less tyrannical than Mademoiselle, where the work was less difficult, the hours less long. The models were first sketched, then constructed. When we wore them, they were in their final form. Only a few fittings were required before the opening day of the collections. In a word, rather restful work. Nothing comparable to Mademoiselle's interminable sessions. Nevertheless, with her, I had the impression that I was more than just a mannequin, a well-turned-out girl, knowing how to walk and smile, a peripatetic showcase, whose cheek is tapped and she is told: 'That's fine, my dear, you were wonderful.'

"It was different with Mademoiselle. Oh! To be sure we could not express an opinion, and our role demanded immobility and silence. But, even so, we participated. The dress was created on us, was *modeled* after our reflexes and the movements of our body. We almost felt the fusion of our skin with that of the fabric, and when the model was finally finished, we had the feeling that it had been made for us, even in a small way *by* us. I have never again had this impression. By reopening her house, Mademoiselle had shown me, right at the start of my career, what fashion was all about and what it really could be.

"Yes, Mademoiselle was someone."

In February 1954, while Mademoiselle was again playing the magical game of fabrics, the atmosphere at Avenue de Neuilly was far from gay. The collection had been expensive and the perfume company had underwritten half the cost. Millions already had been spent, and most of the gentlemen of Neuilly questioned whether this money was well invested. They were flabbergasted by the reactions of the French press. Wasn't it dangerous to continue "wasting" money on a capricious old lady, who, moreover, did not seem to be grateful? Was the sale of the perfumes not going to suffer in the months to come?

The news from the rue Cambon was discouraging. Coco had spent all her French capital in the venture; the rue Cambon firm was on the edge of bankruptcy. The real estate company—which owned 31 rue Cambon—was in difficulty, and the directors of the perfume company envisaged with terror the consequences of the loss of this last building on the rue Cambon, that irreplaceable show window.

Amid the general anxiety, Pierre Wertheimer was blamed. He remained silent, keeping his customary calm. Coco was also his business. Yet there was only indirect news of her. She had given no sign of life since the presentation of the collection. Some of her remarks, which were repeated to him, were not pleasant:

"They, with their dough, must be on pins and needles. In any case, with or without them I shall continue, if it is only just to irritate them. I know they will be only too happy if I fail."

Coco could be all the more unjust since she knew perfectly well that her accusations were not true as far as Pierre Wertheimer was concerned. But wasn't it necessary that she play the role of the perpetual ingrate so that their relations would remain unchanged?

For his part Pierre Wertheimer played his role, which he did with the talent and restraint that Coco expected of him. He had himself announced on the mezzanine of the rue Cambon toward the middle of one afternoon.

Coco was in the drawing room of her apartment, resting for a few moments. For several days her fingers had no longer obeyed her and, deformed by attacks of rheumatism, her hands had lost their agility, so that they were dreaded by the mannequins, whom she often pricked as she pinned. Her features were drawn, and under her hat her face was pale and drawn with fatigue.

"Tell him to come up!"

They met on the staircase between the first and second floors, between the showrooms and Mademoiselle's apartment.

Coco had put on dark glasses, which she rarely wore while working. Were they meant to hide the fatigue showing around her eyes? Dressed in her favorite suit—beige, of course—a hand thrust in her pocket, standing erect, balanced on her left foot, which was placed slightly behind her, in the attitude that she imposed on her mannequins, Coco had recovered her superbly haughty stance. She towered over the imperturbable Pierre Wertheimer by the height of three steps. Several seconds of immobility elapsed, as if she wanted to engrave the scene forever in the mirrors.

"What do you want?"

"I wanted to see you, to talk with you."

"I don't have time. *I* am working. Sit down."

He put his hat and umbrella on a chair beside him, a few feet away from Coco, in the fitting room where she was working.

The hours passed. Pierre Wertheimer silently contemplated Coco. Her fingers had never hurt so much as she made up and unmade a sleeve ten times.

Behind her dark glasses, her contorted, passionate, drained face could be divined. Coco had never worked so badly—the fabric no longer obeyed and hung in grotesque folds on the immobile mannequin. The hands were confused, as if a relaxation of their mucles had given them an absurd and useless freedom.

Night fell. Wertheimer had not budged. Contrary to her habits, Coco had not asked for the lights to be lit.

"Go. That's enough for today. We'll continue tomorrow."

Liberated, the mannequin, the forewoman, and the fitter left. Coco let herself drop into her armchair.

"Come, I'll take you back to the Ritz," Wertheimer said.

Silently, Coco let herself be drawn along the rue Cambon. She walked with her head down, then stopped.

"I'm exhausted. I'm dog tired. And my hands."

Then, suddenly, as though ashamed of this outburst of weakness, she recovered her usual deep, almost rough, and slightly hoarse voice: "I am continuing, I shall continue. They'll end up by understanding."

Her words were addressed to herself. Was she sincere, was she being theatrical? Did she know?

"You are right. You must continue."

Coco said nothing. But on arriving in front of the Ritz, before sweeping into the revolving door, she turned and said the most amazing word that Wertheimer had ever heard from her lips in thirty years: "Thank you."

Pierre Wertheimer's decision was made. He told Robert Chaillet:

"We must continue, even if we have to go through it all again. They all say that I am wrong, but I know that *she* is right."

During the first days, the perfume company continued its financial assistance to the fashion firm; in other words it continued to do what had been agreed upon before the reopening, which was to pay half of the sums necessary for realizing the collections. The Chanel firm of the rue Cambon could not escape from the inflexible financial law that governed haute couture after 1945: the collections—the sales of the models to a private clientele—could not nearly cover the expenditures of a fashion house. Selling the label, making ready-to-wear clothes, were the only solutions available to the Paris designers. The collections themselves had become only a spectacular publicity operation.

Coco obviously did not want to resort to this device exclusively, at least for the moment. She had not been the first dress designer of her time, nor worked so hard to attempt an unprecedented comeback, to become, at the age of seventy, a sales promoter in the service of ready-to-wear manufacturers.

On this point she was in agreement with the perfume company, for whom any sale of cheap articles would be an irreparable blow for the prestige of its perfumes: aside from No. 5, only Coco's haute couture clothes or accessories could have the right to bear the glamorous signature of Chanel.

This concern for maintaining her prestige did not relieve Coco of one regret. She knew she could make money by selling her label. And perhaps there was the nagging and impish desire to take on Parfums Chanel again. It had been such a long time since she had had differences with them!

Claude L. had this to say about the third act of the commercial-financial "play" between Mademoiselle and the gentlemen of Neuilly:

"The fashion house was costing a great deal and the increase in perfume sales that we—and Mademoiselle Chanel—expected did not immediately occur. Then Coco said to us: 'Instead of receiving subsidies that oblige me to keep accounts—and you know how much I detest doing that—I would prefer to sell you my shares.'

"Mademoiselle was extremely clever," added the lawyer, "in that she seemed to be selling you an entire horse. By this I mean that in the beginning she seemed to be selling all the rights to the perfumes, and then, taking a closer look, we discovered that she had only sold the nostrils and one foot, so three feet and the tail remained. 'All right. You want more, I'll sell you what is left,' she said. And we bought another piece of horse, which, by some brilliant new idea of Coco's, was more valuable. But there was always a piece left over with which, sometimes falsely innocent, sometimes violent, she threatened to cause us trouble.

"Once it was agreed that, in any event, we would support the fashion house, whose success at the beginning of 1954 was far from evident, Coco began to say: 'Suppose I were to sell the house to an outsider. Not that I want to, of course, but one never knows what can happen. I am old. I could die from one day to the next.' She didn't believe a word of this; the very idea of her death seemed incongruous to her. 'Certainly, I sold you the perfumes, but the person buying the house might do things that would embarrass you—he might make ready-to-wear clothes, lower the prestige of the label. Now I value this label; after all, it is my name. And then, I like you well enough, we get on so well together.'

"We understood. On May 24, 1954, we bought from her the fashion house, the real estate company, and all the companies carrying the name of Chanel, textile manufacturing, publishing, which no longer represented anything.

"And," specified Robert Chaillet, "we then concluded a new agreement with her. Under the terms of this contract, it was her duty to assist in the preparation of the perfumes from which she already received several hundred thousand dollars in royalties per year. She ruled completely over the fashion house except for the financial end: the models, the collections, choice of associates, etc. Naturally, she remained in her place on the rue Cambon, for which the company paid all the expenses: the Ritz, the secretaries, the domestic help, everything—*everything,* even her telephone calls and stamps."

A fashion house executor confirmed to us: "The fashion house remained hers. She was the boss and if anything or anybody displeased her. . . ."

Freed from all cares, harmony reigning with the gentlemen of Neuilly, comforted by the good news from across the Atlantic, Coco threw herself into making her creations.

Her hands recovered their nimbleness; the fabrics obeyed them as in the old days. Never had she been so serene. She opened her doors wide to her friends and to journalists.

In the spring of 1954, France's eyes were turned toward the Indochinese peninsula—Dien Bien Phu. With peace just declared, the designers presented their collections. And what a surprise! They had let clothes out at the waist, uncorseted the women; breasts and waistlines were put back in their proper places.

Chanel's collection was the last, appearing on August 5. There was a large crowd.

The next day, the general public learned that Chanel had remained faithful to the Chanel line. But—and the press testified to this—it was the future and not the past of fashion design that Coco had inscribed in the large mirrors of the rue Cambon.

Also, the great Mademoiselle's long-lost friends realized that the day was not far off when she, who had been one of the first designers, was, thirty years after her great success, about to impose her fashion law throughout the entire world.

15.

Mademoiselle and Her Peers

AFTER 1955, Coco's success in the United States was spectacular. In France, too, she enjoyed favor, but there her success was less overwhelming. "They" defended themselves and were unwilling to concede the supremacy of her classicism and her tongue.

In the collections of 1956 and 1957 a new order reigned. The New Look had finally run out of steam, dying a slow death. And though the commercial success of the Dior firm was confirmed, its success occurred apart from the style that had launched the house. In those years there existed a certain simplicity in the collections.

After 1958, fashion and styles disintegrated. It was the time of extravagance, excess. Everything had to be changed twice a year. The string-bean line, for example, and the sack followed helter-skelter on each other. Order and good taste disappeared. Nothing remained but innovation, now hailed as the supreme value. Only Chanel continued to do what she had always done, but only she had the United States and the street behind her.

Not only did Coco scorn the devices of fashion—she frowned on Malayalam shoulders, too snug a hip line, the lowered waistline, and blousy dresses, for example—but she denigrated male couturiers.

"Dressing women is not a man's job. They dress them badly because they scorn them."

When she felt indulgent—a rare event—she admired "architectural" dresses as "art objects," cleverly conceived in the art of "dehumanizing woman." "But," she added, "do you like those people in brocade who seen from the front look like armchairs and from the back like old Spaniards? What do they do when they have to lean down to pick something up? Where do they go wearing those things? To 'coquetèles' I'm told. Yet another way of replacing quality with quantity!"

The legends surrounding couturiers annoyed her:

"Those little idiots all pretend to be geniuses. I'm constantly hearing talk about an art to be saved. When in fact couture is a trade and good taste. And an industry that is being killed by pretention. Like fashion, the customers should be able to go down into the street."

Coco bet on the street. On protecting original models she had this to say: "Why not copy fashion? It is a tribute to French genius." Her colleagues and the fashion journalists, of course, snubbed her: "She always does the same thing." She didn't care. She was about to set off a bomb inside the small world of fashion.

On July 25, 1958, she sent her resignation to M Raymond Barbas, president of the Couture Syndicat, the official association of fashion designers.

"Dear Mr. President," her letter began. "I have the honor to submit to you, as president of the Paris couture association, my resignation, which you have been hoping for but which you have hesitated to request of me out of a sense of tact for which I sincerely thank you.

"Thus the conflict that has existed between the association and myself is solved."

She signed her letter: "Chanel." It was brief and to the point. Very Chanelian.

A fight between Chanel and the organization had broken out the year before. Coco, bypassing the decisions taken by the association, had decided not to wait to release photographs of her models. It was revolutionary.

"The stakes in this battle?" said Chanel. "The death, or rather the survival of fashion.

"Fashion designers, who live by publicity—perfectly legitimate, moreover—given them in all the press, claim that they
have the right to secrecy in order to keep copyists from copying.

"As for me, I prefer being copied than seen. It is impossible
for us to prevent our ideas from being taken sooner or later.

"Provided, of course, that neither our names nor our labels
are used. Let's make dresses that give women elegance, youth,
and dignity. All the better if they copy us!"

In the eyes of the fashion designers, who had a morbid and at
the same time apparently legitimate fear of seeing their models
copied by those who, unlike the buyers for the large U.S. ready-
to-wear industry, had not paid for this right, this decision appeared scandalous.

Raymond Barbas commented on Coco's outburst:

> The delay imposed for the reprinting of fashion sketches is not
> the result of a dictum but of an agreement made with the press,
> and this for three reasons:
>
> 1. To protect the interests of the press: documents for publica-
> tion must be made available to all newspape s and publications
> fairly and equally;
>
> 2. To protect buyers and exports: under the present circum-
> stances, the importance of this point should escape no one. Buyers
> who pay high prices for the models do not wish to see them
> reproduced before the time limit for delivery is up (minimum of
> three weeks). It should not be forgotten that every model copied
> represents a loss of money for us;
>
> 3. To protect small dressmakers: there Mlle Chanel is beaten on
> her own ground, for high fashion has already taken up the
> problems of dressmakers in the provinces. The latter, who have
> bought models or patterns for a very high price authorizing them
> to reproduce the original model, have no desire to see them popu-
> larized in the press before they have received their orders.

Chanel did not agree.

"I never prevent anyone from copying me. On the contrary, I
say to them: come and pinch all the ideas you want.

"The result of the decisions taken by the association is that
copies of our models are reserved exclusively to foreigners, and
they don't deprive themselves! As for me, I want the little dressmaker from Confolens and Barcelonnette [that little dressmaker
so dear to Frenchwomen and preferred to ready-to-wear] to
copy me, the poor dear, at the same time as Seventh Avenue

manufacturers. A copy is a tribute to creation. A copy is love! Anyway, the best proof that fashion isn't made to be put in cans is that it goes out of fashion. And very quickly!"

She brandished a letter from a small provincial dressmaker, who in fact may have been the cause of her break with the association.

"Mademoiselle," the young woman had written, "I must tell you that I do not have the means to buy your models for inspiration, but I would like it so much if you would permit me to visit from time to time to look at your collection."

Chanel permitted everything. In the same way, she once received a group of nuns who directed a kind of sewing workroom institution.

That particular afternoon the presentation of the collection was not without its moments of humor. The mannequins pirouetted demurely and, without showing the slightest embarrassment and barely moving their hips, bowed modestly to the row of starched coifs. Coco was delighted and pretended that she could already see all the little Chanel dresses that would ingenuously emerge from the good sisters' workshop.

Throughout the battle of polemics Coco dug in her heels— unflinching in her obstinacy. The press was full of her name. She had become the "grande Mademoiselle."

Why shouldn't the forty thousand French artisans who make a living in couture share in this "plundering from which the whole world is profiting"? she demanded.

Here again the history of fashion would show that Coco was correct. Other couturiers followed her example: Givenchy and Balenciaga. Increasingly fashion became a publicity-getting device whose main objective was to help advertise the prestige of a label, a perfume. In consequence, secrecy came to have no place in an industry that, by design almost, was being run at a deficit.

Michel Gorin, the current president of the association, told us, "Chanel had a genius for publicity. She resigned from the association with a great flourish, but very discreetly she continued to pay her annual dues."

The truth is, while Coco did not want to rock the boat too much, she did want to make her sensitivity to the U.S. market demonstrably clear, especially since she had agreed to go to Dallas, Texas in September of that year to receive from Stanley

Marcus, owner of Neiman-Marcus, the Fashion Oscar that was awarded "the most influential designer of the twentieth century."

Christian Dior had received this award before her—and generally she did not accept awards that were also given to others. In this case, she pretended to forget about Dior. She loved the United States and the Americans loved her. She was full of indulgence toward U.S. journalists, for *they* knew their job. Her friends watched in total amazement as she answered the most ridiculous questions—questions that would have resulted in the immediate dismissal of French journalists. She fended off the most indiscreet questions with a laugh or a joke.

"I'm a hundred years old," she answered when questioned about her age. Or, "It depends on the day."

"What do you eat?"

"A gardenia in the morning and a rose at night."

Laughter.

She left Orly with twenty dresses and suits, seven rows of pearls, and one ruby.

During a grandiose ceremony, organized by Stanley Marcus and held at his ranch, she received a golden plaque.

This is how the United States saw her. On September 25, the *New Yorker* wrote:

"We've met some formidable charmers in our time, but none to surpass the great couturière and perfumer Mlle Gabrielle Chanel, who came out of retirement three years ago to present a collection of dress and suit designs that have begun to affect women's styles (and, apparently, women's minds) every bit as powerfully as her designs of thirty-odd years ago did. We met Mlle Chanel in her suite at the Waldorf Towers, just before she flew back to Paris. She was fresh from three strenuous weeks here in Dallas, where she went to receive an award as the most significant designer of the last fifty years. At seventy-four, Mlle Chanel is sensationally good-looking, with dark-brown eyes, a brilliant smile, and the unquenchable vitality of a twenty-year-old, and when, giving us a firm handshake, she said, 'I am *très, très, fatigué*,' it was with the assurance of a woman who knows she can afford to say it. Since the Chanel look is causing such a stir these days, we took particular note of what its begetter was wearing: a natural-colored straw sailor hat; a natural-colored silk suit, with box jacket and straight skirt; a white silk blouse, with gold cuff links; low-heeled brown-and-white shoes; and plenty of jewelry—a pearl hatpin, pearls and diamonds in her ears, ropes of pearls about her neck, and, on her jacket, an enormous brooch of antique gold studded with rubies, emeralds, and diamonds.

" 'The brooch is of my design, and the dress is nothing, *très sinple*,' she said when we congratulated her on her appearance. 'The cuff links were given to me by Stravinsky, thirty years ago. The occasion? Admiration of course—the admiration I bore *him*.'

"Mlle Chanel said that she had been too busy in Texas to do any shopping but had managed to buy a lot of Texas shirts and hats right here in New York, which she was carrying back to Paris to give friends. 'In America, it seems to me that people look at me in such a nice way,' she said. 'In Europe today, it is as if people had no more time to be nice. I liked very much Texas. The people of Dallas, *ah, je les aime beaucoup! Très gentils, très charmants, très simples.* Never in the least haughty.' Mlle Chanel did a skillful and funny pantomime of a haughty person. 'I had stagefright when I went to Dallas and no wonder, for in truth I was afraid it would be like a huge movie stage, but I found everything real and the people real, like a big family, and the fright went away.'

"We lighted a cigarette for Mlle Chanel and asked her how she had happened to be in retirement so long. Her brown eyes flashed. 'Never was I really in retirement in my heart,' she said. 'During the war, nobody thought any more of making beautiful clothes, and after the war I watched the couturiers, the young men, to see what they were doing. I travelled. I enjoyed life at my country place in Switzerland, but I was bored not having anything real to do. Always, I observed the new clothes. At last, quietly, calmly, with great determination, I began working on *une belle collection.* When I showed it in Paris, I had many critics. They said that I was old-fashioned, that I was no longer of the age. Always I was smiling inside my head, and I thought, I will show them. In America, there was great enthusiasm. In France, I had to fight. But I did not mind. I love very much to battle. Now, in France, they are trying to adapt my ideas. So much the better! But when I see some things they call *"after la mode Chanel,"* I protest vigorously. There are no potato sacks among my dresses!

" 'I must tell you something of significance. Fashion is always of the time in which you live. It is not something standing alone. The problem of fashion in 1925 was different. Women were just beginning to go to work in offices. I inspired the cutting of the hair short because it goes with the modern woman. To the woman going to work, I said to take off the bone corset, because women cannot work while they are imprisoned in a corset. I invented the tweed for sports and the loose-fitting sweater and blouse. I encouraged women to be well-groomed and to like perfume—a woman who is badly perfumed is not a woman! The problem today is *très different*. Nearly all women work, and if they don't work, they want to work. So many women in France drive a little car. This you cannot do with a crinoline skirt. Many of the big fortunes today have crumbled. In former years rich women did not go shopping themselves. Now they do. They have to be practical. Today people travel a lot. The clothes must be light in weight for the flying. But the grand problem, the most important problem, is to rejuvenate women. To make women look young. Then their outlook on life changes. They feel more joyous.'

"Mlle Chanel flicked the ash off the last inch of her cigarette, which she held pinched between the thumb and forefinger of her left hand. 'As for myself,' she said, 'I am not interested any more in 1957. It is gone for me. I am more interested in 1958, 1959, 1960. Women have always been the strong ones of the world. The men are always seeking from women a little pillow to put their heads down on. They are always longing for the mother who held them as infants. Women must tell them always that *they* are the ones. *They* are the big, the strong, the wonderful. In truth, women are the strong ones. It is just my opinion. I am not a professor. I am not a preacher. I speak my opinions gently. It is the truth for me. I am not young, but I feel young. The day I feel old, I will go to bed and stay there. *J'aime la vie!* I feel that to live is a wonderful thing.' "

A month after this interview, Chanel, back in France, was selling seven thousand suits a year. This was her speciality and she was unbeatable at it. No. 5 was still the most popular perfume in the world. She enlarged her leather-goods department and launched her shoulder bag, which seriously threatened the sales of Hermès bags.

Destined to success, widely copied, none of Chanel's innovations was ever lost. She always found the detail that hit the mark.

A dozen or so manufacturers, under licenses to do so from the creator herself, put on the market deluxe "little brother suits," which sold at prices ranging from eight hundred to fifteen hundred francs in boutiques. This profitable operation represented twenty to thirty million francs a year.

Her success never dwindled; her prestige was indisputable. Only a certain coolness toward her remained, or, more exactly, an incomprehension between Coco and the bards of fashion. Not that Coco was neglected. On the contrary, her personality almost overshadowed her creations. For a long time, her designs had transcended fashion's rituals and revolutions. The nature of her designs was probably the source of the misunderstanding.

"A style and not a fashion": But what exactly did she mean by this oft-repeated maxim?

In a famous article Roland Barthes, linguist, sociologist, and author of the most erudite work ever written about fashion and its language (*Système de la Mode*) examined the Chanel style from the intellectual viewpoint:

> Today if you opened a book on the history of our literature, you should find the name of a new classical author: Coco Chanel. Chanel does not write with pen and paper (except in her spare time) but with fabrics, forms, and colors. Nevertheless, it is commonly agreed that she has the authority and flair of a writer of the "grand siècle": as elegant as Racine, as Jansenist as Pascal (whom she quotes), as philosophic as La Rochefoucauld (whom she imitates by giving the public her personal maxims), as sensitive as Mme de Sevigné, and as much of a rebel as the "grande Mademoiselle"* whose surname and function she has inherited (see her recent declarations of war against other designers). It is said that Chanel keeps fashion from falling into barbarism and endows it with all the classical virtues: reason, naturalness, permanency, and a taste for pleasing rather than for shocking. Chanel is well liked by *Le Figaro* where, along with Cocteau, she occupies a place on the fringes of society's accepted culture. . . .

> Chanel's creations are in opposition with the very idea of fashion. Fashion (such as we conceive it today) rests on a strong feeling for the times. Each year, fashion destroys what it has been worshipping and worships what it is about to destroy. The vanquished fashion of yesterday could very well address today's victorious fashion with the unfriendly little message of the dead to the living that is sometimes inscribed on tombstones: Yesterday I

---

*The name given to the Duchess de Montpensier, niece of Louis XIII of France.

was what you are today; tomorrow you will be what I am today. Chanel's work does not take part—or very little—in this annual vendetta. Chanel works year after year on the same model, adding only minor variations, in the same way as variations on a theme are used in music. Her work says (and she herself confirms it) that an "eternal" feminine beauty exists whose unique image will be transmitted to us by art history. She shuns with indignation perishable fabrics, paper, and plastic, which are sometimes used in the United States to make dresses. Permanence, the very thing which kills fashion, is transformed into a precious quality by Chanel.

The Chanel "style" was to influence the entire French fashion world, giving it the limits within which it evolved—until the 1960s. Then came protest; the mini-skirt followed by the maxi. Fashion, no longer directionless, was crazy.

In 1964 a newcomer rocked the Chanel mark. A handsome and athletic man, under forty, a former rugby player, upset traditions: "I am the Matra, the Ferrari," he said. "Chanel is the old Rolls: functional but static."

"There is nothing more ridiculous in all of Paris than Courrèges," proclaimed Coco.

On another day she was asked: "What do you think of Courrèges? Do you think that his above-the-knee fashion will have a following?"

"Who? Cou . . . Cou . . . Oh, yes, that one! You know, fashion is not architecture. An inch above or an inch below does not change the style. If he does not get a better idea. . . . Anyway, I work for adult women. What did you say was his name? Courregès, what a funny name!"

Courrèges, a former cutter for Balenciaga, created a tremendous stir. He gave the mini-skirt its patent of nobility and invented the structured, or trapeze, dress that within a few months had come down into the street and into less expensive shops. His success was prodigious. Chandeliers and stilted parades annoyed him. He considered all that to be of another age. He was the designer of the year 2000 and represented the break with traditional fashion. In his firm everything was white, clean, and athletic. His mannequins presented the collection while dancing the jerk. Right away he thought of exploiting this gold mine by going into ready-to-wear, but he hesitated for fourteen months and finally closed his fashion house temporarily before going into "avant-garde" ready-to-wear. But the bomb had a fallout that would last a long time.

Courrèges' structurism stood in direct opposition to classicism, to the Chanel style. Two visions now met and faced each other, as Roland Barthes showed:

> Within the aesthetic of a garment there exists a certain almost paradoxical quality that unites attractiveness and permanence: "chic." "Chic" requires, even demands, if not a worn-out at least a worn look in a garment: "chic" has a horror of things that look new. "Chic," that sublimated tempo, is the key to Chanel's style. Courrèges' models do not reflect this obsession: very fresh, bright, or even pastel-colored, white, the new absolute, predominate. This resolutely young fashion with its schoolgirl references, at times childish not to say babyish (baby shoes and socks), is continually renewed without complexes for it is designed to dress new women. From Chanel to Courrèges the verb tenses have completely changed: Chanel's unfailing "chic" tells us that a woman has lived (and known how to live); Courrèges' obstinate "new" that she is going to live.
>
> Time, then, which for one is style, for the other, fashion, separates Chanel and Courrèges. On one side there is Coco with tradition and its perpetual inner renewal; on the other, Courrèges with constant innovation. On one side classicism, on the other modernism.

That may have been true in the beginning. Time, however, has passed over Courrèges, and his innovations have become dated. His creations, once endorsed by the street, also became a style. His models have modified the feminine costume beyond just a moment in fashion. Still he was perhaps the first since Chanel to succeed in filling the gap so few couturiers ever filled. Was she conscious of this and therefore secretly jealous? Perhaps. She had stood face to Dior and buried the dying New Look. But with Courrèges the battle was tougher for it took place on ground where she had formerly triumphed: the street, customs, costume. She unsheathed her claws against Courrèges.

For his part, Courrèges confided to us, he admired Coco. Modestly he told us that she had succeeded along the road she had chosen—to change the feminine costume. As for him, his work is still hesitant, uncertain. Much too confident in its own innovations, it is no longer a fashion but a stammering style.

Coco lived quite apart from her colleagues and showed indulgence only for Balmain: "Women from the provinces have to dress, too." And, at first, for Yves St.-Laurent: "He's somebody quite special, that one. I congratulate him. He has had the courage to copy me. He did well. There is a certain admiration in a copy. The more he copies Chanel, the more success he'll have."

But when he ceased to be inspired by her, she dropped her kind sentiments.

She detested Cardin, his designs, and his highly developed commercial sense. Yet of all the young high fashion designers he was the only one to keep up a tradition, that of patron of the arts, which Coco herself had raised to the level of an institution. One evening she met him.

André-Louis Dubois, who remembered it well, told us:

"Something quite funny happened with Cardin. She had gone to the opening of a play. During the intermission everyone got up. Someone presented him to her—hubbub—maybe she got or maybe she didn't get the name, she chatted with him for a few minutes. Then she came over to me.

" 'Who is that charming young man?'

" 'Unfortunately, it's Cardin.'

" 'Well, he's charming. As a man, of course. As for fashion, that's an entirely different matter. He'll ruin fashion with his ready-to-wear.' "

She never forgave Jeanne Moreau, her customer and intimate friend of four years, for her romance with Pierre Cardin. She considered Moreau's act an unforgivable infidelity.

About Paco Rabanne, whom she called the "Metallurgist," she said: "It gives me shivers down my back when I think that they put bolts on women and cover them with aluminum, nails, and a coat of mail."

When she learned that Castillo, who bragged about having been a tailor for four years in her firm and who claimed that he owed all his knowledge of fashion to her, was joining Lanvin, she said, haughtily and with feigned surprise, "A noble Spaniard! You know very well that if there had been a noble Spaniard among my personnel, I would have known it."

Through a "strange" set of circumstances, the hour of the presentation of her collection coincided several times with that of the Lanvin-Castillo firm. And she reproached them for copying her, for not copying her, for making mini-skirts or maxi-skirts. For compromising French fashions.

She thundered! "Never, until today, had I ever heard anyone dare to ask if fashion was made in Italy or in the United States. We have lost our place because men are inventing fashion. They don't know what to do anymore. When they think they're creating something new, they design old Chanel. Couture is going to founder—after I'm gone, of course."

She talked about some of her young colleagues with the condescension of a chef scolding his scullion: "A collection consisting of a hundred and fifty models is obviously a disgrace. The dresses can't be sold and you need too many mannequins to present it well. I don't like mini-skirts because they're not correct. I have some friends who aren't particularly eccentric, but they dress so short that it is embarrassing. Today women don't dress to please men; they dress to startle each other. They show the most incredible disdain for their male companions. Look at them in a restaurant: they're offered flowers, the menu is handed to them, they take out their compacts and start daubing their noses."

Fashion's meanderings and the extravagances of her colleagues annoyed her profoundly. Soon she was no longer satisfied by an occasional statement to journalists she met at collection time. She needed to make "her" declaration of war.

The occasion presented itself at a press conference she gave when it was announced that the musical *Coco* was to be staged. On February 13, 1967, little was said about the play when Coco, surrounded by microphones, received the journalists of the press and radio at the rue Cambon.

She had neglected nothing. They sat in the salon and drank champagne; she sat in state on the famous sofa, dressed in a sand-colored suit.

She talked a little bit about the musical, but much more about her colleagues, whose lives were naturally of no interest to Hollywood. She had never before gone so far in her criticisms.

"Fashion today is nothing but a question of skirt length. High fashion is doomed because it is in the hands of men who do not like women and wish to make fun of them.

"It used to be," she added, "that women at the age of forty traded youth for grace and mystery. That was an evolution that left them intact. Today they take on the youngest women with ridiculous weapons. All they need now is a ribbon in their hair and a schoolbag on their backs.

"And even for young girls, I find that the mini-skirt is 'dirty.' I'm not talking about modesty, of course. But one already collects so much dust and mud on one's legs in Paris, must one now have it on one's thighs?

"Today if one is not a 'swinger,' if one has no desire to twist and shake at Régine's, one might as well give up. People are surprised that I no longer go out in the evenings. The idea that if I did go out I'd be treated as a social locomotive makes me throw up. In my time women were compared to flowers, even to sausages, but never to 'locomotives.'

"The swingers? It's all their fault if the world is so sad, with their stupid dances, their taste for mediocre things. Why today a girl isn't even invited to dance. Everyone dances for himself, trying to ape his partner as if they were savages.

"Men dress like women; women like men. They're destroying love. As a result, no one is ever in a good mood; no one is satisfied with what he has. I know: I have three hundred and fifty women who work with me. Boredom of every kind has become an institution. Before the war I never heard anyone talk about complexes or about depression. All right, we were sentimental. Perhaps it was foolish, but it filled our lives, and that was much better."

By their very extravagance, by their carefully measured allusions, these statements stirred up a wave of resentment among the fashion designers. It was considered correct to show respect for Mademoiselle, and they continued to do so, but they peppered the compliments that custom and her age required with snide remarks. Of course, no one had the bad taste to insinuate that nothing in Mademoiselle's past qualified her to set herself up as an arbiter of morality.

It was a typical Parisian quarrel, almost well mannered. Indignation was expressed by certain well-chosen and well-calculated phrases. Ted Lapidus: "Mademoiselle Chanel has a fantastic talent. What she thinks about mini-skirts comes as no surprise to me. If one is an eccentric like her, one has eccentric ideas. As for me, I still think that the mini-skirt works."

Maggy Rouff: "It's a personal stand. Mademoiselle has always chosen to stay aloof from the great movements of fashion. So she insists on her own style? Fine, let her have it. No one will take it away from her."

Pierre Balmain: "Mademoiselle Chanel can drop all the

bombs she wants if that amuses her. I don't feel that anything she says concerns me."

Guy Laroche: "I like women so much that I dress them—like women. What I find strange is the wish to make skirt lengths go down, in a time when they're going up. That's just provocation."

Jean Dessés: "I admire Mademoiselle Chanel a great deal. But I find that her statements are unworthy of her. With all due respect, I say to her, 'Mademoiselle, you would be better off if you kept quiet.' "

Marc Bohan (Dior): "Mademoiselle Chanel? I was just about to say something, but I won't, out of respect for her age. She's been defending the same fashion for thirty years now and dressing women of all ages the way she dresses herself, which is perhaps not always what they want."

M Barbas (president of Jean Patou): "What youth wants is the prime consideration. I cannot accept what Mademoiselle Chanel says, for in our profession there are men who love women and wish to see them look pretty (such as myself)!"

Robert Ricci (Nina's son): "There is an age for being a swinger. Let everyone look out for his own interests."

Paco Rabanne: "She's contradicting herself. Who, in 1925, invented the tailored skirt? Fashion has become more masculine since women like her took a hand in it."

Louis Feraud: "Chanel is sincere, but women have chosen. And we love them. The proof is that my boss is on his third wife, and I'm getting married in three weeks."

Philippe Heim: "I don't want to be bitchy, but Coco Chanel is a designer who will never see twenty again. The driving force of fashion is youth. And when she says that designers don't like women, the fact that our house has been passed on from father to son refutes her."

It is not easy to tell off a woman who in 1925—at a time when Courrèges was learning to make mud pies—invented the tailored skirt.

Courrèges, who was often the butt of Coco's shafts, kept quiet. Even though he did not know her, he sensed that his quarrel with her was something that went far beyond the frilly and narrow world of fashion.

More reserved than his colleagues, Pierre Cardin attempted to raise the level of the debate and to place it in the perspective of fashion history:

"It is regrettable that Mademoiselle Chanel chooses to ignore the history of costume. But she does know that every period has been marked by a certain style of dress imposed by the tendencies and tastes of the times, which the designers can do no more than express, each according to his manner. . . .

"Mademoiselle Chanel has every right to be against the short skirt. Nonetheless, this time she is far from having the unanimous agreement of her colleagues.

"I also regret particularly that Coco Chanel does not show a little more indulgence toward the young designers, who show so much for her."

Cardin and all the couturiers of his generation—Marc Bohan, Paco Rabanne, Yves St.-Laurent, and Louis Feraud—failed to see in what way their fashion "killed love" and in what way Mademoiselle Chanel's famous suits exalted it.

"How can she accuse us of making women masculine?" Cardin exclaimed. "Was she not the first, in 1919, when she was just getting started, to kill off the woman of 1900? Was it not she who invented the modern woman? Wasn't she the first to cut her hair, to throw away her corset, to shorten her skirts, to bring her waist down to her hips? Chanel's line in 1920 was undoubtedly hideous, but it made the sporty woman, the practical woman.

"The snip of the scissors that cut Chanel's hair," Cardin added, "made thirty-five thousand beauty salons spring up all over France. So why should she come and rebuke us today for stirring up a revolution?"

His last comment, somewhat more philosophic, was: "Mademoiselle Chanel can always accuse us of detesting women, but what counts after all is that women themselves do not detest us."

The battle had been joined, and her eventual victory was far from apparent. Although in the United States and elsewhere, sales were still going up, in France they were leveling off. But Coco's mind was on other things.

She received an honor she had not expected, from behind the Iron Curtain. Why was she invited in 1967 to present her collection in Moscow? It has never been made clear.

Coco was flattered, but she hesitated, finally deciding not to present her collection in person. She did, however, send a delegation of seven mannequins, led by the director of the fashion house, M Pierre Tranchant.

Coco, exultant, was almost apologetic:

"This amuses me. I think this experiment is worth making. I've only had one aim in life: to send my models out into the street. And now here they are on Red Square."

For two days the models were displayed before thirty-five thousand people, who had paid two rubles each to see them. From then on Coco had to admit that Soviet Russia had a certain amount of good sense: Russia's working women were against the mini-skirt.

On his return to Paris, Tranchant made a report on the first official trip of a Western couturier to Moscow:

"No one in the U.S.S.R. can afford to dress in high fashion, not even in ready-to-wear as we think of it. But an evolution is taking place. I even think that in the future we might be asked to act as fashion advisers for the Ministry of Light Industry, which is in charge of couture.

"In any case, the Russians plan to come to Paris for the winter collections.

"The only trade agreements we came to concerned the perfumes. Chanel perfumes, which for a year now have come under an import agreement, will from now on be sent in greater quantity to the U.S.S.R. But here again, the market is a limited one due to insufficient buying power."

From a strictly commercial point of view, the trip was a flop. But it was quite another matter when it came to prestige. By showing her collections in a country whose very economic structure excluded even the notion of high fashion, Coco had established her creations as part of the patrimony of humanity. She had a point when she felt superior to her colleagues—except for one, for whom she almost admitted her respect, before she quarreled with him, that is. Though she may at times have said awful things about him, she would not stand anyone else doing it unless encouraged by her.

Why him? First of all, he demanded respect, for several reasons, all of which involved professional respect, goodwill, and envy.

He sold his models at higher prices than she did hers, and they sold very well. There was another thing: silent, unobtrusively disdainful and discreet, Cristóbal Balenciaga may have accomplished what Coco herself wished she had been and had done. He was a solitary personage when it came to his professional life. Like Coco he did not like journalists, but, in contrast to her, he never received them. She was a personality, a sacred cow. He was a myth.

Did this reserved gentleman, whose models excluded all sham and who resolutely shut his door on the press, really exist? One almost suspected that he didn't until a reporter finally succeeded in ambushing, or rather in photographing, him. He talked to us about Coco, whom he had first seen from afar in 1920 in San Sebastián when he was a young, unknown Spanish couturier. He told us about their friendship, their quarrel.

"I met her shortly after she reopened her house. I had been told that she wished to see me. I was delighted. We often had long discussions. When we did not agree, she always respected my opinions. She joked; she seemed so young:

" 'Cristóbal let's get married,' she said.

" '???'

" 'You don't mind if I tell the journalists that we are getting married?'

" '???'

" 'Don't you want to? Too bad, it would have been the wedding of the century. We could have gone into ready-to-wear together. We really would have driven the others up the wall!' "

Then came, almost inevitably, their quarrel. Could she really ever forgive Cristóbal Balenciaga for inspiring such respect in her?

"We had dined in her home. At two o'clock in the morning she said: 'Cristóbal, I want to visit your fashion house.'

"We made a date for the next day, Sunday, on Avenue George V. She arrived, looking lovely despite her age, dressed in a white shantung suit and a blue hat.

"She visited the house, reorganizing everything in a few minutes and with a few words. Then we went to lunch in St.-Cloud. During dessert she spoke about a press conference:

" 'Don't you want to come?'

" 'Coco, you know very well that I don't want to see them.'

" 'Oh, yes! Too bad, I would have liked it if they had photographed us together. Actually, you're right. What a lousy business we're in! I am so tired.'

"Half-joking, half-complaining, she confided to me how lonely she was, how she wanted to give up couture. 'It's my last collection.' Several times in the course of the day she again mentioned, without insisting too much, her plan to have me accompany her to the rue Cambon to meet the press. Then she complained about how tired she was. We dined that night at the Espadon and left each other greater friends than ever. At least I thought so. I had cheered her up.

"The next day she received the press. I read later in the newspaper what she had said to them:

" 'Yesterday I saw Balenciaga. Poor Cristóbal, he was so tired that I wonder what kind of a collection he'll be able to put together.'

"I was deeply wounded. She called me three times. I had her told that I was not there. I never saw her again. I regretted it, and I think she did, too."

That, too, was the way Coco was. Solitary, sick with solitude to such a point that it brought out the meanness in her.

16.

Mademoiselle at Work

THERE was a 'Chanel' constant," René de Chambrun has told us. "The constant was her love, esteem, and respect for work, especially work well done. She was, to be sure, hard on others, but she was hard, very hard, on herself.

"Her symbol was a pair of scissors, her work tool. I had some made for her in Baccarat crystal."

"My art," said Coco, "has consisted in cutting off what others added."

Mademoiselle is at work.

In the corner she has chosen, next to the platform, the chairs have been pushed aside, leaving an empty space in which wait, much like courtesans in a king's anteroom, Mme Raymonde, the working studio director and Coco's closest collaborator, the forewoman, the tailor, whose models are about to be passed in review that afternoon, a few other minor employees who in a few minutes will hold out pins and take the ripped-off sleeves that Mademoiselle will hand to them. ("No one has ever ripped off a sleeve like Mademoiselle.") Farther away, in their dressing room, a few mannequins sit.

A smile from Chanel. ("Today she looks in a good mood.") A few remarks, neither kind nor caustic, made to create an ambience, followed by one or two reflections on the weather.

"Yes, Mademoiselle." "All right, Mademoiselle." Few answers. First of all she didn't hear them, and, too, everything should be sacrificed to save time so that things could be done before nightfall. Stoic, resigned, and already weary, a mannequin stands there, dressed in a pink suit. It looks completely finished. Mademoiselle does not want to see her yet. Once more the forewoman brushes with a hesitant hand, almost regretfully, the impeccably mounted sleeve before the Boss's ruthless eyes reveal its faults to them with the magic of a domineering word, especially since this afternoon a photographer and journalist are present. ("She's going to give us her circus number again!")

"Let's get to work . . ."

As Mme Raymonde hands her the scissors, the tape on which they hang catches for an instant on Mademoiselle's hat, a black boater, its crown covered with innumerable marks left by the pin she has pushed in it every morning for months now, as a nun pins her coif. The tortoise-shell-rimmed glasses are perched on her immense nose, its dilated nostrils dominating the thin-lipped mouth, impeccably outlined, almost scarred, by the vivid red lipstick to which Coco has remained faithful despite the passing years and fashions.

Everything is ready. Or almost. Under Mademoiselle's incensed glare, Mme Mortreux, director of the showrooms, is discretely ushering into the next room a customer who has had the presumption to come while Mademoiselle was officiating. Of course, Mademoiselle had told her director ("but nobody listens to me here!"):

"I don't want you to take any more orders. We're now preparing the collection, and I want to have all my people available."

Alas! The Chanel firm is also a business enterprise. Sales have to continue and workrooms kept busy.*

The intruder having disappeared, the mannequin performs a few pirouettes, shows her back, her profile. A few steps away, the

---

*The personnel of a fashion house is divided into workrooms. The Chanel firm has eight, of which four are "creating ateliers" where models for the collections are fashioned. The four others simply reproduce models for the customers. Each workroom consists of about thirty people: apprentices, assistant second seamstresses, second seamstresses, assistant first seamstresses, first seamstresses, all under the supervision of a forewoman or of a tailor assisted by a second.

forewoman, in her white blouse, waits for the verdict. Or rather knows it already. The photographer is ready.

"But it's impossible! How dare you show me this?"

The sleeve flies. A few snips of the scissors into the lovely pink suit: in a second or two the seams of the model, just basted, have been undone. Hardly anything is left except a few unrelated pieces of material, stuck raglike on the mannequin who, but a few moments ago, had seemed elegant.

To the sound of Mademoiselle's necklaces jangling as she moves, the astonishing business of refitting the sleeve begins, slowly and precisely, watched by the mannequin and the bemused forewoman.

"I told you yesterday. You've got to take that pleat out. Why don't you obey me? [It wasn't at all certain that in fact she had said that yesterday, but why argue? It would only draw out the session.] Why do you want to keep all that? Cut it off and let's forget it. What woman would wear this thing? To have all this paraphernalia against her skin? Not I in any case. Nice and straight here. I already did it yesterday. . . ."

Sometimes in the course of her meanderings the fateful words "that reminds me of . . ." surge forth, producing a general sigh of consternation, except from the latest arrival to the Chanel firm. For her oft-repeated stories are interminable; anecdotes known in all their variations to those around her elicit nothing but an absentminded "Oh! Mademoiselle" or "Fine, Mademoiselle!" She interrupts her work, takes off her glasses, sits down, and talks. "The Ballets Russes, Biarritz, Deauville . . ." The mannequin who has been abandoned in the middle of the rug like a greasy pole the morning after the village fête, fights against a desire to dump everything.

"That's not all. Come back to work." Mademoiselle resumes her work.

She remounts the sleeve, gets down on her knees to check the hem ("What is the use of a hem? Women aren't going to grow!"). Her hat has not budged.

Finally the mannequin is sent off with an almost-kind word, meant to make up for everything.

In the late Mademoiselle's apartment, her employees in their white blouses sat under the sheaf of golden wheat, next to the Venetian black whose shadow was projected on the Coromandel screens nailed to the walls, and they remembered. Mademoiselle's shadow still haunted this sumptuous, almost baroque, decor.

You feel it with Mme Manon, first among the forewomen, who joined the rue Cambon in 1933 as an apprentice and returned in 1953. Today she is continuing Chanel's work.

"Mademoiselle always created alone. She chose her own materials and ignored the designers. To us, her forewomen, she used to say:

" 'You're going to do this. You're going to do that.'

"And if by chance one of us thought up something on our own, she'd leave its execution to someone else. Nothing could come from us. She did not want anyone creating along with her. And if we added a little knickknack, she'd say:

" 'Just look at that. If I gave them their head, they'd keep adding and adding, but that's not elegance. Elegance is line.'

"She refined things. She was a good boss, but a severe one, exacting very high standards for the finishing of work. Yet she had very human reactions, bursts of kindness: if somebody were ill, she took an interest, though always discreetly. Two months before the collections, when new fabrics arrived, we started work on the models. She would call us together: 'Forewomen in the studio!' And she would say to us: 'You're going to cut this and that. Prepare me a suit. [Her gestures indicated exactly what she wanted.] 'When you've got it falling correctly, come and see me and I'll give you the trimmings. You might give me a sleeve with a little width.' She never provided sketches; she always explained everything orally. She'd say: 'Above all, make sure it hangs correctly.' When we finally had it hanging right, we'd bring it to her, and she would take her scissors and start cutting, always without a sketch. It was extremely tough on us. Often we had to undo everything the day before, sometimes even a few hours before, the collection. She would say: 'Too bad. We'll show this suit basted, but it's got to be redone.' We would do it over three times, even four times, for it never suited her taste. It was very hard.

"Then she'd say to us: 'You haven't understood a thing. You don't know how to work.'

"A word, a smile, or a pat on the shoulder, and everything was forgiven. . . ." There was a moment of silence, then Mme Manon continued:

"In spite of everything ['everything' pronounced with a deep sigh] she is irreplaceable. In dressmaking, if you've never gone through Chanel, you've missed something. It's an entirely different lesson, another way of seeing things. She had a technique that was entirely her own, not to be compared."

Mme Raymonde, lively and sprightly, with a youthful smile, who can bring Mademoiselle back to life with a gesture, a word, told us:

"I joined Chanel's ten years ago. Jean Dessés, for whom I had been working, had just closed his doors. Mademoiselle interviewed me on a Friday.

" 'It's decided. You'll start Monday.'

"I was slightly apprehensive about working for a woman. But she was so extraordinary, so intelligent. She felt things, guessed our bad moods.

" 'What isn't going right today? You're not in a good mood.'

" 'Mademoiselle, we've got problems . . . that model, time.'

" 'But that's of no importance. I know that you always do your best.'

"And that made up for all our difficulties. We were under the spell of her charm.

"We began the intricate work of preparing the collections in the studio.

" 'Mme Raymonde, when do you think you'll be able to show me some fabrics?'

" 'Well, Mademoiselle, I think it will be some time in May.'

" 'When you receive them, tell me and I'll come up to the studio.'

"She would come up to the studio, sit down, and tell us all sorts of stories. She talked about her past life, shooting, and salmon fishing. The collections were forgotten. Finally, she would say to us:

" 'Ah, have you understood? I don't feel like looking at fabrics. I'll do it tomorrow.'

" 'Of course, Mademoiselle. It doesn't make any difference. . . .'

"She evoked memories of the past very simply. She talked of her youth, the aunts who brought her up; she recalled her last moment with her dying mother. She saw her only for a few minutes, long enough to kiss her. She talked about the people she had known. Cocteau, Picasso, Sert. She could be quite mordant.

"The next day she would come back to the studio. She chose all the fabrics herself. At first, I didn't even dare take them down.

" 'Pick out a piece of material to make a blouse to go with this suit jacket.'

" 'Mademoiselle, I don't know which one you'd like.'

"So she'd plant herself in front of the rack of materials and would take one out. She never made a mistake. Some of the very exclusive ones were made in Scotland. She had explained precisely what she wanted beforehand. She never sketched. When she gave us a jacket to do, she said:

" 'You're going to cut a jacket in this fabric. Do you think it nice, does it really please you?'

" 'Yes, Mademoiselle.'

" 'Put the waist here.'

"Her gestures were always precise. She was at her most inspired when she stood before the already cut material. Then we started undoing. All the models were in her head.

"Then she would call the tailor to the studio.

" 'Choose some fabrics. Tell me which one you like.'

" 'Ah, Mademoiselle, that one is marvelous.'

" 'Good. Put it there.'

"Invariably she would say to me: 'Give the material he likes to another cutter.'

"She would never have tolerated my making the least objection to her choices.

"Then we would go to the salon, where we worked out all the details. There, her scarf tied to the side and her hat on her head, Mademoiselle remained impassive under the lights. We came and went, exhausted by the heat. She stayed on until nine o'clock at night, until near exhaustion.

" 'What would I do, Mme Raymonde, if I didn't have my work? I wouldn't see you anymore, any of you, and I don't know what would become of me!'

"And with false innocence she'd add: 'You know, I don't need to work anymore in order to eat.'

" 'Well then, Mademoiselle, you're not as lucky as we are. For we work in order to eat as well as for pleasure,' I answered once.

"Then she would burst out laughing."

Coco seemed to find relaxation in the euphoria of creation. In spite of this, her personnel remained on their toes, for her rages were like flashes of lightning and often totally unexpected.

"When Mademoiselle was on the staircase, no one dared come down. And, Mme Raymonde added, "I used to say to the others: 'Why? I don't understand you.' In fact, one day, shortly before her death, I ran into her on the ground floor around one o'clock in the afternoon.

" 'Well, you've certainly got nerve! Here you are leaving just as I arrive,' she said.

" 'I'm going to have lunch, Mademoiselle.'

" 'And you're not sneaking out?'

" 'Why should I, Mademoiselle?'

" 'Just to be like the others. They really make me laugh.' "

Claude de Leusse has described for us Coco's morning arrivals at the rue Cambon. One senses in her person the former queen of high fashion that she was not so long ago, when as a mannequin, she presented the Chanel collection in the famous salons. She has a delicate face, blue eyes full of candor as well as charm, and a well-modulated, slightly hoarse voice. The words flow easily as she plucks the stories from her memory, talking with great simplicity and a touch of gaiety in her eyes. She is a tall, handsome woman, a wholesome flower. She wears no makeup. Her hairdo would not have pleased Mademoiselle Chanel: long chestnut brown hair coiled just above the nape. She is dressed in a very simple skirt, a little black cashmere sweater with a scarf around the neck. No jewelry, no frills. Today, Claude de Leusse works for *Women's Wear Daily,* the U.S. fashion bible. She recounted:

"Every morning Coco arrived between twelve and twelve thirty at Chanel's. She was always superbly dressed and impeccably groomed. She had remarkable health, absolutely remarkable! Later, when I was working for *Women's Wear Daily,* whose offices are also on the rue Cambon, I sometimes used to meet her on the point of quarter to one. She'd start to talk and talk, right there on the sidewalk. I didn't dare say: 'Excuse me, Mademoiselle, but I've got to go.' Sometimes our conversation lasted until three o'clock! She was always just as fresh as a daisy. As for me I was exhausted, my eyes were down to here. . . .

"When I worked as a mannequin we were always on the lookout for her arrival. For about ten days she'd arrive at a quarter to one, and so we wouldn't come until twelve thirty. Then, on the eleventh day, she'd get there at a quarter past twelve and the tempest would break out: catastrophe. Actually it was a little like boarding school. The one among us who had been chosen as lookout informed the others of her arrival via the Arab telephone from the ground floor to the upper floors, the salon, the press office: 'Mademoiselle is coming! Mademoiselle is coming!' The first thing we did was to put on lipstick. She couldn't stand the girls without makeup. Mademoiselle made her entrance. We always delegated someone to find out if she was in a good or bad mood.

"Mademoiselle went into her office, saw this one and that one, the house came to life."

Mademoiselle's rapport with her mannequins was always very complex in nature. They represented her court, with its corridor intrigues and plots. She liked being surrounded by these beautiful young women as though she herself were rejuvenated by them.

Claude de Leusse evoked a feeling of a very special atmosphere:

"We lived with Mademoiselle Chanel, but actually we worked very little, about two hours a day, except of course during the collections. We often lunched with her. She'd invite one or the other of us. There was a golden rule: when we came out of the dining room we couldn't repeat a thing, otherwise Paris would have been in an uproar! She talked a lot, and she was fascinating, though mean. She told nasty stories about everybody, especially about her best friends.

"She hated to have any of us refuse to have lunch with her. She'd invite the same mannequin once, twice, three times in a row, then on the fourth day she'd drop her and ignore her completely. Our domestic problems, the health of our children, none of that interested her. She didn't want to know anything about it. If, one day, one of us said to her, 'It's terrible, Mademoiselle, but today I can't have lunch with you, I've got to go home,' she would become absolutely furious and not talk to that person for weeks. She was very jealous, very possessive. She couldn't stand what she called 'the bourgeois way of life.'

"Whenever she saw that we were tired and had circles under the eyes, she would say: 'No matter what you do, no matter how many hours you spend dancing or drinking, you will never dance as much as I used to, nor will you ever drink as much champagne as I have.'

"Then she would add: 'If you're sad, if you're unhappy in love, make yourselves up, take care of yourselves, put on some lipstick, and *attack:* men hate weeping women.'

"She told us the story of her life not once but one hundred and fifty times. Yet I had the impression that she told it after her own fashion. She embroidered and changed things around to her advantage. She had a fantastic imagination and ended up by believing what she had invented. She confused fact with fiction.

"She was very feminine and adored pretty young women. But when she didn't like someone anymore, it was awful. Because she was so shy she used nastiness as a defense. She made use of her charm, and, Lord knows, she had plenty of it. I've seen several girls go up to her office determined to tell her off. In moments like these, she welcomed them with a smile and put on such an act of seduction that nobody dared utter a single disagreeable word—except one day when a young English girl had the audacity to tell her exactly what she thought. Mademoiselle threw her out of her office and shouted insults at her from the top of the staircase. . . . But, deep down, she rather respected the people who stood up to her. She detested 'doormats.'

"She was a mixture of greatness and pettiness. I'm thinking about the way she treated her employees, especially the minor ones. She was merciless.

"She tried to promote rivalries between her mannequins. For example, she'd start to work on six models on the same girl; then suddenly she didn't like the girl anymore, and—presto!—she would put the six models on another girl who didn't deserve them because she hadn't worked.

"She was extremely wary of people she didn't know. She knew absolutely everything that happened to us, pretending, of course, that she was totally uninterested. She also knew everything that went on in Paris but never talked about it.

"She got mad forty thousand times with the same people, made up with them, only to have another fight with them.

"She used to say to us about marriage: 'Do you realize that if I had gotten married, I'd find myself today with an old husband to look after.' "

Age was illness, ugliness, and death—all things that Coco feared. She didn't talk about them; she ignored them. Not that she lacked courage. Once when she had fractured a rib, she wanted to get out of bed to finish her collection.

Maybe it was because she had too many sad memories: the death of her mother, the disappearance of her father, being brought up like an orphan. Too often in her life, Coco had seen illness bring on decrepitude. She couldn't stand it. Without mercy she turned away the sick from the rue Cambon, as though, superstitious, she feared that their very presence might cast an evil spell.

Michèle Cazaubon, Coco's former star mannequin, came back in 1953 as director of the studio for Chanel's reopening. Mme Raymonde told us the story of how she first assisted and then replaced Michèle Cazaubon.

"Michèle fell seriously ill. Her heart would start beating wildly at the slightest effort. When Mademoiselle found out about it, she came up to see me: 'You know, I can't keep Michèle.' I was so shocked that she couldn't help but notice it. 'Don't worry. I'll pay her. I'll pay her the entire time she's ill. But I don't want to risk her dying in the house.'

"Michèle died shortly after, at fifty-seven.

"One day," continued Mme Raymonde, "I felt a little faint. Mademoiselle was told about it and telephoned me immediately to enquire how I felt. The next day, when I ran into her, she said: 'I consulted my doctor. Since you didn't collapse, it wasn't a heart attack. You know that if it were your heart, I wouldn't keep you!' "

That was Coco. She warded off the risk of death through ostracism. The same was true for ugliness or whatever displeased her:

" 'My dear, you're really too ugly. . . . I can't keep you.'

" 'But, Mademoiselle!' "

The young girl, one of the prettiest mannequins in Paris—at least she had been and would soon again be as soon as her hair grew back—almost choked with indignation. She had cut her hair on Mademoiselle's orders. Short hair was extremely unbecoming to her, and Mademoiselle didn't hesitate to dismiss her.

Coco's constant preoccupation was long hair. "It hides the nape and the neck, two of the loveliest things a woman can show," she announced, laying down the law.

Claude de Leusse was luckier.

"When I arrived, I had very long hair," she told us. "She was horrified. I succeeded in keeping it for two and half months. Every day she would say to me: 'How can you stand that chignon? You look as though you were a hundred years old! You're terribly out of fashion!'

"One day, I went to Alexandre's and asked him to lend me a short-haired wig. I put it on and went home. Charles, my husband, was heartbroken. 'You've taken off the best you had!' Eight days later I went and had it cut off anyway. Mademoiselle wanted her mannequins all to have the same hairdo. a thick bang and a bare neck.

"When she saw me thus transformed, she didn't say a thing. She never gave compliments. One knew that everything was all right when she started telling stories."

Just as she never gave compliments, Coco hated to be contradicted. Everything was done to spare her the least annoyance. All visitors were instructed in the golden rule: "Always say, 'Yes'!" That's exactly what a young law student, Mahlia, did one day.

The first time she crossed the threshold of the rue Cambon, she hoped to show Chanel, whom she admired, a piece of material she had woven during her holidays on a makeshift loom. She didn't get beyond the doorkeeper's lodge and went away with a heavy heart, leaving behind her sample.

The next day she received an imperious call from a secretary: "Mademoiselle wants to see you immediately."

Mahlia had to cross at least ten barriers before being allowed into the Holy of Holies. At each stop she was warned by several people: "Don't forget, always say yes to Mademoiselle. She can't stand to be contradicted; it would put her in a bad humor for the rest of the day."

Finally she had the terrifying interview. From under the famous boater, Mademoiselle's black eyes sized up the young woman. She tilted her head and smiled: "I liked your fabric. Do you have a workshop?"

Mahlia blushed and just as she had been advised to do answered, "Yes."

"Could you bring me five yards of this fabric tomorrow?"

"Yes," Mahlia again answered, trembling.

That entire night and the whole next day, the young girl wove and wove on her old loom. By the next evening, exhausted, she had kept her word.

Since then, Mahlia's fabrics—for she now has a workshop and employs twenty women—have dressed Mme Pompidou, Jackie Kennedy Onassis, the Baroness de Rothschild, and Mademoiselle herself.

Mahlia recalls many anecdotes:

"One day Mademoiselle went over to a vase of flowers. She plucked a flower, then another and still another. When she had her hands full, she crushed the petals, mixed them all up, and showed me the result. 'That's what I want,' she said in a tone that brooked no refusal.

Her talent as a colorist was never denied.

"For me, Chanel was above all a colorist," M Tranchant said —high praise coming as it did from the man who, from 1956 to 1967, fought an artful battle against Mademoiselle as the director of the fashion house, in charge of administrative and commerical affairs: all things in the art of which Mademoiselle was superbly ignorant. He had one—in the eyes of Coco—unpardonable fault: he had been put there by the perfume company. Theirs was a quiet and underhanded battle, not lacking in humor.

"In all the time I was there, from 1956 to 1969, I dined only twice in her home. I was paid to put up with her during the day and to work with her, but not to entertain her in the evening! Furthermore, after working all day, I was very hungry. But Mademoiselle Chanel—this was a passing fancy—couldn't stand real eating at table. She considered it vulgar. The last time I dined with her, I remember that we had lamb chops. Normally, you were supposed to nibble one with two salad leaves. I took the butler aside and asked him to bring me three chops and lots of vegetables. Chanel couldn't believe her eyes. She never invited me again."

M Tranchant is very critical about Coco's talent: "She wasn't the creative genius she was cracked up to be. She always repeated the same models, changing only the details. She wasn't really a dressmaker. She had a great knack for ripping everything apart and sending it back to the workrooms to have it put back together again. The most precious assets of the Chanel firm were the forewomen, who were real professionals.

"One day Mademoiselle hired a dress designer. What was the

use? The only thing she allowed him to design were paper flowers, with which she decided to decorate the salon. In fact, they were beautiful flowers, and I remember selling some to Daisy Fellowes for more than six thousand new francs!"

M Tranchant's remarks are a trifle harsh. Could Coco have lasted fifty years in a world known for its uncharitableness if she had had so little talent? If the forewomen were unequaled professionals, wasn't it, after all, she who had hired and trained them, inculcating them with the incomparable Chanel taste? No one denies that there was a certain amount of "show" in Coco's work, especially her habit of fashioning her models on the mannequins. But does this diminish her creativity? She didn't know how to sew? Does Picasso know how to make paintbrushes?

The relationship between M Tranchant, the technician, and Coco, the inspired genius who looked down on commercial and legal "details," was inevitably strained. Nevertheless, it was very profitable for the Chanel firm.

It came to an end in 1967 after M Tranchant had committed a crime of *lèse majestè*: he hired a tailor from Balenciaga's, M Salvador, a forewoman, and several other persons from the workshops of that prestigious firm on Avenue George V, which had just shut its doors.

The action seemed very shrewd. For by creating two new workshops on rue Cambon in the building next door to number 31, M Tranchant saw a way to capture part of Balenciaga's clientele.

Was Coco poorly informed (only by chance did she discover that enlargements were being made to the premises to accommodate the "usurpers"), or was it that she delighted in thinking herself persecuted? Were the perfume gentlemen really thinking of replacing her? Were they seriously going to try to "make Balenciaga" on the rue Cambon?

She ranted and raved, fired M Tranchant, boycotted his successor for a year, and refused categorically to let the newly hired personnel work.

In fact, there had never been any question of the two new workshops doing anything but Chanel work, just as the firm continues to produce Chanel under Gaston Berthelot.

Probably it pleased Coco to pose, once more, as the victim of the Wertheimers.

The other side of the Coco establishment were the models.

"Remember that you are young and beautiful, and that you are wearing my clothes. Look at those women from the press who decide about fashion. They are fat, ugly, and badly dressed."

That was in 1959. Breaking with fashion tradition, and resuming her prewar tradition, Coco had stopped hiring professional mannequins. As Claude de Leusse told us:

"I joined the Chanel firm as a mannequin in 1959. It was, I think, four or five years after the reopening. Chanel said to herself one day: 'I want to show my collection on the women who will wear my models. After all, in England, duchesses are mannequins, so why not in France?' It made a terrible scandal in my family. My mother-in-law cried over it! They would say to me: 'How can you parade like that with everybody staring at you?'

"I remember the opening, the day we presented her collection for the first time. We were all scared to death! Mademoiselle came into the dressing room to encourage us. She gave us a push and for better or worse we made our entrances. We were completely out of our minds."

Coco was delighted. This wasn't like her revenge on high society after World War I, but it gave her a certain satisfaction.

"I have mannequins who are society ladies. If they gossip, I throw them out.

"I mean by this, of course," she added: "If they gossip with anyone else but me!"

After 1959 Coco's dressing room was filled with celebrities. Young women of the aristocracy, especially, dressed in Chanel, whose grace was reflected in the mirrors of the showrooms. During the sixties, the dressing room became a real heraldic registry. And even though they wore nothing but Chanel, their blazons suited their haughty bearing: Claude de Leusse (*De gueules à deux brochets adossés d'argent, accompagnés de trois croix de Malte d'or, 1 en chef et 2 en flancs. Supports: deux lions*); Jacqueline de Merindol (*D'azur, à une hirondelle d'argent volant en bande*); Mimi d'Arcangues (*ecartelé au 1 d'argent a un arbre arrachè de sinople et un lion de gueules passant au travers de l'arbre; au 2 et 3 d'azur a une croix d'or; au 4 de gueules, à trois pigeons d'argent, rangés sure une terrasse d'or, et, sur le tout d'azur, a trois chevrons d'or.* Supports: *deux lions).* Also present were Odile de Croy and other beauties of the French nobility. So it went.

It was a court with its own protocol, intrigues, and favorites. Coco liked to cultivate a climate of jealousy, arousing likes and dislikes inside her little world. She needed to be surrounded by pretty women. In their youthful company she could dissimulate her age. She distributed favors and friendship with parsimony or generosity, depending on her mood, and in return asked for something akin to filial affection. They were the daughters she had never had, whom she would like to have had.

There was nothing else, in spite of the insinuations. As she confided to one of her lawyers: "Do you think it's fun to be taken for an old dyke?"

The most beautiful ornament of this court was Marie-Hélène Arnaud, a commoner and Coco's favorite child.

"I joined Chanel's not only as a mannequin but as a collaborator. I immediately caught on that she didn't like to be given ideas. Nor did she like it if someone took on a certain importance. She accorded certain prerogatives, which she really believed she was 'giving,' but the Chanel firm remained her private domain. Every so often she listened to suggestions I made, but one could never try to give her advice. She gave the advice. Even when I went out, she would say: 'I would have put on that . . . I would have worn white muslin . . . black velvet.' She enjoyed giving advice."

In photographs taken at that time, this splendid young woman was always at Coco's side.

People gossiped. "She's the heiress, Coco's successor." Marie-Hélène Arnaud wanted to leave.

P.M. recounted:

"One fine day Chanel got the impression that Marie-Hélène was about to escape her. She had suddenly begun to manifest a certain desire for independence. She was becoming less pliable.

"Chanel decided that in order to keep the girl, her father should be hired. So he was engaged as general director of the fashion house for two years. He was a professor but took on his new job with a great deal of good humor. It didn't prevent Marie-Hélène's departure. On Chanel's insistence he had been hired for ten thousand francs a month. Tranchant, who at the time was director, knew perfectly well how to do his job and moreover didn't need this gentleman. But he had to give in, furious though he was, to Mademoiselle Chanel's wishes.

"When Marie-Hélène announced that she was tired, needed a vacation, and left on a cruise on the yacht of an American movie producer, M Arnaud behaved in a very elegant fashion. He came to see me and said: 'My contract is still good for another year and a half. But maybe we should discuss it. My daughter having left, most certainly for good, I really don't want to stay on here. I don't wish to exploit the situation. So, if you like, why don't we say that my contract expires in six months and it will be just fine.' "

In fact, M Arnaud had accepted a position in Chanel because he had been told by well-meaning friends: "Your daughter is going to become director of the firm. She'll be the successor. . . . she needs someone to help her."

"Everybody believed that, in fact, Marie-Hélène had been designated by Chanel, who herself told it to anyone who wanted to listen.

"But Mademoiselle didn't mean a word of it and said it only to keep Marie-Hélène with her."

Marie-Hélène explained to us, very simply, why she left: "Everything was marvelous. I loved Coco, but at one point I said to myself: 'There's no reason why in ten years I shouldn't still be climbing these stairs.' At my age, it didn't seem right not to try something else, that's all! It had never crossed my mind that someday I might replace her, as people said. It would have been awful to live with that idea in mind.

"We never got mad at each other. We never quarreled. Even though, it seems, she was a woman who could easily have a falling out with this or that person. I never tried to influence her— which is probably why we got along so well. When she felt that someone was trying to influence her, part of her nature reared up like a wild animal. She kept her distances. But with me, on the contrary, she could even pretend to herself that she was training me. She had no wish to see me become too important. Yet she was the one who first gave me a certain importance. Later she wanted to take it back. I didn't want to fight with her. I preferred to leave.

"After that I saw very little of her. I founded my own business. I made dresses for five years. Then I gave up because, as you can well imagine, it is very difficult, these days, to go into that kind of business in Paris. And, then, I was offered a good position. I am delighted. I have interesting work; I travel, and I don't run the risk of getting in a rut, as might have happened had I stayed with Chanel.

"There, I haven't much else to tell you. Chanel's daily life was very simple, almost routine in fact. She was a fascinating woman who played an important role in my life. She taught me a great many things. Among them, true elegance, which consists not in having a closet bursting with clothes but rather in having just a few well-chosen numbers in which one always feels at ease."

Marie-Hélène's departure caused Coco a great deal of pain, which she sought, as usual, to hide beneath a mask of sarcasm and banter: "The dear little thing asked for six months' vacation. It seems she no longer wants to be a mannequin. But what else? She doesn't know how to do anything else. In fact, she's nothing more than a shy little bourgeoise."

Marie-Hélène Arnaud had been repudiated as though she had never existed. Coco found insupportable the idea that anyone could suppose that she could have a successor.

A few years later she asked Bettina, Prince Aly Khan's last companion, to present her collection.

The press and the photographers crowded around Bettina, but Coco could not conceive that anyone could survive her, in the world of fashion or in her firm. Or maybe she simply could not imagine that one day she would die.

17.

Mademoiselle Day by Day

Oɴᴄᴇ more she had triumphed: 1970 saw the last outrages of a derelict fashion founder upon the rock of women's lassitude. Skirts returned to a more reasonable length: that of Coco Chanel. In the rue Cambon, sales had never been so high: sales figures were up 30 percent over those of the preceding year.

She no longer talked of retiring—or very little! Her traditional excuse "It's my last collection" seemed no longer appropriate. Everyone smiled. Indomitable, imperious, impatient, she pondered questions of her immortality.

"Death? It's too stupid. . . ."

As for retirement—useless to think about it. Her Swiss villa remained deserted. Mademoiselle was turning over in her mind several plans that, had they been realized, might have brought about changes in dress similar to those brought about by Chanel after World War I. Coco envisaged nothing less than creating collections for women *and* men.

"Finally she abandoned the idea temporarily. But she did not renounce it altogether," a director of the fashion firm told us.

"Did she sometimes think about the future of the firm?"

"Certainly not. She was much too egocentric: 'Or else I'll close shop.' And since business had never been as good . . . Death? Out of the question! Illness? She would continue to work as long as she was capable. After we could think about closing."

Her energy amazed and exhausted everyone. P.M. said: "How did she keep up her health? A mystery! She went to bed very late. She entertained almost every evening. As soon as you arrived in her salon you would be served whisky or vodka. She drank a little sometimes. At table there was wine, champagne, liqueurs. She talked nonstop, stories that had become familiar to everyone, fascinating when heard for the first time, but tiring after a while."

A fabulous storyteller with a fantastic memory, Coco willingly recalled her memories. Often she lost herself in lengthy asides before returning to her main story line: anecdotes, triumphs, loves—Balsan, Capel, Westminster, Reverdy—friends—Picasso, Misia Sert, Dali—the Ballets Russes.

"Good God, why do I talk so much?" she asked Jean Cau, the journalist and novelist, one day.

"Because you are shy, Mademoiselle!"

She admitted this to be true. Paradoxically, and never did she allow this emotion to show, everyone intimidated her: a mannequin, a minor employee, a delivery boy. "Fortunately, no one or almost no one knows this," she said.

Sunk in her leather sofa, she talked, triumphed, fulminated, often bitterly.

"Her dinners were hard to take, for Mademoiselle could talk for hours. Finally, when you thought it was over, you got up to leave, thanked her, and put on your coat—only to find yourself detained on the second-floor landing for another half hour. Since she slept in the Ritz, she came down, too. You came out on the rue Cambon, and arm in arm you'd accompany her to her hotel, just a few hundred yards farther. In front of the three steps leading up to the revolving door, out in the cold, you'd spend another good half hour listening to her.

"And," added P.M., "it started again in front of the elevator door. She would hold the door open while people waiting to go up became impatient. 'Let them wait!' she'd say."

She wanted to put off the hour of solitude, steal a few from the pressing memories, lurking in the shadows of her room, that waited to haunt her until she fell asleep, usually at dawn, heavily dosed with sleeping tablets. In her room at the Ritz, far from the Coromandel screens, the wooden deer, the silver and gold lions, and the old leather bindings, she could no longer cheat. She was alone, desperately alone.

She called her Ritz apartment her "student's room." Actually the perfume company, which paid all bills, rented a small suite—a drawing room, her room, and her maid's room. This suite was on the rue Cambon side. Coco had only lived there since the Liberation; before the war she had lived in another suite overlooking the Place Vendôme.

Long after the war, Lady Abdy, back from Mexico after an absence from Paris of eighteen years, paid a call on her old friend.

"I went to see her at the Ritz, rue Cambon side, for she had changed apartments. I shall never forget her bedroom with its white walls. The furniture belonged to the hotel. There was nothing of her own, not a single painting, not one personal object of value. On the bedside table there was a small alarm clock. On two ordinary red screens belonging to the hotel she thumbtacked the postcards that her friends sent her from all over the world."

"You see," she said one day to Lady Abdy, "those are my trips."

Her trips! She didn't even leave Paris on the weekends, the way most of her friends did.

"On Sunday afternoons, she used to sit on one of those small wrought-iron chairs in the Tuileries Gardens, accompanied by François, her faithful butler. They spent part of the day there together. She dreaded and hated Sundays!" André-Louis Dubois told us.

Trips back into time: one of the postcards represented the large square of Issoire. Michel Déon had sent it to her when he was on a trip to Auvergne.

Late into the night, Céline, her maid, waited up for her. Mademoiselle saved the last confidences and recriminations of the day for her. She was the last bulwark against the anguish of a restless slumber. Céline put out the light and locked the door of the room.

In her mid-sixties, elegantly dressed in a navy blue Chanel suit and white Chanel blouse, Céline talked to us with great emotion about Coco, but without ever losing the sense of distinction possessed by those who have only worked in the "best houses."

"Before entering Mademoiselle's service, I worked for [none but the most distinguished people]. I came to her in 1966. In spite of her character, I always got along very well with Mademoiselle. She called me Jeanne, the name of one of her former maids. Sometimes she joked: 'When we get old, we'll each have a little baby carriage, and we'll push each other.'

"Mademoiselle woke up very early in the morning, sometimes around six. After her breakfast (black coffee, sometimes oatmeal), she stayed in bed until eleven o'clock reading books, newspapers, and her mail and sorting the many requests for help that she received. She chatted and it was the only moment of the day when she was more or less relaxed. Around eleven o'clock she started to get dressed; it took a long time and she always finished by spraying herself generously with No. 5. Around one o'clock she left for the couture house, where I accompanied her if her secretary, Lilou Grumbach, didn't come to get her.

"She read a great deal; the books that she received or had someone buy for her. When she came home early, she watched the television, systematically absorbing all the programs until the television went off the air. Yet Mademoiselle criticized everything and drowned the 'rock' singers with sarcasm.

"In fact, she said terrible things about everyone, sparing only a few of her old friends: André-Louis Dubois, whom she always respected, Serge Lifar, and Claude Baillen, the confidante of her last years. The others? 'They dine with me to save money.' She ran them all down—and complained when they had not come to see her in a long time."

Very few of Coco's prewar literary and artistic friends were left. There would be the occasional visit from a Salvador Dali, a Lucchino Visconti. Serge Lifar explained:

"She had—and always had—a very sharp tongue. She demolished people behind their backs. You could be absolutely sure that as soon as you left her, she would start saying the worst things about you. That's why she lost almost all her friends at the end of her life. . . ."

Georges Auric, one of her "lost friends," told us:

"How she changed! As she got older, she became a different person. That is why I rarely saw her during her last years. It made me feel ill at ease. Every time I met her, she would ask me to come to see her. But I didn't want to become part of her little circle of intimates, so limited and, it must be admitted, rather suffocating. She had Jacques Chazot repeat to her the latest gossip. I had absolutely no desire to find myself at the Ritz between Chazot and a rather ferocious old lady!

"She had tremendous wit, which she used at the expense of her friends and the people around her. During her last years, her irony became extremely caustic. She became very nasty, attacking everything: the period, things, and people. I preferred to remember her the way she used to be, the incomparable Coco Chanel!"

Coco entertained no illusions about the little circle that surrounded her and in which her old friends felt so ill at ease. She even went quite far. She confided to Céline: "They come to get something out of me. But today I won't give them a cent!"

Yet to her phobia of being fleeced was added her pathological fear of being alone. Never imagining that she could be loved for what she was, she bought people, finding bitter satisfaction in displaying her scorn toward those whom she could not do without.

Not to owe anything to anyone: "It is better to give than to receive"—she had kept the good sense of the Auvergne peasant, a taste for well-kept accounts and a horror of debts. Thus she excoriated her youth spent as a poor and abandoned orphan. Nothing, neither life nor people, had ever taught her that relations between human beings could be purely disinterested. She had to pay off those she sometimes referred to as the "presences," thus giving them a significance other than her desire to feel them close to her.

To Serge Lifar, her friend for nearly fifty years, she said, after a falling-out of short duration: "Stay with me: I'll leave you everything. You'll be the richest man in the world."

Witty, funny, charming, gossipy, and enamored of social gatherings, Jacques Chazot greatly amused Mademoiselle. He told a journalist: "Mademoiselle was lavishly and spontaneously generous. One day, I admired a very pretty sapphire ring, designed by her, and she gave it to me. 'If you like it, take it.' After that, I didn't dare compliment her on any of her things."

At times stingy, tough with those who owed her money, often very generous to friends, Coco had only a sketchy idea of the value of money. All her expenses were paid by the firm, and she never carried more than a few carefully folded ten franc notes to be used as tips.

M Tranchant told us a curious anecdote on this subject: "One day I accompanied her to the airport. We were with the actress Suzy Parker, who had presented the 1954 collection. Mademoiselle Chanel suggested we have coffee before getting on the plane. We had plenty of time. So we all three went to the bar. As I was about to pay, Chanel insisted that Suzy Parker pay the bill.

" 'No, I want Suzy to pay!' she said.

"Suzy did just that and as we were getting up to leave Chanel asked her: 'What did you leave as a tip?'

" 'I don't know, one or two francs,' answered Suzy, rather taken aback.

" 'When you're with Chanel, you don't leave one or two francs as a tip!'

"Very regally, Chanel left a ten franc note on the table."

The first time she won at the races, Coco decided to give her jockey, Yves St.-Martin, a wedding present. After making inquiries as to what he wanted, she presented him with a portable television set.

"Two thousand francs!" she said. "It certainly isn't a giveaway. Well, it's done. But I should also give his bride a 'little something.' "

"And so," relates a witness, "she grabbed her jewelry box, and almost haphazardly selected an emerald worth at least three million francs. For her it was just one of many stones."

Though she could be generous, she was very possessive. She didn't like to share her friends. As we've seen, she dropped Jeanne Moreau when the latter became romantically entangled with Pierre Cardin, "that destroyer of fashion." She resented Jean Cocteau for being more famous than Pierre Reverdy* and her sentiments toward him turned to bitter hatred when he became friends with Francine Weissweiller.

"It was unbelievable," remembers Serge Lifar. "She had manuscripts of his, dedicated books, irreplaceable things. One day, around 1947, she got it into her head to burn it all. An auto-da-fe! Fortunately I was there and thus able to save quite a few things."

She had helped Cocteau financially before he attained success, and she had saved him several times from drugs. She never forgave him for no longer needing her.

"When he died in 1963, Coco called me as soon as she got the news: 'Serge, come quickly! Cocteau is going to be buried!' She attended the funeral and, afterward insisted that we dine

---

*Pierre Reverdy and Jean Cocteau remained the best of friends, however.

together. We went to Barbizon, I don't remember the name of the restaurant. In any case, it was one of the best. We ate sumptuously and drank champagne. She was beaming. 'He is gone. He is dead.' She couldn't stop repeating these words. And yet, when he had been admitted to the Académie Française, she made it a point of honor to give him one of the largest stones for his academician's sword!"

Before the war, Cocteau had drawn a striking portrait of her:

"Her spectacular liaisons, her rages, her nastiness, her fabulous jewels, her creations, her whims, her excesses, her kindness as well as her humor and generosity, all these were part of her unique, endearing, attractive, repulsive, excessive, and very human personality."

Later, he added two lines in which he summarized his own fate: "Coco? She looks at you tenderly, then nods her head, and you're condemned to death!"

But if the scathing remarks about Cocteau, Picasso, Dali, and the others, that she made during her last years fill us with indignation, we should never forget that she knew these people and helped them long before official opinion turned them into peerless paragons. She recognized their genius at a time when official criticism saw them as nothing but obscene buffoons. So can we cry sacrilege about a few cutting remarks?

Around Coco, whether in her apartment on the rue Cambon or in the grill room of the Ritz, at the mercy of Mademoiselle's rages, sometimes provoking them, sometimes appeasing them, vigilant, thoughtful, at times obsequious and always devoted, stood her ladies-in-waiting. Dressed in "Chanel," they mounted guard around Mademoiselle. *Lilou Grumbach,* the secretary, who had been hired and fired a thousand times: a young and pretty woman, slightly bohemian, Lilou is the wife of the journalist Philippe Grumbach and the sister of Serge and Christian Marquand, both film directors. *Claude Baillen,* daughter of a psychiatrist, friend, confidante, devotee, confessor, and *eminence grise* of that great priestess of her own cult, Coco, in her "temple" on the rue Cambon. *Jacqueline Citroen,* daughter of André Citroen, childhood friend of Jacques Wertheimer, a press agent whose name was mentioned in connection with Coco's succession.

Then, too, there was someone who did not quite fit into this very Parisian milieu, and whose presence at table sometimes inhibited the rest of the guests, Mademoiselle's faithful "mameluke." She forgave him the bad taste with which he sometimes dressed: light beige trousers with a black jacket. He kept the imperturbable calm and good sense of the French peasant, which he brought with him from Cabourg, his native town in Normandy, and which, paradoxically, enabled him to feel perfectly at home in Mademoiselle's refined and rarified milieu. Strong, with a red face and a monk's serenity, he was Mademoiselle's secretary, and she appreciated his meticulousness even after she had discovered him cleaning her jewels with his clumsy hands. He helped her, gave her her medicines at the prescribed hour, escorted her in her solitary Sunday walks, and was always there when the ladies-in-waiting had gone off with husbands or children. François—his real name was Jean-François Mironnet—became indispensible. He was there, and with sufficient patience, on any occasion.

A former butler at the British embassy, François entered Mademoiselle's service as a majordomo. One day she announced to her friends before sitting down at table: "François is now my secretary!" And with that he sat down at table. Pascal, the new butler, served.

Naturally there was lots of gossip, which did not bother Mademoiselle, who had developed a real affection for this patient and uncomplicated man. If people wanted to continue spreading tales about her when she was over eighty, it made no difference to her. She was used to it; it had always been so.

Then François got married. "To a trollop!" shouted Coco, jealous as usual. He became less available and took evenings and Sundays off.

She accepted the change without ever really forgiving him. Afterward, she was almost always alone when, on Sunday afternoons, she went to sit on her wrought-iron chair in the Tuileries Gardens.

She still had her hates. Fierce, monolithic, sometimes grotesque.

"It's not possible. You're going to see that old dodderer, that paranoiac?"

This outburst left Serge Lifar cold. Even though it resulted in a bitter quarrel of fifteen days' duration with Coco, he decided to go to the Elysée anyway where he and other artists had been invited by General de Gaulle.

She did not like the General. His neutralist foreign policy threatened to affect the sales of Chanel products in the United States.

Deep down, did she resent the fact that official France ignored her, never having offered her that little bit of red ribbon that she probably would have enjoyed refusing with a flourish? Perhaps. As far as she was concerned, she was not being shown much gratitude, for had she not done everything to defend her country's reputation by upholding the traditions of haute couture? But then, France's first lady, Mme de Gaulle, was not her customer. She was dressed by Jacques Heim.

"I'd like to see de Gaulle going down the Champs Elysées in chains. . . ." Thus she adopted the secret wish of several hundred thousand fellow citizens for whom France's misfortunes had begun at the Liberation. She remained the "1944 purgee" with her rancors and prejudices. But the General's departure in April 1969, his retreat to Ireland, and the grandiose dignity with which he accepted his defeat provoked her admiration: "He shouldn't have been dismissed that way. You'll see, he'll be mourned when he dies."

His sudden death at dusk one fall evening inspired in her a cry that hid a secret wish: "I would like to die like he did."

In the meantime, she *was* invited to the Elysée. Claude Pompidou had been her customer for a long time ("My dear, one does not wear red when one is the wife of the President of the Republic.")

"It was in June 1970," André-Louis Dubois told us.

"Mademoiselle arrived in the President's private dining room, on the second floor of the Elysée. She was slightly surprised by the very modern decor that met her eye: a Knoll table, a Vasarely rug. Dressed in a straw-white Chanel suit, she was extraordinarily at ease, making conversation with Mme Pompidou, while the President, very interested, even intrigued, by her personality, listened, intervening rarely in the conversation—as is his habit. It was delightful meal. Mademoiselle, very flattered to be invited by the President of the Republic, forgot about the 'Chanel style,' which consisted in pushing people around by pushing words at them. She was exquisitely civil. We stayed quite late, and the word 'fashion' was never mentioned.

"Yet when we left, she stopped for a moment and contemplated the façade of the Elysée, then she turned to me: 'You know, I have gone by this house a thousand times, I even lived nearby. Well! I never imagined that one day I would be invited here!'

" 'Why?'

"And Coco answered regally: 'In my day, one did not invite one's dressmaker!' "

And the dressmaker climbed back into her Cadillac. She drove off with her chauffeur—pardon us—her "mechanic." Coco always referred to "my mechanic" and never to "my chauffeur."

That was how she was.

18.

Mademoiselle and the Solitude
of the Famous

SHE was ageless. She had become a personage, almost an institution, whose witty remarks, edicts, maxims, and anecdotes were periodically collected by a delighted press. Once and for all she condemned everything she saw or heard about.

Her colleagues, of course, first, last, and always:

"They don't like women. . . ."

. . . the mini-skirt?

"That idiotic fad is the limit. . . ."

. . . the pill?

"How do you expect children not to hear about all those stories?"

. . . fashion journalists?

"They ought to go back to school and learn what fashion is all about, cutting, fabrics. . . ."

. . . De Gaulle?

"That old swinger?"

. . . Brigitte Bardot?

"She's much too sloppy for me to waste my time giving her fashion advice."

. . . movies?

"They're always talking these days."

. . . youth?

"Youth must be replaced with mystery."

. . . old age?

"Horrible!"

. . . solitude?

"It's dreadful."

. . . marriage?

"It lasts too long."

. . . her friends (especially those she could not do without)?

"Always using me."

. . . The United States (even though *she* would understand if Chanel closed her doors)?

"The country of cheap goods, that's the horror of it."

. . . France?

"Its money is no longer worth anything."

. . . the French?

"When I am abroad and meet an agitated type with a frantic look in his eyes, he doesn't have to open his mouth. I recognize a compatriot immediately."

. . . Elizabeth of England?

"I would like to dress her. That good deed would not go unrewarded on Judgment Day."

. . . Algerians?

"Why did we give them Algeria?"

. . . doctors?

"They begin by kissing your hand and then. . . ."

. . . her seamstresses?

"They rob me blind."

. . . her mannequins?

"You think it is fun to kneel in front of these girls. To begin with they smell bad."

. . . Maurice Chevalier?

"An old man who sings, 'She had wee little tits.' "

. . . student protest?

"They should be sent out to break stones on the roads."

. . . Nureyev?

"If you've known Nijinski, you have no desire to see Nureyev."

. . . Nijinski?

"Aside from his great leap in the *Specter of the Rose*. . . ."

She no longer liked anything or anybody—except for a few memories (Pierre Reverdy, the duke, Diaghilev). She could love only the dead, for they could no longer talk back, and—of course—Coco Chanel, that personage whom she so lovingly fashioned for posterity, playing on humility—"I'm just a poor little seamstress"—and pride—"When I'm dead, who will be able to do this?"

By "this" she meant her dresses and suits, which she would work on for hours long before she "prepared" the collections in front of a group of carefully selected journalists. It was her big number. They always left completely spellbound, drunk with her words and gestures: "I saw Coco Chanel at work," they'd murmur.

In contrast, Coco would snap: "The idiots, I could have done any old thing. They would bleat anyway."

She didn't like journalists (especially fashion reporters) and found it difficult to forgive them for having made so much fuss over the small couturiers' mini-skirt and especially for having partially ignored her before her big success in 1970.

"You see, most of the women who edit fashion magazines don't know how to do their jobs. Most of them don't know a thing. They launch any old thing into fashion without ever worrying if it will be becoming to women. That's why I saw a woman going out to a party dressed in oilcloth!

"I know of some women's magazines who in their desire to exploit several fields have opened their own boutiques, all over the place. This naturally forces the editors to think about business first and then about fashion."

The exception to this condemnation were U.S. journalists, for Coco was indulgent of the United States, which had followed her more than any other designer.

"In America, it's different, it's much healthier. Editors of women's magazines really do their job. Their principal concern is for fashion, and they are interested in all segments of the fashion world (manufacturers of fabrics and accessories as well as couture houses). That's very healthy. They work for Seventh Avenue and that's fine."

A fantastic publicity-getter, she knew how to receive journalists, to detain and fascinate them. And yet it was well known that "Mademoiselle does not receive journalists." She needed them just as they needed her. She adored this personage of hers whose every word sparked, causing scandals. She was a sacred cow in every sense of the word. And she never disappointed her public.

The declared enemy of ugliness, vulgarity, and sham, she had drunk at the very source of the spirit of arts and letters, and better than anyone she could unmask the ridiculous and the fake. Also, laying down the law on morals and mores may have helped her forget some of those secret wounds of her youth.

She did not lack for platforms from which to speak, and she had nothing better to do than to serve her fame. To live longer? Was that possible? Maybe Coco had already ceased living a long time ago, except perhaps at night, when stretched on her white bed in her attic room, her eyes desperately sought dawn's first glimmer of light. She had nothing left outside her public life and her Swiss millions: few if any relatives, almost no friends, nothing but a play in which to perform. Only Mademoiselle and her fashion firm remained, each pushing for the greater glory of the other, the projection of an image for the edification of future generations.

It was easy, for Coco was good copy. She was much in demand for television, musical comedy, and newspaper articles.

It was only in 1968 that she agreed to appear on television. And it was almost by chance and because Jacques Chazot had asked her. Of course, she had a purpose. She wanted to strike a blow at mini- and maxi-skirts in front of millions of viewers. Her last collection had sold 30 percent more than the preceding one.

And, of course, she may simply have been tired of always refusing.

"I don't mind showing life in a real French fashion house," she said. "Many people have already asked for permission to film me. I've always thrown them out. Including François Reichenbach. I can't stand the idea of a man who films Brigitte Bardot coming into my establishment. I detest vulgarity. But I trust Jacques Chazot. He is a nice young man."

"The nice young man" was overjoyed.

"Mademoiselle has just given me the most fantastic present."

Jacques Chazot, the Opéra-Comique dancer, the man who waltzes with debutantes, he whom one never sees without Françoise Sagan or Bernard Buffet, whom some consider indispensable at a party and others an unavoidable sponger, had for several months been turning over in his head an idea: a television series on famous women.

When he proposed his idea to the French television service, the directors took their time in coming to a decision. Meanwhile,

Chazot, who had known Mademoiselle for five years, saw her almost every day. Chazot explained Coco's willingness to appear:

"With me she knew that nothing would be distorted, that she would see and hear exactly what she would say. And then, too, I think that friendship had something to do with it."

At least we can be sure that she felt safer with Chazot then with the talented and indiscreet Reichenbach, who characteristically caught on film the fleeting, telling glance and who used his cameras to reach the inner soul.

Finally the French television service woke up and agreed to the proposal, but all the television crews were in Grenoble for the Winter Olympics. The filming would have to be postponed. Chazot and Mademoiselle had agreed to have the interview two days before the collection and to film the collection. Fifteen days were too long to wait. He had to find another way. Guy Béart suggested that he produce the program himself and hire a cameraman. The deal was quickly concluded.

No rehearsals, no set questions. The filming started at three o'clock, with two cameras and one sound man. Chazot and Mademoiselle talked for twenty-five minutes. Her last sentence was: "Well, if they're not pleased with this, what do they want?"

It was decided not to cut anything from the interview. Inside the cutting room, Chazot listened and ran the film over and over again. He was frantic. Every fifteen minutes he telephoned Mademoiselle. She comforted him.

"Don't worry, my little Jacques, I'm sure it will be very good."

Two days later the film was run for Mademoiselle. Jacques was worried; he brought Françoise Sagan with him. The lights went up again. All Mademoiselle said was: "It is very good. If you don't sell this film for lots of money, you're an amateur, and I hate amateurs."

Chazot still did not realize that he held a gold mine in his hands. The French service immediately used the program as a special, throwing out its regular schedule.

The Americans wasted no time in inviting Chazot over to England to discuss business. The Germans, Italians, and English followed suit. Chazot was forced to hire an agent. He refused to speak about the sums offered him.

"If I talk, the tax collector and the cadgers will come running," said society's favorite sponger.

Already he was planning his future programs: Callas, Grace of Monaco, Marlene, and, of course, Sagan.

"It won't be easy for the one who goes after Mademoiselle. She was fantastic. She dominates the screen. In any case, thanks to Chanel, I know that when the days come when I'll no longer be able to dance, I can do something else."

In her room in the Ritz, Coco watched the small TV screen as Mademoiselle Chanel wrote off hairdressers, jewelers, other couturiers, fashion magazines, ready-to-wear manufacturers, nightclubs, television, night owls, Courrèges, women, China—everything.

A: I hate mini-skirts, I think they're immodest, I think they're ugly, I can't understand why women wear them. There's not a man who likes them. So what is the point of making them? Whom does it please? Why show knees, which are rarely pretty. It is pretentious and without modesty, two things I abhor. I haven't met a single man who has told me mini-skirts were pretty. . . .

Our fashion magazines constantly disparage us. Ready-to-wear, this and that, all of which should be limited to certain neighborhoods, certain purses; it should not make up a fashion magazine. We are living in a dreadful nightmare.

Q: Mademoiselle, do you think that fashion such as you conceive it is an art?

A: Not at all, it is a trade that should be carried out with a great deal of rigor. It is a style and not a fashion. I think fashions change much too often. What is the point of having a different fashion for winter and spring? I do not approve of the Mao style; I think it's disgraceful and idiotic. In such a sad age as this, the idea of amusing oneself with such games, with such formidable countries, I think it's dreadful.

Do you think that a woman looks younger when she shows her knees and her thighs? I think that it ages her, and moreover makes her look ridiculous, which is the most absurd thing of all.

It will end, for I think that the ridiculous disappears or it kills, and that is awful. In times such as ours, women owe it to themselves to be very feminine. They don't help; they burn everything. They drink too much, women drink much too much. They think it makes them intelligent.

After the program was shown, she received a huge amount of mail, all approving.

"And all that just to see a woman of sixty play the role of a woman of eighty-six with dances and songs. This must be the beginning of the counter-revolution," wrote a famous critic.

Katharine Hepburn was the star in a musical comedy about Coco. On November 13, 1969, when the ticket office of the Mark Hellinger Theater opened, the waiting line stretched around Broadway.

Two hundred fifty-three costumes, 53 actors, 35 musicians, and $900,000; producer, Frederic Brisson; costumes and sets, Cecil Beaton; book, Alan Jay Lerner; music, André Previn. Everything was ready for a huge success! Six weeks before the opening, planned for October 18, the ticket office announced that advance receipts had set a record: over $2 million.

Will she come? Or won't she? Coco hesitated, blew hot and cold, had an evening dress made (the first in years). Finally she decided not to go, giving her health as an excuse.

In fact, she was not very enthusiastic about the project. She had accepted because she couldn't overlook the terrific publicity inherent in the production of such a musical comedy. But she remained rather half-hearted about it.

Frederic Brisson first had the idea in 1962 while on a trip to Paris. Coco did not finally agree until 1965. It had been difficult.

"Rosalind Russell, 55, and Mademoiselle Chanel, 84, fell into agreement as well as into each other's arms," reported an over-zealous press agent. The announcement was a bit premature, for Coco caught herself: "Rosalind Russell? She's too old." A few days later, Rosalind Russell, who happened to be Brisson's wife, announced that she had given up the role.

Coco wanted the action to take place in 1913: "my best period." But the Americans had already decided and their choice —1953— was irreversible.

The musical takes place in Paris at the rue Cambon. When the curtain goes up it is 1953, immediately following her first post-war collection, which was so severely criticized by the press and snubbed by the French. When the final curtain falls, it is three months later and the atmosphere is one of general euphoria, the result of the U.S. buyers' enthusiastic reception of her new collection. Like the good sheriff in a Western, the buyers rehabil-itate her models, as in fact happened. Yet it bored Coco to hear it all sung on Broadway. Film flashbacks throughout the play permitted the heroine to see on the screen the men who had played such important roles in her life: the Grand Duke Alexandrovitch (Dimitri), Charles (Boy Capel), the Duke of Glenallen (Westminster) Lesage (Paul Iribe). Naturally these were very rapid flashbacks, for Coco did not wish her private life to be too lengthily dwelt upon.

The high spot of the show was the finale, a spectacular parade —a backward glance at fashion seen through the dresses created by Chanel from 1916 to 1970. Not a detail, not a jewel, is missing, even down to the perfume, the famous No. 5, which wafts from the stage down to the audience.

As the star Katharine Hepburn was proposed. Coco agreed, flattered that one of the most popular actresses in the United States had been picked for the role. Katharine Hepburn would not be too old!

But many things did annoy Coco, especially some of the outrageous statements made by Brisson's press agents, whose releases were, in her opinion, much too faithfully copied by the French press:

"Katharine Hepburn has spent entire days observing Coco. She walks, talks, and knows how to rip apart a fabric just like Mademoiselle Chanel. Until now Chanel was the only one who could rip apart in that way."

Actually, Coco and Katharine dined together only once.

"Coco asked Henri de Curiel, genealogical expert, to draw up her family tree. It seems that his researches were conclusive: the couturière's antecedents go back as far as Saint Louis."

"Soon they'll have me descending from Joan of Arc. Well, as long as they don't burn me on the stake at the finale," Coco grumbled.

What about the costumes? It was, of course, impossible not to have a controversy over the costumes designed by Cecil Beaton. Immediately after the opening the fashion critics tore into Cecil Beaton, who had designed close to 250 costumes in the Chanel style for *Coco.*

The fashion critics accused him of having designed clothes that were different from those designed by Coco Chanel. Cecil Beaton answered that they were exactly what Chanel would have designed, had she designed them for the stage. A theater is not a drawing room or a boulevard. Theatrical costumes, as well as the entire theater itself, must interpret reality, not copy it.

On this delicate point, Coco kept her mouth shut, at least in public. But she wouldn't go to New York.

The show was a success, thanks to Katharine Hepburn, who was terrified but acted wonderfully.

"It's dreadful. My singing voice is the most painful thing I've ever had to listen to. I must have been drunk when I accepted this part," she said.

Yet no other star was as capable of playing this role as Hepburn was. Parisians privileged enough to call Gabrielle Chanel "Coco," instead of "Mademoiselle," are no more numerous than Americans who are allowed to address the "African Queen" by anything but a respectful "Miss Hepburn." The right to use "Kate" belongs to a handful of intimate friends. In the world of show business, where first names are more often used than last names, Katharine Hepburn is an outstanding exception.

Mlle Chanel and Miss Hepburn both had become legends in their own lifetimes. In 1969 the theater made it possible for one to perpetuate the legend of the other.

"I've always thought we were alike, Coco and I. I've always thought we were both women who never let themselves be intimidated by the world, who never changed style just to conform to public opinion. Like me, she is practical, a fighter and yet vulnerable. Her talent for survival fascinates me. She has taken some very tough blows but she has never hesitated to stand in the front lines," Katharine Hepburn said.

From the day that she accepted the role of Coco in a musical comedy, Katharine Hepburn, who had never sung, started to work on her voice eight hours a day.

After a six months' run, Katharine Hepburn left the show. Over ten actresses, tried out for the role, declined to take it on, declaring themselves incapable of dancing and singing for two and half hours on stage. Finally, a French actress accepted: Danièle Darrieux. She enchanted the critics and had a tremendous personal success. Yet if most successful artistic interpretation is the result of a close identification between the model and her stage counterpart, in this case it was the opposite. Never had a heroine and her interpreter been as different, one from the other, as Gabrielle Chanel and Danièle Darrieux in fact were.

The pampered child of an upper-class Bordeaux family, Danièle Darrieux, as François Mauriac wrote, "belonged to that group of adolescents who, in Bordeaux, knew how to do everything: compose a Bonnard picture with a bouquet of wild flowers, receive with perfect tact, an art worthy of the 'Grand Siècle,' rich shipowners or pretentious members of the vineyard dynasties."

When barely fourteen years old, Danièle Darrieux triumphed in her first film, *Carnet de bal.* A brilliant career opened up before her: it looked as though everything were going her way. She has a faultless talent, and backed by innate gifts, her range as an actress is very diversified. Everything in life has been easy for her. To interpret Chanel represented a real challenge. She succeeded. Perhaps because she was French and elegant she understood Coco and was able to breathe life into the part.

But the "Hepburn miracle" did not reproduce itself, and audiences dwindled. *Coco* closed on Broadway. Darrieux came back to France. A few months later Katharine Hepburn agreed to go with the show on a tour of large U.S. cities. Again it was a triumph!

In August 1970 Coco showed what was to be the last collection she herself would present to the three hundred privileged enough to have been invited. Here, too, it was a triumph: "One of the most beautiful collections," said one critic. Best of all, fashions had returned to the Chanel length; there were few or no mini- or maxi-skirts. It was a return on the part of practically everyone to a kind of "classicism," but not without a certain boldness. Seventeen years after her comeback and after her triumph in the United States, Coco at last was the uncontested queen of France.

The excitement of the collection over, she returned to her immense solitude. Few friends, many acquaintances.

Again she had won. But was she any happier? A year earlier she had finished her televised interview with these words: "A woman who is unloved is a worthless woman, no matter what her age: young, old, mother, mistress, anything you want. A woman who is unloved is a lost woman. She can die, it isn't very important."

There was nothing left for her to do but to die. And she did, but with great chic.

19.

Death

THAT day, for the first time, I heard her talk about her death. It had suddenly seemed to her to be a possibility. She, who had never spoken about it," Robert Badinter, her lawyer since 1967, told us.

That day, December 24, 1970, Christmas Eve, reminded Coco of her unhappy past.

"I hate holidays," she said. With the workshops on the rue Cambon closed, she was just a very old lady alone with her destiny and thoughts, idle and useless. She exhausted herself with boredom. Far from the frenzy of creation, she watched the hours slip by. Death now became a possibility.

Death had often struck down those whom she had loved. She remembered: "In the next room, my mother was dying. We walked on tiptoes."

Then there was Julia, the unhappy sister. Antoinette, the sister whom she had loved and protected. Boy Capel, Misia, Westminster, Balsan, Dimitri, Gérard Mille, her favorite decorator and Maggy van Zuylen.

She had often witnessed death.

"Listen . . . listen. In three days, God's soldiers will shoot me," screamed Raymond Radiguet, the overloved child of literature and glory, to a horrified Coco as he was dying. In Venice, Diaghilev, ravaged by fever, had only been able to smile at her.

On the terrace of La Pausa, Iribe had died in her arms, suddenly struck down after that tennis match.

"Yes, that day," recalled Robert Badinter, "she was really strange. Curiously distant and yet at the same time close. She confided certain things to me. She told me that she wished her fortune to help encourage young artists, and to bring succor to the unfortunate.

"I never saw her again. My relations with her? Always excellent"—Maître Badinter smiled ironically—"even though I am a Jew. I always tried to calm Mademoiselle and especially I tried to make sure she was happy."

On that December 24, stores crowded with last-minute shoppers displayed a new perfume in a bottle identical to that of its elder: No. 19. Almost fifty years after No. 5, this last perfume was like a farewell to all women—an exit such as Mademoiselle alone could make.

"She suggested the formula and supervised the perfecting of it with extraordinary care and vigilance," Robert Chaillet told us.

"The perfume company was not terribly enthusiastic, nor, for that matter, were the distributors, who feared that it might torpedo No. 5. At first Mademoiselle insisted; later she demanded. And, once again, she was proved right. Sales of No. 5 continue to go up while No. 19 is making its way with a younger clientele.

"Every week for over a year, I brought her three different perfume bottles marked 1, 2, 3. She sprayed herself with them from head to toe and then she wandered around the fashion house waiting for reactions. If the salesgirls said, 'Oh! Mademoiselle smells good!' she was delighted. If nothing was said to her she would telephone me, furious, 'This perfume is awful, I don't want any. It stinks! Nobody noticed it!'

"She made another test. There was always a wood fire burning in her drawing room. She would put perfume on the fire shovel, and if it filled the room with a fragrant smell, it was good."

Finally the formula was found; all that was left was to find a name.

"We thought of many things. At first, Mademoiselle wanted to call it 'Coco,' like the musical comedy. We didn't all agree. 'Coco' did not mean much. It sounded a bit like 'Communist,' like 'My Coco,' 'rococo,' 'cocaine.'

"In short, it was not a very pleasing name.

"One day, having already ordered labels with the name 'Coco' on them, she decided that in fact it was not at all suitable. So she named it No. 19."

Why No. 19? Coco explained why shortly before her death, to Carmen Tessier.

"It is the date of my birthday, August 19. I was born under the sign of the lion. I am a Leo, and like him I unsheath my claws to prevent anyone from hurting me. But believe me, I suffer much more when I claw than when I am clawed.

"Well, what do you think of this perfume," she said, spraying us again. "Imagine, because of it a man stopped me in the street. Coming out of the Ritz, I suddenly felt a hand on my shoulder and I turned around to see an unknown face. I was just about to tell him off in no uncertain terms, when he said to me, with an American accent, 'Excuse me, I am with two friends who want to know the name of your perfume.'

"I said to him: 'Follow me, all of you.' So I took them to Chanel's where they recognized me, for they had seen the musical *Coco* in New York. To be stopped in the street by a man at my age, that's not bad, is it?

"But how old are you, Mademoiselle?"

"A hundred, of course, and forever."

Forever—just a few more weeks. Just time enough to launch her last perfume, to finish her collection, and to dictate her last wishes about the disposal of her fortune. Coco Chanel's affairs were in order.

"No one had ever seen it. It was a cheap little wallet of the sort you could buy in a popular bazaar. Very worn, it was buried in the bottom of her bag. Inside there was a yellowed photograph of my father taken during his military service and a few holy pictures, some of which were very old. On the back of one of these: 'In case of serious accident or urgent hospitalization, I request near me the presence of a Catholic priest. This is my express wish. Gabrielle Chanel, 31 rue Cambon.' "

With great emotion Mme Gabrielle Labrunie, Coco's grand-niece, the daughter of André Palasse, told us about this discovery. In her mid-forties, Mme Labrunie has features and an expression that bear a marked resemblance to the person she used to call "Aunty Coco," and for whom she was "Tiny." Like her aunt she has a rare distinction, the opposite of fake "elegance," that insists upon a precise and descriptive manner of speech.

Coco was her godmother. Her godfather was the Duke of Westminister (until his death, he sent Tiny a present every year).

Having always kept herself in the shadows, Tiny was one of the few people whom Coco often saw alone, far from future memorialists and the usual entourage. She revealed to us a Coco whom we had suspected without ever really finding, for she had eluded us just as she had evaded all those who had known her: a warm Coco.

"I remember, when I was seven or eight years old, playing with a balloon in her room at the Ritz. Years later, I came to see her with one of my sons who was then about six or seven. She asked him if he was doing well in school.

" 'How do you spell rhinoceros?' My son hesitated, but I saw Coco thinking it over—suddenly she changed the subject. She probably was not sure how to spell it herself. The next day my son received a fabulous album all about animals published by Delagrave. The rhinoceros was circled in red ink."

A laughing Coco.

"I remember her one evening before the war. She was getting ready to go to a costume ball given by Etienne de Beaumont. The theme for the evening was 'The Forest.' Her costume, a dress meant to look like a huge fern, had just been brought to her. When she had put on all that gear, she burst out laughing.

" 'I look absolutely ridiculous! No, really, I can't see myself dressed like this.'

"She took off the costume, slipped on a pair of trousers and a navy blue sweater and covered her face with black. She loved to put on blackface. The only thing she kept was the fern-shaped bolero."

A jealous Coco, very much attached to her family.

"She had a very strong character. So did I. When I was young, I had frequent disputes with her. I didn't let myself be pushed around. One day after we had exchanged rather heated words, I said: 'I don't need you or your money. I can earn my own living.' I left, banging the door, and went to the firm's accountant to tell him not to send me the monthly allowance that my aunt, generous as she was, gave me. Then I came back to tell her: 'But you're crazy. I didn't want that.' And I left.

"A few months later, her maid called me up on the telephone. 'Mademoiselle speaks often about you. You should come and see her. Not seeing you makes her sad.' Of course, Coco had asked her to call. I went the next day. She greeted me exactly as though we had parted the day before without ever mentioning our quarrel."

An apprehensive, unhappy, and vulnerable Coco.

"During the last few years she became extremely fragile. One had the impression that a puff of wind could knock her over. Even though she pretended not to notice it, she suffered from the servility shown by those around her and understood perfectly well that they were not always completely disinterested. She became embittered. She could no longer stand being contradicted, and I was always very careful not to argue with her for fear of harming her. One day she took me by the shoulder and said: 'Actually, it's you who has been right in life. You are much happier than I am. You have a husband and children. I have nothing. I am alone with all my millions.'

"Few people really understood her. 'She was against everything, believing only in herself,' said those who thought they knew her. They did not know her well. Her 'against everything' was her defense, her armor. Beneath it all she was very sensitive, very vulnerable."

A Coco who was about to depart—on Sunday, January 10, 1971, around 8:30 P.M.

Hotels and circuses have one law in common. Nothing, not even death or taxes, must stop the show. That night in the Espadon, the grill room at the Ritz where Coco dined so often, the waiters performed the same unchangeable ballet around the crowded tables.

Nothing distinguished their gestures from those they performed daily. Except perhaps. . . .

Over there, near the entrance, almost outside the room ("Eating in the middle of other people's food smells," Coco often said. "How awful!") near the glassed-in bay, her table was empty. Head waiters, waiters, and helpers swerved from their course as they approached, keeping a respectful distance between it and themselves.

They had just learned the news: Mademoiselle is dead.

Up in the room, with tears in her eyes, Céline had just finished dressing Mademoiselle in her favorite suit: green, pink, and beige, its colors slightly faded. Then she pulled the sheet up to her heart. On the night table, Stravinsky's icon was bathed in subdued light filtering through an old-fashioned pink crepe-de-Chine lamp shade.

A few drops of liquid still dripped on the carpet from a now useless syringe. Camphor. The doctor later approved of Céline's actions: "I could not have done anything more myself."

She had returned from a drive in the car late in the afternoon. Once more, the long Cadillac had driven through the Paris streets, which that day were drenched in pale sunshine, much too cold to heat the bones of a very old lady.

Céline recalled: "When she came in, she said, 'I am very tired.' She lay down on her bed in her clothes. I couldn't get her to take them off. Only her shoes. She watched the television for a few minutes and then asked me to turn it off. She lay there in the twilight, drowsing. I never left her room.

"Later she sat up. 'I'm going to eat here,' she said. She read over the restaurant's menu.

" 'I'm suffocating . . . Jeanne . . . the window.' I rushed over. 'It hurts.' She held her hands over her chest, her face taut. I grabbed the syringe. She tried to break the phial without success while I bared her hip. I struck the needle in. She pushed the syringe herself. As I was taking out the needle she murmured: 'So that's the way one dies.' I knew immediately that it was all over. I rushed to the phone. When I came back to her, she was absolutely still. I closed her eyes."

In the office where we had been talking, Céline finished her tale. Her glasses were damp with tears.

The funeral took place in the church of the Madeleine, on Thursday. The religious service surprised certain people. Even among her intimate friends, very few knew her true religious sentiments. The coffin was soon covered by masses of mostly white flowers: roses, gardenias, orchids. On top, in vivid contrast, lay two wreaths of bright red roses: one from Lucchino Visconti; the other from the fashion association.

The homage rendered her by the association was unanimous. All were present: Balmain, Castillo, Balenciaga, Marc

Bohan, Michel Goma, Yves St.-Laurent. Paco Rabanne and Courrèges came. Only Pierre Cardin was missing, unable to attend, but he sent someone to represent him. Perhaps all these couturiers, none of whom had been spared at one time or another from Coco's attacks, felt gratitude toward her, for by upholding the standards of couture she had brought credit to all of them.

In the first row, to the right of the coffin, the mannequins, dressed in Chanel suits, stood throughout the ceremony. Behind them, forewomen, seamstresses, and helpers expressed their silent tribute to the Grande Mademoiselle.

Even before the ceremony began, the church was full. The crowds joined Paris society, and in the throng friends and intimates had a hard time getting through: Serge Lifar, André-Louis Dubois, Carmen Tessier, Salvador Dali, Lady Abdy, Madame Henri Bernstein, Jacques Chazot, several Rothschilds, Robert Bresson, Jeanne Moreau, Juliette Achard, Hervé Mille, Bettina—everyone.

Only the inflexibility of protocol prevented Mme Pompidou from attending the funeral.

What would become of the fashion house?

It would continue; this was announced very quickly.

On January 26, there was a crowd at the rue Cambon such as had not been seen since the reopening in 1954. It was Mademoiselle's last collection.

Even the mirrored staircase was jammed with people, unknown faces, for that matter, who during Mademoiselle's lifetime would never have dared to brave this inner sanctum, reserved to the intimates only.

The press of the world held its breath. With the first model, a pink suit, everyone felt they were viewing an apparition. Nostalgically, they watched the long parade of pink, beige, and white suits—some with short jackets, others with longer ones—dresses, fake lumber jackets, tunic skirts, knitted two-piece outfits, coats, dresses with deep kick pleats, beautiful evening dresses made of organza and English embroidery. All the accessories—the refinement of the blouses, the belts, the long sparkling watch chains, the ties, the boater, and the catogan—recreated the magic of an era that even the mirrors failed to capture.

Dressed in a black suit with white collar, seated in the crowd between Mme Zorine, wife of the Russian ambassador and Mrs. Watson, wife of the U.S. ambassador, sat Mme Pompidou, who had insisted on being present.

Coco's work is now continued by her forewomen with the help of Gaston Berthelot, a former designer for Dior. But it is still the Chanel style that the famous house on the rue Cambon presents every six months.

Today Coco Chanel rests in the Lausanne cemetery, whose entrance bears two verses of the Gospel according to St. Matthew, engraved in the stone. To the right: "Watch therefore, for ye know neither the day nor the hour." To the left: "Blessed are they that mourn: for they shall be comforted."

On her tomb, white chrysanthemums framed by clipped yews have replaced the yellow and blue pansies. The flowers change according to the seasons.

Soon a stele will be erected behind the grave. "My aunt," Mme Labrunie confided to us, "always said: 'When I die, I don't want a stone on my head. Should I wake up, it would prevent me from getting up.'

"Her name, *Gabrielle Chanel, 1883-1971,* will be engraved in the pink marble stele. At the top, five little lions' heads, her sign of the zodiac, will be carved in the stone in the shape of medals. These heads will be like those on the buttons she used for some of her suits."

Mme Labrunie, who was wearing a Chanel suit, showed us one of the buttons. "At the bottom of the stele, a little cross will be carved into the stone."

What has happened to Coco's fortune?

Coco had promised so much, and her "friends" were so numerous. For a while, a few of them cluttered up the waiting room of the Paris representative of her executor, who lives in Zurich. Practically all the Chanels of France and Navarre showed up.

What follows is Coco's will in all its brevity:

Probated before the Justice of the Peace of the Lausanne District Court, on the 17th of February 1971.
[signed by the justice of the Peace]
This is my last will and testament.

I designate as my sole heir and legatee the Coga Foundation of Vaduz.

[here followed by the name of the executor.]

Lausanne,
11 October 1965.
Gabrielle Chanel

Coco had never been able to get used to the idea that her hard-earned money would some day end up in the coffers of a government of which she did not approve. Moreover, had she not done enough for France, more than the vast majority of her compatriots? Did she not bring into the public treasury huge sums in foreign currencies, especially dollars, every year?

In France she was merely a privileged client of a deluxe Paris hotel and the director of a fashion house owned by a Swiss company; therefore, she had declared her residence to be Lausanne. Upon her death, Mademoiselle's fortune was left to the Coga Foundation (*Co* for "Coco"; *ga* for "Gabrielle"). A trustee, the executor named in the will, Mademoiselle Chanel's Zurich lawyer, sits on the board of directors of the foundation.

His representative in Paris explained to us in detail the terms of the will.

"It is the duty of the foundation to dispose of Mademoiselle's fortune according to the wishes she expressed on different occasions to her executors, her lawyers, and her closest friends, among them André-Louis Dubois. We often asked her to write them down, but she always refused. She refused to talk about her death.

"Nevertheless her wishes are perfectly clear and the foundation has a double mission.

"The first involved the continuation of what she did during her lifetime for members of her family and of her immediate circle [former servants, employees, and needy friends]. In short, 'Mademoiselle's pensions' must continue to be paid. This poses no problem.

"The second is a much more delicate matter: Mademoiselle wished that a large part of the fortune she had accumulated through her work be used either to help suffering people or to encourage young artists.

"She often said: 'New talents will have to be encouraged.'

"She also said that she considered it a dreadful hardship not to be able to use one's hands. She felt this all the more strongly because she herself had suffered from temporary paralysis of her right hand.

" 'Something will have to be done for artisans who are victims of accidents.'

"She was especially interested in those who like herself worked with their hands.

"These were Mademoiselle's last wishes. The Vaduz* Foundation can take care of all private charities with no difficulty. As for dispensing help to young artists, it will probably be necessary to set up an organization, with headquarters in Zurich, or better still in Lausanne, Mademoiselle's legal residence, to authorize persons competent in the artistic field to distribute sums of money to a selected number of young artists.

"How should this be done? Should one or two fairly important prizes be awarded in the glare of publicity or should a greater number of more modest and less publicized grants be made to a greater number of young artists?

"The executor is in the process of setting up as flexible a system as possible in order to assure that Mademoiselle Chanel's last wishes be honored: to continue to help those closest to her, to encourage young talent, and to help handicapped artisans."

Mme Labrunie, Coco's grand-niece, worries.

"Now that my aunt is gone, I would like her generosity to be carried on, but with great discretion. I don't want anything to be done in a spectacular way—a Chanel Prize or a Chanel Foundation. My aunt often expressed the desire that her name be forgotten after her death. She accepted a certain amount of personal publicity in the interest of business. Today it makes no sense. Furthermore, a Chanel Foundation would especially benefit the Chanel firm by endowing it with a certain moral prestige. Everybody would think of a Chanel Prize as being offered by the firm rather than by my aunt."

To find out more we went to Zurich to see Coco Chanel's principal executor, her Swiss lawyer. In the Dolder hills, in a discreetly luxurious villa overlooking the city, we found ourselves in the presence of a short, slender man. In his seventies, he looks ten years younger. He has a subdued voice and his blue

---

*Vaduz, Lichtenstein.

eyes look straight out at you from behind spectacles. Despite his apparently jovial manner, one senses an unyielding iron will.

For a long time, he was lawyer for several Hollywood greats, among whom were Carl Laemmle, Sam Spiegel, Joseph Pasternak. "Then, one day, I realized that if I continued having clients from the movie world, I would soon die of a heart attack!" he said.

"In the course of my long career, I have only had two women clients, one is the head of an important Zurich business and the other was Mademoiselle Chanel, my client for thirty years. During all that time we never had a single disagreeable word.

"When Coco came to see me, she relaxed. 'How do you expect me to be happy in Paris?' she would say. 'I am surrounded with nothing but hysterical women and pederasts!'

"Mademoiselle loved Switzerland, which to her represented security in all its forms. I think that Switzerland reassured her. Here, her greatest luxury was to drive across the country in her car, stopping to look at the scenery or to lunch in a tavern."

Her lawyer is extremely reticent when he speaks about Mademoiselle's affairs and fortune.

"Nobody ever knew that I was her lawyer. It is the rule in our profession never to give the name of our clients. I can talk to you about her now only because she is dead.

"Chanel did not have luxurious tastes. She could have lived between four white-washed walls, with only a bed, a chair, and a plain wooden table.

"One day in 1965, she came to see me and told me that she wished to draw up her will. It was the simplest will I have ever drawn."

Her lawyer told us what he thought of Mademoiselle's relations with Pierre Wertheimer:

"Had Wertheimer not existed, we would have had to invent him. He had the gift of annoying Coco. Then her fighting spirit showed itself. Attacking Wertheimer gave her an incentive. It may even have been at the source of her creative genius.

"Let's say that she detested him cordially, and that when he died she missed him a great deal!"

"And the foundation?" we asked.

"Chanel's wish was to have no publicity after her death. The money she left [ten million dollars or so, they say—perhaps more] has a purpose and it's working."

Her lawyer had very little more to add. He said: "During the last years of her life Mademoiselle Chanel often repeated to me: 'All I want is tranquility. I hope that they will let me rest in peace after my death.' I respect her wish."

In Paris, the rue Cambon continues. The Chanel style cannot die. It will live on, as though, reflected in the mirrors, Mademoiselle were still there to inspire the models.

Epilogue

In the preface of his *Life of Napoleon,* the nineteenth-century French writer Stendhal notes: "Everybody agrees that the narrator should tell the whole truth. But in order to do that, he must have the courage to enter into the minutest details. It seems to me that is the only way of overcoming the reader's distrust."

Coco Chanel lacked the courage to enter into those minutest details. She never really told Chanel's story.

So, discarding literary disguises, we started out in search of things past, in pursuit of the real Chanel, to find that swarthy and taciturn little animal, so at ease in her peasant childhood redolent of the clean aroma of waxed floors and saintly habits; for that thirteen-year-old peasant named Gabrielle was the only person who possessed the power to reveal to us the secret of Coco and the truth of Mademoiselle. It was she who confided to Truman Capote: "Cut off my head and I am thirteen years old."

She trailed her youth behind her like an incurable torment: thirteen, the age of childish caprices and womanly passions, sudden outbursts of anger and of irrepressible wild laughter, sly smiles and moments of heartfelt generosity, "life and death" oaths and the perverse cruelty of the innocent.

However, with time's passing, the cruelty, at first innocent, becomes indecent. And so the little girl who was having fun has turned into an old queen who abuses others for her own amusement. One example: the testimony of Serge Lifar regarding the death of Coco's intimate enemy: "She telephoned me: 'Serge, come quickly! We're going to bury Cocteau!' That evening, we dined sumptuously and drank champagne. Coco was radiant: 'He's gone . . . he's dead!' "

One may be horrified by such joyous cynicism, by the stony heart of an icy monster of eighty. But that would be to misunderstand the joy with which she clapped her hands. Such ferocity is found only in those childish hatreds arising between two schoolgirls angry "to the death" because of a chocolate bar, a toy, a sarcastic remark. That age is without pity. Thirteen-year-old school girls quarrel on a life-and-death basis. It is easy for them to do so since they do not yet know anything about life and are ignorant of everything about death. Real cruelty would don Tartuffe's mask, not the cynical laugh of a "little girl" of eighty.

Coco's secret lies in her fidelity to a poverty-stricken and orderly childhood, imbued with security behind the high walls of boarding schools that also sheltered dreams of glory and escape.

Coco's secret is her obsession with early terrors, the poignant and mysteriously haunting memory and fear of solitude and silence, the nightmare of an empty room in the night.

"A woman who is not loved is nothing, no matter what her age may be: young, old, mother, mistress, what you will, a woman who is not loved is a lost woman. She may as well die. It doesn't matter."

Coco's secret is that little girl holding out her hand while dreaming of that person who would one day grasp it. But success is intoxicating, with friends who flatter you, power that hardens you, passions that break you. The heart finally dries up. Mademoiselle succeeded in everything except life. She won everything except the happiness of loving.

Applying the maxim of an obscure writer, "If you want to live independently you must become neither mother nor wife," she rejected any inclination for marriage. At Moulins, at the Ritz and for the rest of her life wherever she went, she remained the lonely boarding school girl.

Drowning her misery in daily work, Chanel departed on January 10, 1971. It was a Sunday. Only a Sunday could kill her.

Index

1 2 3 4 5 6 7 ← P Y → 9 8 7 6 5 4 3